jump point

How Network Culture
Is Revolutionizing Business

Tom Hayes

New York   Chicago   San Francisco   Lisbon   London   Madrid   Mexico City
Milan   New Delhi   San Juan   Seoul   Singapore   Sydney   Toronto

1 2 3 4 5 6 7 8 9 0   DOC/DOC   0 9 8

ISBN: 978-0-07-154562-4
MHID: 0-07-154562-X

This publication is designed to provide accurate and authoritative information in regard to the subject matter covered. It is sold with the understanding that the publisher is not engaged in rendering legal, accounting, or other professional service. If legal advice or other expert assistance is required, the services of a competent professional person should be sought.

McGraw-Hill books are available at special discounts to use as premiums and sales promotions, or for use in corporate training programs. To contact a representative please visit the Contact Us pages at www.mhprofessional.com.

This book is printed on acid-free paper.

This book is dedicated to Samuel and Elizabeth,
my beautiful wife, Estelle,
and
my mother, Athena

Contents

Acknowledgments vii

Introduction ix

PART ONE　The Jump..1

1　The Paradox of Rapid Change 3

2　A Brave New Network...29

3　The Next Market Spaces 49

PART TWO　The Five Discontinuities 69

4　The Attention Wars 71

5　The Permanent *Now* 91

6　The Augurs of Amplitude 105

7　Mashup Culture 119

8　Trust Is the New Money..139

PART THREE　The Next Curve 159

9　The Bubble Generation 163

10　Jump Point to Growth 187

11　Future–Perfect–Tense...211

Notes..237

Index 251

Acknowledgments

Writing a book is an enormous undertaking, and I am grateful to the many people who, in one way or another, contributed to this one.

Big thinkers from the business world gave me both inspiration and guidance throughout the process, among them Ted Leonsis, Tim Draper, Stowe Boyd, Debi Coleman, Lawrence G. Roberts, Tomi T. Ahonen, Eric Horvitz, Mark Whitty, Brian Brownie, and Jamais Cascio. Also a core set of brilliant academics kept me on point: many thanks to Andrew Odlyzko at the University of Minnesota; Tamas Vicsek at Eötvös Loránd University, Budapest; David Levy of the University of Washington; and Pauline Ratnasingam at the University of Missouri.

Deep appreciation goes out to my colleagues at Enea, Johan Wall, Per Akerberg, Hakan Gustavson, and, most especially, Virginia Walker, John Smolucha, and Linda Thompson.

My agent Jim Levine and the team at the Levine Greenberg Agency proved again why they are the best in the business. Jim worked hard to give this project life from its earliest stages, and for that I am tremendously appreciative.

I am eternally grateful for the unrelenting support of my editor at McGraw-Hill, Jeanne Glasser, who along with publisher Herb Schaffner maintained faith in this project from the very beginning.

This book would not have come together as quickly, or as well, without the help and encouragement of my friend, and a gifted author Michael S. Malone. Mike was tireless in talking out my ideas with me, reading the work in progress, and advising me all along the way.

Most of all, I am grateful to my family; Sam, Elizabeth, and my wife, Estelle, a talented writer in her own right, for their unbending belief in me and for putting up with the many long, late hours it took to write this book.

Introduction

In mathematics it is called a "jump discontinuity." In engineering, this is known as a "step phase change." In climatology, they call it an "abrupt delta." I call it a *Jump Point*—a change in the environment, in this case the business environment, so startling that we have no choice but to regroup and rethink the future.

The economic history of the world is punctuated by Jump Points. The tricky part has been identifying them at the right time. Very often, we mistake the arrival of a stunning new invention for the Jump Point: we get mesmerized by a new innovation, think the world has changed the day a new technology leaves the lab. But that is rarely, if ever, the case. That is not the Jump Point.

Instead, technology revolution is a fitful process. New technologies take time to be absorbed and diffused. We are a curious species; it is human nature to tinker, and experiment, test, and play. And most inventions improve with application, adoption, and time. Therefore, most Jump Points occur well after the enthusiasm settles and the parade has passed.

Real Jump Points most often arrive after we grow complacent about that invention, when the technology becomes routine and unremarkable, after the novelty has worn off and the technology has gone mainstream. It is then that rapid change finally happens.

In our lifetimes, that is exactly what happened with the Internet. It spawned a mania when it was introduced to the general public. At the time, circa 1992, it was envisioned as the antigravity device, time machine, and fountain of youth of our age. Wild promises were made, and even wilder business plans were written.

Eventually, the hype got so far out in front of the promise that the latter could never catch up. It wasn't until almost a decade later, after the bubble burst and the parade moved on—that is, when the rest of the world turned its attention elsewhere—that the real work could take place. That's when things got serious.

Jump Points throughout history have occurred when technology, economics, and culture converged to produce transformational change. The Jump Point for the Internet—the subject of this book—will happen when the Web soon welcomes its third billionth user. That milestone will mark the first time in human history when all the world's producers and consumers are unified in a single, integrated global system. Soon, all three billion of us will communicate, collaborate, and community-build—buy, sell, borrow, and invest—together without middlemen, brokers, or gatekeepers.

And that will be one of the most explosive combinations in human economic history. The resulting economy will be big, *really* big—of a scale the likes of which we have never seen before. Hundreds of millions of the world's disenfranchised will now take a seat at the table. They will make, sell, and buy things. They will, by their efforts, enrich the common wealth in new and unimagined ways.

But, it's not going to be one big nirvana. There will be plenty of challenges to go around, as we welcome in the next cohort of contestants. There will be new tribes, new criminals, and unimagined new problems to deal with. And unlike the old economy, there will be no escaping them. No more retreating to the First World to hide.

The same network that will create a giant seamless economy will also make the world smaller than it's ever been. Six degrees of separation, 19 clicks away? Forget about it. We are, all of us, about to get a lot closer than that. That's a good thing, except when it's not. People everywhere are getting a taste of power now, and they're keen on changing the rules. Introduce a few billion more people to the equation, and you can expect commensurate change. You can expect a flood of new consumers coming out of previously disconnected corners of the globe.

Also get ready for a spate of strange, new megamarket communities to form around people's quickly shifting wants and whims. Increasingly, the balance of power will shift to these new coalitions and armies of opinionated consumers.

And, hard as it is to believe, that's the *small* stuff. Prepare for time to disappear, space to collapse, and the old trusted rules of the road to go out the window.

If the past is a guide, very few social conventions, institutions, or companies will survive the Jump Point intact.

The freeway to the future is littered with the business cards of the blindsided. Even when they see it coming, even when they think they're ready, too many organizations, history shows, simply don't prepare, adapt, and adjust. Inevitably, that will happen again with this Jump Point, and the broom of change will sweep out many of today's best-known companies and most-revered brands.

This book is designed to help you and your company make the coming Jump and come out alive on the other side.

This book asks some big questions. For example:

- Just how destabilized will global markets get when every person on earth is connected to every other person without intermediaries, regulators, or arbiters between them?

- Does chaos reign, or do producers and consumers find new, orderly ways of interacting?
- What happens when the classical impediments to growth—scarcity, imperfect information, and distance—are reduced or eliminated?
- What happens when ideas—and products—can spread through this neural network with the brutal speed and pervasiveness of a viral outbreak? Or, conversely, when too many choices produce a consumer "whiteout" of information overload and analysis paralysis?
- Will the old rules of law be spurned by predatory free radicals and open-code warriors?
- Who wins and who loses when many of the old, orderly laws of business are wiped out by a virulent new form of *pandemic economics*?
- Is your business ready to compete in this coming chaotic environment?
- Most of all, are you prepared for the Jump?

Jump Point is a book for people who want to better understand and anticipate the new, often strange forces driving the next global economy.

The coming economy will actively involve more people than at any time in history. More people produce more ideas, opportunities, and wealth. And more competition. Winning in this new environment won't be easy. There will be serious implications for both organizations and individuals. Challenged will be our old assumptions, business models, and even rules of law.

After the Jump, discontinuities will upset that status quo. These will force companies to rethink and regroup. The changeover will set off a mad scramble for the future. Here are some things you will find in the chapters to follow:

■ An examination of how network effects, agglomeration economies, and organic solidarity are working together to create new markets of massive scale and fluidity.

■ A look at how social media communities like YouTube and MySpace, as well as massively multiplayer online games and crowdsourcing sites, are ushering in—and preparing us for—a new way to live and interact. Also, an examination of how and why these sites have grown so fast, what drives the "group-forming" impulse, and what the implications are of collaborative behavior on a global scale.

■ Why labeling the world as "flat" is a dangerous mistake. The post-Jump world will be anything but. Expect instead a gyrating roller coaster of expansion and contraction— massively user-led markets that can change on a dime, shift on the fly, spawn new markets overnight, and kill them off in half that time. Small players can explode into global domination overnight, and market leaders can disappear just as quickly.

■ A look at the Bubble Generation, the young, connected consumers who have already made the Jump. These early adopters are leading a radical reshaping of the business landscape with each click, text message, video download, and podcast. Mobile, connected, demanding, and opinion-ated, this new wave of alpha consumers is already impact-ing every business everywhere. What the BubbleGen wants and buys today will shape the way we all will do business tomorrow.

■ An exploration of the new management challenges brought on by pandemic economics. How operating in continual real-time will make institutional information processing and decision making more challenging than ever. Major challenges for organizations will include *response latency*—the inability to act on and react to real-time external events with clarity and decisiveness. Why too much information will likely kill more companies than too little.

- The anatomy of a Blockbuster—why some products will become pandemic market-makers by root-tapping the power of person-to-person (P2P) and many-to-many viral dynamics. How Blockbuster products and services will overwhelm competitors with rapid customer acceptance and rule-changing results.

- A profile of the coming consumerism—a delicate balance between the wisdom of groups and the tyranny of mobs. A look at the downside risks from what has been called a "dictatorship of idiots."

- A consideration of the dark side of the next economy, including new threats to—and from—our current conception of intellectual property, and the devastating effects of "mudflation"—the rapid devaluation of property, caused by overly fast, overly hot markets, and behavioral economics and irrationalities.

Ignore the Jump Point and you may not see it coming. Dismiss it, and you may miss the leap entirely. Resist it, and you will be left to the graces of history.

PART ONE

The Jump

This is not the end. It is not even the beginning of the end.
But, it is, perhaps, the end of the beginning.
—WINSTON CHURCHILL

It is no longer a metaphor, or a feature, or a mere conveyance. It is not a "plus" market, alternative channel, or new means of distribution. Today, the network *is* the economy. After the Jump Point, words like *Internet*, *Web*, and *online* will gradually disappear from use. They will be superfluous.

This first part of the book looks at how we got here and considers the implications of a networked world where three billion people—the world's entire workforce—will soon be unified in a single economic system. What's important to remember while reading the following pages is that this global network, like all networks, has distinct properties and behaves in unique—sometimes even counterintuitive—but ultimately predictable ways. Knowing this, as we approach the Jump Point, we should be unsurprised by the network's natural characteristics and patterns of behavior.

For example, it is futile to deny that information wants to be free and wants to flow as a virus flows through a host population. It is pointless to overcontrol information or to try to hide it. And it must be acknowledged that the fastest-moving, most efficient viruses are always helped along by their hosts. In the new social-driven economy, user-generated content, news, rumors, and referrals are the good viruses that fuel future growth and vitality. These and other important allowances set the stage for the Jump Point.

In the chapters that follow in this part, we will look at how all of the forces, many of them disguised or misidentified, are already in place around us to create the Jump Point. The challenge now is to recognize them for what they really are . . . and prepare ourselves for what will be the most radical social, cultural, and commercial shift in our lifetimes.

1

The Paradox of Rapid Change

Technology revolutions always take longer than predicted, but arrive faster than anticipated.

—MICHAEL S. MALONE

Finally. After more than a decade of blue-sky hype, the dot-com run-up, the dot-com bubble, specious business plans, snake-oil value propositions, math-challenged balance sheets, projectile hamsters, talking sock puppets, and every conceivable form of rapture and exuberance, the end of the beginning is near.

It will happen early in 2011, probably before summer. It may be a Chinese sheepherder in a ramshackle border town in Mongolia, or a bank intern in a Chelsea coffee shop, or a student in a Buenos Aires *cabinas publica*. This person will perhaps be the first in the family to go to school, learn to read, or make a living wage. He may be the scion of a wealthy family, or the daughter of a truck driver. Perhaps this person will have saved for years to buy a telephone, or must walk for miles to use a computer. It will matter little what language this person speaks, if words are even spoken at all. And as to his or her religious background, value system, or ethical underpinnings, it will not matter one whit.

This person will be remarkable for not being remarkable. And if anyone is watching, his or her first connection to the World Wide

Web will seem like a small thing. But it will mark a turning point in the human experience.

This man or woman, boy or girl, will be the third-billionth person to join the networked global economy.

Whether by cell phone, Internet, or satellite, by pushing a few buttons, or by punching a few keys, by using the everyday technology that surrounds all of us, he or she will set off a trip wire that announces the largest interconnected, integrated web of communications and commerce in history. This person will represent the completion of a huge network involving the world's entire workforce. And the arrival of this last "node" will signify the end of the era of discrete, disconnected economies, and the start of an infinitely bigger and more dynamic system.

Consider this: it took 100,000 years; 300 generations; the domestication of animals; the invention of money; the craft system and mass production; the rise of the city and the modern state; the invention of the steam engine, the internal combustion engine, atomic power, the telegraph, telephone, motion pictures and television, flight, the computer, the Internet, and wireless telephony; and the birth of representative democracy, common law, and market capitalism to arrive at, in 2001, an integrated market of one billion human beings.

Only six years later, in 2007, the second billion arrived. And, at an astounding rate of acceleration—about 70,000 new people linking in every day—the third billionth person will join in just a few years from now. That historic milestone will signal the end of business, markets, work . . . and life, as we know it.

At that point, one-half the world's population—its entire productive work force—will be united in a truly global marketplace of products, capital, and ideas: the largest economic engine in the history of the human adventure. *Finally.*

The true history of technology is 10 percent invention, 90 percent adoption. No doubt about it, we live in an unprecedented time of history.

Technology, culture, and economics are all coming together in just the right way to create the biggest, most dynamic wealth-creation network the world has ever known. The mass adoption of personal computers, the Internet, and mobile telephony, combined with the ready use of voice, data, video, and e-mail communications, are forging a powerful, new global nexus.

This is what a great Jump Point looks like—a nonlinear growth surge in the adoption of a technology. Such watersheds are about more than technology breakthroughs; a Jump Point is a fundamental shift in the way society and the world works. The Internet is now reaching that critical mass point when its true impact can be felt.

Writes economist Carlota Perez:

Similar productivity explosions and bursts of financial excitement leading to economic euphoria and subsequent collapses of confidence have occurred together before. They are interrelated and interdependent phenomena; they share the same root cause and are in the nature of the system and its workings. They originate in the way technologies evolve by revolutions, in the peculiar manner in which these great upsurges of wealth-creation potential are assimilated by the economic and social system and in the functional separation of financial and production capital.

The main contention is that the full fruits of the technological revolutions that occur about every half century are only widely reaped with a time-lag. Two or three decades of turbulent adoption and assimilation elapse from the moment the new set of technologies, products, industries and infrastructures make their first impact to the beginning of "a golden age" or "era of good feeling" based on them.

There have, of course, been other periods of technology discontinuity in human history. Some nine thousand years ago, craft specialization in the Neolithic period led to major changes in the formation of early society. The development of individual skills like milling, metallurgy, and brick making allowed people to move from sparsely populated settlements into villages and then to build cities. The Jump Point of this era was the creation of the world's first true city, Catal Huyuk, in what is now south-central Turkey.

The first organized cosmopolitan city-state, Catal Huyuk started out humbly, a settlement on a migration path, a few huts located near a clean water source. Soon, more structures went up and more people passing through opted to stay. Over time, people far and wide heard of this bustling place and sought it out. Gradually, a new form took shape: a city. While typical settlements of the time may have had a dozen or so residents, Catal Huyuk became home to 10 thousand citizens living within its walls, the largest-ever concentration of humans to that point. This unprecedented degree of human scale and density required people to learn new ways of interacting. The new city-state paradigm required new forms of social and political organization, such as central administration and laws; it created social hierarchies; and it spawned a complex, diversified economy that included long-distance trade.

The "urban revolution" that began at Catal Huyuk spread through the world, ultimately changing the way humans developed and how we live today. And the unintended consequences of that urbanization—regionalization, conflict, alliances, and warfare between states—survived as well. In the late Middle Ages, a mechanical revolution took place in Europe. In clock making, the invention of spring-driven mechanisms provided an important alternative to the bulky, weight-driven mechanisms of the period. Weight and pulley clocks had arrived on the scene a hundred years earlier, but the spring-driven escapement was a major breakthrough, allowing for smaller clocks (later watches) and making possible personal ownership of timepieces.

Again, this Jump Point came not from a technical switchover, but a social one. Until the early 1500s, clocks were found primarily in church steeples. They were basically signaling devices to call people to Mass or religious celebrations. The proliferation of easier-to-install, spring-driven clocks led to more publicly owned clocks in town squares throughout Italy. Since these clocks weren't operated by the church, the townspeople were free to operate them on "absolute" or constant time, as opposed to canonical time.

Before the proliferation of these public clocks, people worked, ate, slept, and went to church according to the patterns of the sun and moon. After the clocks appeared, the day was divided by regular increments from the time of rising to the hour of rest. This capability allowed for a common frame of reference and an efficient coordination and scheduling of activities. In turn, a common understanding of time brought order to a world governed by happenstance and subjectivity. It is hard to imagine the great social, scientific, and economic breakthroughs that followed were it not for the adoption of absolute time that started with Italy's public clocks.

New technology can take time to reveal its real purpose. The Newcomen steam engine was invented in Scotland in 1712, initially as a water pump. It took decades for it to be seen as anything else. It wasn't until the end of that century that steam-powered machinery based upon the Newcomen engine, such as the power loom, was introduced. These inventions in turn helped transform late eighteenth-century England from an agrarian economy to an industrial power.

Even then, the paradigm-bashing Jump Point made possible by the steam engine did not occur until 1814—a century after Newcomen's invention—when an American, Francis Cabot Lowell, combined various steam-powered technologies in a new way. His textile mill on the banks of the Merrimack River in Massachusetts was the first *integrated* application of the technology to provide an end-to-end production line.

Not only did this act bring the Industrial Revolution to America, it brought *linearity* to the industrialized world. By sequentially lining up equipment that took raw cotton at one end and rolled out finished cloth at the other, all under one roof, Lowell introduced such concepts as the factory, the assembly line, and process flows to the manufacturing world. Just as significantly, the Lowell Experiment introduced the concept of linearity to the rest of society. This idea—that we start at square one and progress down the line—shaped everything from modern bureaucratic organization to our public school systems.

As these past moments illustrate, it is not the invention of the technology that causes the Jump, but rather the *diffusion* of the technology and its application in new and meaningful ways. In other words, the real impact of a technology is rarely realized when it is introduced, but rather when it is widely adopted and used.

It was not the development of brickmaking that reshaped civilization, but the use of those bricks to make cities and walls. It was not the invention of the automobile that changed society, but the critical mass point at which its popularity created a need for paved roads, traffic laws, and signal lights. That's when our mobile culture really got its start.

As with the steam engine, it can sometimes take years for an innovation to take off. The postage stamp was first used in England in 1840. As smart an idea as it was, it took 50 years before it was widely adopted throughout Europe and the United States. The telephone was a mere voice recording device when it was patented. It took several decades before its widespread use created a new paradigm in communications.

Researchers typically plot technology adoption on a gradual S-curve. First on the adoption curve are the innovators, the adventuresome risk takers who make the initial discovery. Next will come the early adopters, the social leaders and "influentials" who want to be out ahead of the pack. They are followed by the early majority, those people who deliberate as long as possible but finally come around, followed by the late adopters and laggards. Afford-ability is usually the holdup for the last groups.

In the case of the Internet, after its own quarter-century lag, global adoption is now accelerating at a rate we have never seen before. The ramp from the first to the second billion connected peo-ple took less than eight years. The ramp from second to third bil-lion adopters, will take only half that time. A Jump as high and fast as the Internet is undergoing will produce more than a few nose-bleeds. We are literally going to "feel" the Jump; it will be palpable.

We will soon see signs that things are changing—strange new pockets of demand, new competitors, and new tastes entering the consumer mainstream. This development is to be expected. Econ-omists say the coming run-up will be followed by a period of dis-equilibrium and discontinuity, followed again by a return to equilibrium and the beginning of a new growth period. Getting through each of those stages will be as great a social and business challenge as we have ever faced.

Several factors are converging to accelerate the arrival of the next Jump Point. First, the early majority has settled in and is becoming quite comfortable with information technology. Mobile phones, personal information appliances, and the Internet have become routine for people in the industrialized world. In fact, we can't imagine life without these devices. And, because we know a lot more about the power and limits of the Internet than we did, say before the dot-com bubble, we are more certain of what we can and cannot do with it. There are a few applications that won't fly or are not practical, but for the most part, we have seen that the Internet is real, entirely useful, and transformative. Those qual-ities have resulted in greater investment being made in hard infra-structure and more innovation in applications and content—the second factor. In particular, in the area of telecommunications, trillions of dollars have been spent on satellites and the fiber backbone over the last two decades. Today, 80 percent of the world is covered by mobile networks. The first cell phone call placed from the Himalaya-sheltered summit of Mount Everest in May 2007 is a measure of just how far we have come. The third factor is the way existing technologies like cell telephony, digital imaging, and the Internet are beginning to converge into more convenient packages.

The once run-of-the-mill mobile phone has today morphed into a "network appliance," allowing people to do everything in the palm that they once did on a personal computer (PC) or laptop. Slightly larger displays and keyboards transform new Web-enabled phones into full-fledged Internet devices. Add Google's mobile Gmail, the mobile versions of social sites like Twitter or Jaiku, and the ability to build a mobile Web page using a service like Winksite, and you have the best of all worlds. Now, you don't need to be tethered to a desk, laden with heavy equipment, or dependent on industrial-strength power supplies to be part of the networked economy. If you have a mobile phone, you are part of the network.

The final factor is that the very same technology that is making it easier to connect is also making it cheaper to do so. The price of admission to the global economy is dropping rapidly with each new generation of mobile phone and computers.

This outcome is in keeping with Moore's law, the metronome of the Information Age. An observation made 30 years ago by Intel cofounder Gordon Moore, the "law" asserts that computing power doubles every 18 to 24 months while during the same time its cost is halved. A unit of computing cost one million dollars when Moore made his observation in 1964. Today, a unit of computing costs one penny.

That reliable pattern has been a major factor in the widespread affordability of technology around the world. As each new generation of semiconductor chips rolls off a fabrication line, the prior generations become cheaper and cheaper. Plenty good enough to meet the needs of the world's computation and communications needs, the dropping price of these older chips also reduces the costs of everything along the information continuum, from laptops and bandwidth to telephone base stations and handsets.

Meanwhile, on the software side, open platforms, such as Linux, and the open source movement have driven down the cost of code while also tapping into some of the best minds of our generation.

From No Phones to Net Phones

While the underlying technology has been advancing, the market has not been sleeping.

There are several important public and private initiatives under-way aimed at bringing low cost (less than two hundred dollars) laptops to the bottom of the economic pyramid, but market-based solutions are rolling out even quicker, especially for Web-enabled mobile phones. According to Forrester Research, the number of PCs in the world won't hit two billion until 2015; but *non*-PC Internet devices—including mobile phones—will boom from today's 100 million to more than 14 billion as early as the end of 2010.

Telecommunications titans, such as Nokia, Motorola, and Ericsson, are already manufacturing ultra-low-cost phones expressly for the developing world. Additionally, efforts led by the GSM (Global System for Mobile communications) Association, the trade group for the mobile phone industry, are making affordable, universal network access a growing reality. The industry's goal is to have a $30 phone and a $5 monthly calling plan available for anyone who wants it in the underserved developing world.

According to the analysis group at Lehman Brothers Banks, lowering the price of a phone by just $20 in many poorer countries could increase its affordability by 43 percent. Based upon that rate of affordability, the GSMA forecasts Web-enabled mobile phone adoption to easily reach the three billion mark by the Jump Point year, 2011, attaining an astounding *five billion* worldwide users by 2015.

Already, by summer 2007, 1,000 new mobile phone customers were signing on every minute of every day—65 percent of them in the developing world.

What is the likely impact of such rapid Web phone diffusion? A 2005 study of 21 developing countries by Leonard Waverman of the London Business School, showed that an extra 10 mobile phones per 100 people in a typical developing country leads to an additional 0.59 percentage points of growth in gross domestic product (GDP) per person. With millions of new phones arriving every year in the developing world, we can expect to see life-changing benefits showing up everywhere.

Internet use also has been shown to conclusively impact trade and economic growth. For example, a 2004 study by the Brookings Institution showed a dramatic connection between Internet adoption and economic and trade growth after 1996. Among other findings, the study suggested that a 1 percentage point increase in the number of Internet users in a country increases total exports by 4.3 percentage points and exports from low-income countries to high-income countries by 3.8 percentage points.

Because of the dropping cost of a ticket to the show, the concern among some people has shifted from a "digital divide" to so-called participation inequality. As the phrase implies, advocates worry that the Internet playing field may not be as level for the newly assimilated as for those who have been online for years. Language, customs, familiarity, and efficient practices (like search) are possible barriers to meaningful adoption for the new entrants, particularly for people who can neither read nor write.

But here, too, there are efforts to make the Internet experience simpler and more universal. Tellme, purchased in 2006 by Microsoft, has a voice-driven platform that allows users to speak instead of use a keypad. International efforts, like the W3C (World Wide Web Consortium) Web Accessibility Initiative, are working to make it possible for people to use language alternatives, pictures, and symbols to access the Web.

The Lincoln software system for smart mobile phones, also developed by Microsoft, shows the possibilities of an Internet unencumbered by language barriers. The system enables a user to take a photograph with a smart phone and then use that photograph to browse the Web. The system matches the photograph that the user has taken against a database of tagged photographs, thereby avoiding keyboards and even language. As more pictures of more items organically get tagged by users, the utility of such a language-neutral system will only grow.

Winnie Mangaliso is symbolic of the technology transformation taking place in South Africa.

Having spent a lifetime as a domestic worker in and about Cape Town, Winnie now makes her living as an entrepreneur. One of millions throughout Africa who have signed on with a company called SharedPhone, Winnie operates a very cost-effective and simple mobile pay phone business. The turnkey "business-in-a-box" cost her only 1,500 Rand (about $200) and she is now earning 1,700 Rand a month providing neighbors with cheap and easily available pay phone services.

For those who don't have a phone or even a bank account, a service like SharedPhone is a convenient lifeline to the world. When her neighbors don't want to hike over to the local *spaza* shop to use a traditional pay phone, they can stop by Winnie's shack and, for the equivalent of a few cents per calling minute, can talk with family and friends, conduct business, or send a text message.

Though only set up for voice or text today, SharedPhone is working on a Web-enabled handset that will give Winnie's customers access to the entire World Wide Web and to vital markets for local crafts, such as eBay and Overstock.com.

"This is a product which has changed my life," Winnie says on a SharedPhone blog. "For the first time, I feel that I am my own boss."

While SharedPhone programs are rolling out in Mozambique, Zimbabwe, Lesotho, Uganda, and throughout Africa, it is not the only sign of a telecommunications revolution on the continent.

Growth of phone and Internet subscribers in Africa, particularly Sub-Saharan Africa, has been mind-boggling. For example, according to the World Bank, mobile subscribers in Nigeria grew from 370,000 to 16.8 million in just the last four years. Newfound access to the capital, markets, ideas, and consumers of the rest of the world is expected to promote rapid and robust growth in many disenfranchised corners of the globe.

Consider the groundbreaking work of Nobel Peace Prize winner Muhammad Yunus and his Grameen Bank and phone companies. By aiming programs specifically at village women, these companies are helping "phone ladies" in Bangladesh, or their *sari sari* counterparts in the Philippines, to start mobile phone businesses financed by low-cost microloans. Through such innovative efforts, Grameenphone is empowering millions of people to self-sufficiency and beyond.

According to author Nicholas P. Sullivan, phone ladies in Bangladesh, for example, can earn from $750 to $1,200 per year, compared to an average per capita income of $415. The extra $400 earned each year, multiplied by 250,000 village phones in Bangladesh alone, adds $100 million to the village economies. And that, Sullivan emphasizes, still doesn't account for the productive use of the phone or income generated by selling goods and services through the phone.

Scale Changes Everything

We have never before known an economy as big and diverse—either in absolute or relative terms—as the coming post–Jump Point world will be.

Before, when we spoke of a global economy, we were talking largely of a Western economy, of trade and commerce involving a relatively small fraction of the world's people living in the industrialized world. Until now, the vast majority of people everywhere else have been relegated to subsistence-level local or regional trade, or to largely exploitive, one-way trade.

C. K. Prahalad's book *The Fortune at the Bottom of the Pyramid* documents well the stratification of the old global economy. At the top of the pyramid one finds the world's wealthiest people, less than one-half percent of the population. The next two tiers account for another two billion people, including a growing global middle class in rapidly developing nations like China and India. At the very bottom are the four billion poor and disenfranchised, people living on less than $5 a day. People at the bottom of the economic pyramid, Prahalad argues, are poor because they lack access. Since they don't have ready access to the vast flows of global capital, they cannot convert their considerable assets—labor, work product, and resources—into wealth.

Now all that is changing, as even the poorest among us will soon find the price of admission to the global economy within reach. Cheaper solar panels will light up rural areas. Electric generators run on human waste will provide power to city slums, extending the working day, deterring crime, and increasing Internet and mobile phone use. When that happens, things start to get really interesting. We can flip the pyramid.

When all the world's producers and consumers are united by common information technology, the focus of the pyramid can change to *access*. With the majority of people granted access—via Internet, mobile phone, or other network appliances—the fat end of the pyramid will represent the connected majority, the small bottom will contain the shrinking ranks of the unconnected. And with their access, the newly enfranchised will be able to rapidly improve their living standards. A study of 100 countries between 1991 and 2001 showed that income per capita, years of schooling, illiteracy rates, the urbanization rate, telephone density, electricity consumption, and regulatory quality all improved significantly with increasing access to the Internet.

Is such a rapid reversal of fortune really possible?

Yes. Just look at China. China's population of abject poor—those making subsistence wages—dropped from 250 million people to 26 million and falling in the span of a decade. Today, China is on path to become the world's largest economy within a decade.

It should also be noted that the benefits of a bigger network are not one-way. People on the bottom of today's pyramid do have assets and the potential to create more wealth. With more people living within capitalist regimes than at any time in history, there are now more entrepreneurs, inventors, and business renegades alive today than have ever lived. Welcoming them into the networked world will enrich the economy for all.

It took the entirety of the human experience to achieve the billion-person global economy, which, even then, only engaged a bit more than 15 percent of earth's population. The next waves of people linking in can change everything. More connected people results in more choices for all, more combinations and permutations of people producing, consuming, and trading goods and services—more raw growth.

In the immediate aftermath of the Asian Tsunami in 2004, sardine fishing off the coast of Kerala in southern India came to an abrupt halt. Just when the hard-hit villages needed the food the most, there were rumors circulating that the fish were somehow poisoned by the upheaval of the tidal wave.

After a few days, the rumors subsided, those with intact boats resumed fishing, and makeshift markets reopened. One big difference was that no boat now went out without a mobile phone on board. After such an epic trauma it was understandable that the fishermen and their families took some comfort in staying in touch. But the mobile phones have had an additional consequence that has contributed to a radical change in the local fishing industry.

Even before the tsunami, sardine fishing in Kerala had been a tough way to make a living. It was either feast or famine. Some days the schools of "oil" sardines were nonexistent, resulting in little supply; other times the runs were plentiful. But, a good day for one boat usually meant a good day for all, and those days would produce a sardine glut in the beachfront market stalls. Puttering the small wooden boats from market to market in search of better pricing—or a buyer at all—was time consuming, and with a perishable product on board, this often meant excess fish were simply dumped at sea.

But then something interesting happened.

With the mobile phones on board, the fishermen came to realize they could call the coastal markets while they were still at sea. Rather than sell their fish at beach auctions, they could call around for the best price along a wider swathe of the coast. This has produced better efficiencies and the dumping of fewer hauls. Information technology improved access—and that in turn is making a difference at all levels of commerce on the coast of India.

The New Math: 1+1=3?

How much bigger will the global economic pie be after the Jump Point?

It's a tricky question. The answer is imprecise; a product of several extrapolations. Current measuring tools are inadequate to the task; it is not as simple as forecasting each nation's gross domestic product and adding it all up. There is harder math involved.

Fortunately, economists agree on a few things we can use to make some forecasts, at least of the potential scale.

First, it is well proven that population growth throughout human history has resulted in technological and economic progress: more people, more ideas, more money. By that view, the raw growth in the online population will reasonably result in new outcomes—new technologies, products, and wealth that will spur future economic growth.

Second, technology itself has always been a catalyst for economic growth. Economists have long studied the effects of technology diffusion on economic performance, from the wheel to the nanobot. However, measuring the impact of information technology is more complicated than, say, the steam engine or even electricity. Every improvement in information flows is a benefit unto itself, but better information also improves everything it touches, including supply chains, distribution flows, and labor. Abundant knowledge means that good ideas, practices, and policies are shared faster and bad ones shelved quicker than before.

Third, there is the added value of the networks themselves. But, if fairly evaluating the benefits of discrete information technology is hard, measuring the real and potential value of an information network, particularly a large and complex one like the Internet, is even harder. In fact, the imperative to understand the dynamics of complex networks today has spawned an entirely new discipline around it. Combining mathematics, physics, biology, and sociology, the new science of *complex networks* provides a very good lens on the behavior of the coming economy.

Professor Geoffrey B. West and his team at the Santa Fe Institute have compared the behavior of large social structures, cities, and corporations to biological patterns. They have studied the relationship between economic growth metrics—patent activity, talent pool, wages, and GDP—and population size, and found a distinctive "power law scaling relationship."

According to West, "a doubling of population is accompanied by more than a doubling of creative and economic output. We call this phenomenon 'superlinear' scaling: by almost any measure, the larger a city's population, the greater the innovation and wealth creation per person."

So, bigger is better, but how much better?

One way to answer this is to combine Moore's law with Metcalfe's law. Coined in the 1990s by Robert Metcalfe, inventor of Ethernet, the observation basically goes like this: *the value of a network goes up as the square of the number of users.*

In other words, the value of a network—like the global economy—grows exponentially every time someone new joins in. If the value of two people linking up is 4, the value of four people linking up is 16, and so forth. By Metcalfe's reasoning, the global economy, with a gross domestic product of $65 trillion today, could *quadruple* by 2011.

Of course, Metcalfe was speaking as a hardware guy about the value potential of physical connections. We also need to consider the human factors.

Reed's law offers another view. Coined by Professor David P. Reed of the Massachusetts Institute of Technology (MIT), the observation states that the *utility* of large networks—particularly social networks—scales exponentially with the size of the network.

Reed says, "While many kinds of value grow proportionally to network size and some grow proportionally to the square of network size, I've discovered that some network structures create total value that can scale even faster than that. Networks that support the construction of communicating groups create value that scales *exponentially* with network size, i.e. much more rapidly than Metcalfe's square law."

Reed is suggesting that some connections are simply more valuable to a user than others—those that provide entrée into a bigger community for instance. And then, there are the so-called spillovers and the unintended consequences of network profligacy; the human intangibles, like all the new geniuses and catalysts that pop up in the network—the 15-year-old savant in Bangladesh who may grow up to one day cure cancer or the Lebanese entrepreneur who's got an idea to slow global warming.

These x-factors cannot be discounted, particularly as a benefit of attracting new participants from the frontiers. History shows that the great leaps forward usually come from the hungry edges, not the center. The "edglings" will bring with them many new ideas and much fresh thinking.

Another view comes from a team at the University of Minnesota led by Professor Andrew Odlyzko. According to Odlyzko, a mathematician who heads the university's Digital Technology Center, as a network grows, its value increases proportionally, not logarithmically, at a substantial rate—although he believes at a slower rate than either Metcalfe or Reed asserts.

Speaking of the next networked economy, Odlyzko says, "Indeed, any kind of technological, managerial, or other type of innovation can give rise to a situation where 1+1 is more than 2."

A major problem with "laws" concerning network value is that they discount the power of association itself. Joining a network is much more than buying a mere utility; it is about creating value through things you can only do in a community of interest: form groups, send and receive messages, browse one another's recommended favorites and suggestions, and bounce and riff ideas. The network permits activities that create a compound value that is both collective and unique for each network participant. In that sense, each new participant offers others in the network the chance to create value that did not—could not—exist without the network.

Again, more people mean more options, choices, combinations, and possibilities. One thing we do know: the coming economy is going to be bigger than the sum of its parts.

Economics of Abundance

There is yet one more factor, a fourth one that will set the value of the new economy: *price*.

The tumbling cost of access makes an important difference, as the resulting scale-up occurs more quickly and produces broader-based benefits than any simple algorithm can capture.

This outcome is something new. What traditional economics fails to appreciate about the Internet is that information technology generates a greater output from a given set of inputs. By making it possible to exploit resources that were not exploitable before, the network is expanding the resource base for all. The third billion represent not only more people and more possibilities; they represent people who would not have had access at all before the network era.

Additionally, traditional economists like to split the world into wants and physical objects. Because objects are subject to scarcity, in the old view, the only decision people are left with is how to allocate scarce resources to maximize wealth.

Enter Paul Romer and the New Growth camp of economic theory.

Romer, an economist at Stanford University, has in recent years proposed a whole new view of economic growth for networked times. Romer also divides the world into two: physical objects and ideas. In his view, objects include everything around us, from automobile factories to atoms. These objects are apt to be scarce and subject to the law of diminishing returns, which suggests that costs will rise as input increases.

But these objects, Romer argues, are not the real drivers of economic growth. Instead, new ideas, embedded in technological change, are what really move the economy.

Unlike the old view which was defined by scarcity and limits, the new networked world offers unbounded opportunity: new ideas beget new products, new markets, and new wealth. Old Growth theories ask us to allocate scarce resources among alternative uses. New Growth says that neither resources nor alternatives are scarce. Because humans possess a nearly infinite capacity for new ideas and new ways to reconfigure physical objects, we live in a world of abundance. By coming up with new ideas on how to use a platform such as the Internet, for example, humans can boost productivity, spawn new opportunities for profit, and ultimately drive economic growth.

The Third Billion

As people around the world rapidly come online and start to interact directly with one another, we can expect both positive and negative outcomes. As economic historian Eric L. Jones observes: "In India and China, where village isolation lasted almost to the present day, the spread of radios, televisions and mobile phones means that huge populations are suddenly and for the first time being granted access to market prices, land ownership, and national and global culture."

We are about to experience the greatest social reckoning since the eleventh century, when the First Crusade linked Europe and Asia Minor. The first billion people are the world's middle class, those with means and education who are invested in the legal and regulatory structures that guide the orderly running of markets.

The next waves are decidedly not middle class. Many will have leapt from near-medieval circumstances into the thick of the modern economy in a single bound. There will be consequences when the economy scales, but society trails.

Optimists can see the positive synergy in the next waves, the richness of their cultures, the power of their collective imaginations and ambitions, and the world-shaking new ideas and inventions that still lie locked up in their minds and hearts waiting to be unleashed. Their world is about to be changed forever—and in return, they will transform our world as well.

But there will be a darker side: the predictable influx of thieves and scam artists, combatants and terrorists, not to mention added volatility in markets. The world may well become a more dangerous place before it becomes safer, and certain regions may very well witness the dystopian culture clash dramatized in the famous street scenes of the sci-fi movie *Blade Runner*.

One thing is for certain, the coming world will be very different from the one we know now, inhabited by new arrivals very different from us. Consider that a typical citizen of the third billion will have

- Never seen an airplane close up, much less flown in one
- Only seen food refrigerated at a trading post or government building
- Watched a television but never owned one
- Ridden in a gasoline-powered vehicle, but never owned, driven, or even been in a car
- Never been in a classroom, owned a book, or read more than a few signpost words
- Never owned or even used a personal computer
- Brewed his or her own "beer"
- No indoor plumbing, and not be aware of what toilet paper is
- Never used money
- A deep spirituality, and, even if Christian, Buddhist or Muslim, that faith will be mixed with animism, voodoo, shamanism, and a belief in signs, auguries, and fate
- Fearlessly welcomed new technology but seen it as a form of magic
- Probably eaten bat meat but not a Big Mac

And this unlikely person will be online with you in the next 1,000 days.

2011 and Everything After

We are crossing the threshold into an astonishing, frightening, and, in many ways, unprecedented era in human history. And, even for those of us in the West who have become accustomed to rapid change, this future is coming toward us at a breathtaking, even disorientating, speed.

Five years ago, for all of the talk of digital revolutions and globalization, the world still seemed compartmentalized and predictable. It was still possible to speak of a world divided by levels of modernity: the first world, the developing world, the third world. Politically, there was the West, which now included the old Soviet Empire and the Tigers of the Pacific Rim; a developing world led by an emerging India and China, and the problematical places like Africa and the Middle East, where the few bright spots like South Africa, Jordan, and Qatar were overwhelmed by the endless chaos that roiled over the rest of the region. Inequities in wealth distribution were unfortunate, but the march of progress would take care of all that. After all, the linear path of world prosperity had always been about more growth and more opportunity, and eventually those left behind would be cared for.

For the businessperson, the path ahead was clearly marked: grow your business at a steady pace, take full advantage of established distribution channels, implement the latest marketing tools, stay on top of technology so you don't get blindsided, and outperform your competitors in price, quality, service, and support.

Just a few years ago, we assumed the global adoption of the Internet was pegged to the PC at a nice, steady rate of growth. Five years ago, looking to the future, the combination of Pax Americana, broadband wireless communications, digital computational technology, and global consumer marketing and distribution offered the potential for decades to continuous improvement in the lives and lifespans of the world's poor, while their growing taste for consumer products and service would further enrich the developed world's economies, in the process rewarding smart entrepreneurs and efficient corporations.

Sure, we thought, there would still be regional conflicts, and local tyrannies would remain, but history would be moving against the totalitarian side of human behavior. Democracy, already spreading around the globe to a degree unimaginable even two decades before, would continue to grow—and the combination of consumer capitalism and access (via satellite dish and the Net) to a free press seemed a potent antidote to both dictatorships and peoples' republics.

Now the future doesn't seem so predictable.

The problem is not that these portents are wrong. On the contrary, their promise of changing the world for the better still seems valid. But, as is always the case with technology, the underlying structures changed as well. For example, consider computers: even as we were assuming that the PC would drive the growth of the Internet, it was already being supplanted by other, cheaper devices. Today, mobile phones and other network devices are driving the mass adoption of the Internet at a much faster pace than we ever predicted. And that development, in turn, nullifies most of our other assumptions about the world.

The result is that change is now coming so fast, and at a magnitude and complexity that no one seems to have predicted, that it is almost impossible now to make plans, develop strategies, or conduct risk assessment. What we expected to be a big but predictable new wave of consumers/producers/voters/players on the world scene, has turned into the biggest commercial tsunami ever recorded; filled with the debris and backwash of a thousand cultures, bearing down on us with paralyzing speed and threatening to disrupt everything we know.

In his book *The World is Flat*, Thomas Friedman calls this period "the great sorting out." That is an understatement. Indeed, we have much to rethink and make sense out of anew. What makes the coming economy so thrillingly—frighteningly—different is not only all the new people coming onboard but also the powerful new forces they will unleash that will govern us all.

Ours will no longer be the orderly market of classical and neoclassical theories, the "magnificent dynamics" espoused by Smith, Malthus, Mill, and Keynes. Instead, the emerging structure will likely be a chaotic amalgam of decentralized agents, nodes, and confederations, a market that will mimic viral forms found in biology, an environment characterized by rapid, unchecked growth, geometric progressions, and unpredictable combinations and permutations.

In order to truly understand this new environment, we have to understand the nature of networks and groups and the new geometry of opportunity. To understand our life and times after the Jump Point, we need to assemble a new economic lexicon. We need to adopt fresh thinking; like New Growth and Complex Network theories; sociological concepts, like organic solidarity (which help explain why people form and join the social groups they do); and microbiology—particularly the study of fast-moving viruses—because networks resemble viral environments.

Download This

- About 70,000 new people join the connected global economy every day.
- In less than five years, three billion people will be part of a seamless connected global economy—The Jump Point.
- In less than five years, the value of the world economy will increase significantly—growing between two and four times larger—as more consumers and producers connect to one another.
- The assumption that the Internet is a PC-driven network has been proven wrong; its diffusion will be mobile device–driven, and at a much quicker pace.

- The new world will be anything but "flat" as global competition will become more brutal and unforgiving than ever.
- The giant cohort of new consumers will not be homogenous, predictable, and static, and they may not even be paper-trained. People will organize themselves in new types of online communities. They will likely be more loyal to these affinity-based communities than their real-life communities . . . or their own countries.

A Brave New Network

We have come to see that we live in a small world, where everything is linked to everything else.

— ALBERT-LASZLO BARABASI

The city of Alcobendas, just north of Madrid, is not the first place you'd expect a telecom revolution to start, but that is exactly what Martin Varsavsky is doing there. As founder of Fon, a company dedicated to building the world's largest wireless local network (WiFi), Varsavsky has discovered a brilliant way to tap into the viral nature of the new networked economy.

Founded in November 2005, Fon is a "community-empowered company" aimed at building a worldwide network of one million WiFi hot spots by 2010. It's a lofty goal, to say the least, but Versavsky is one of Spain's most successful serial entrepreneurs, and he has won backing from Web heavyweights Skype, eBay, and Google. Some wonder if advancing technology—and competitors such as Whisher and WeFi—might derail the "Fon movement," but Varsavsky plans to expand the company's service into emerging technologies like WiMAX, and keep his movement growing.

What's so revolutionary about Versavsky's approach?

On the face of it, nothing. Fon appears to sell routers and a phone service to a subscriber base. But in reality, Fon is a giant social network. When you buy into its service, you receive a router for your home or office. If you opt to become a Fonero (it is optional), in exchange for making your hot spot available to fellow subscribers who may be visiting your area, you too get to use the entire global network any time you are out and about. In other words, pay once for home service and you can connect from hot spots around the world. Adding to the social dimension, members can personalize the log-in page that other subscribers see when they use a Fon Access Point. A little biography or guide to local highlights makes the experience all the more engaging and sticky.

Fon is an archetype of the new people-driven network; more hotspots result in greater user choice and convenience; meanwhile, the network gets more valuable as more people join. That is the very definition of the *network effect*. And what's most clever is that the network is being built by the subscribers themselves, therefore, Fon can grow faster at a fraction of the cost than the big network players can because the latter are saddled with billions of dollars of investment in their own infrastructure.

Can Fon attain its goal of becoming the largest WiFi network in the world? Look to the Skype example. An online "telephony club," before being acquired by eBay, Skype grew virally, member getting member, to become the second-largest fixed landline phone operator, with over 100 million users, in just 18 months—something that took its competitors more than a century.

The Secret Life of Networks

Technology is a tool of social revolution. Twenty years ago, the imperative was a transformation of industry and society from analog to digital. More recently we have seen a transition from centralized to distributed networked models.

The coming revolution will change the equation again as consumers make the shift from receivers to connectors. With the network infrastructure in place, people now have the power to do more than just receive information; they can choose whether or not to evaluate, reshape, add value, and pass the information along to others in the network. This power shift from receiver to connector is a driving force of the next economy.

In the world after the Jump Point, the network is everything. To really understand what you will be up against, you need to understand how networks work. You don't need to be an expert on complex networks. Nobody really is. But, you do need to know the basics, as well as the unique properties, of networks that can either work for or against you.

Eight Principles of the Network

1. Networks are made of connected "nodes."
2. Nodes connect directly to each other.
3. Some nodes have more connections than others.
4. The more connected a node is, the more valuable it is.
5. Information in a network moves like a virus, from node to node.
6. Nodes spread information according to self-interest.
7. Big networks contain smaller networks.
8. Networks want to grow; the bigger, the better.

The study of complex networks is a relatively new discipline or, rather, multidiscipline. It is a hybrid science, combining, among other things, mathematics, physics, engineering, biology, sociology, and economics. At its core is an understanding that we are all connected in a vast network of life. Our natural ecology is a network, the human body is a network, and each of us is part of a social network of interdependent relationships.

Networks are composed of interconnected or linked members called "nodes." In a broadcast system, like television or radio, the nodes are one way; the recipient nodes merely catch a message with a receiver.

In a network like the Internet, the nodes are two-way. That means there is expected to be reciprocity—a feedback loop—

between the linked participants of the network. They can relate to each other, talk to each other, and share information. In the network called the global economy, we are all, each of us, nodes. Soon there will be three billion of us interacting among and between ourselves. We can choose to share information with each other, we can choose to buy and sell to each other. And, we are free to group ourselves together in new ways that benefit us.

A complex network is made up of smaller networks. So, for example, if our global economy is a web of varying interrelationships and types of connections, the Internet is a giant network of networks. The important thing is that all components of the networks must be able to link together. And, thanks to a smart decision made three decades ago, they do.

The Network of Networks

The roots of the Internet go back to the 1960s, when it emerged as part of a project on "internetworking" within the U.S. Advanced Research Projects Agency (ARPA). At that time, the idea of creating an interconnected computer network was very appealing to academics and researchers who wanted to share ideas and stay on top of the work of colleagues. During the 1960s there were numerous efforts aimed at producing computer-to-computer communications networks. The concern at ARPA was that these parallel efforts might produce a balkanized array of networks that could not communicate with each other.

In 1973, two researchers, Robert Kahn at ARPA and Vinton Cerf at Stanford University, collaborated on an architecture that would permit these separately emerging networks to communicate with each other. The resulting Transmission Control Protocol and Internet Protocol, known as TCP/IP, provided a common platform of network-to-network communications which opened the way for the supernetwork we now know as the Internet.

Today, e-mail, data, audio and voice, and photo and video files all move easily between millions of computers, networks, and the entirety of the Internet using the common interface of TCP/IP. While every computer system isn't necessarily connected using Internet Protocol (some are private and secure from the public), ultimately, all computer networks eventually link up by some means to the Internet. That one decision, to create a standard linkage protocol, made the networked global economy possible.

Corporate and commercial sites and communities such as MySpace, Orkut, Facebook, and LinkedIn are subnetworks operating inside the Internet, with smaller circles of "friends" and associates forming groups inside them. Empowered nodes can choose with whom to form a group or community. That vast constellation of interlocking networks within networks is a driving dynamic of the new global economy and social order. Circles within circles create entirely new ways to organize markets, as we will see in the next chapter.

Net Complexity

If the sheer complexity of seemingly unlimited combinations and permutations of interrelating nodes isn't confusing enough, nodes in the network are also "Boolean," creating added complications.

Boolean or binary networks get their name from the nineteenth-century English mathematician, George Boole, who first deployed binary ("on-off, yes-no") operations to develop a logic now known as Boolean algebra. The state of a node, either on or off, adds additional complexity to the network because it changes performance and the speed and efficiency of information flows. As an example, you may have a friend in your social network, but if she is offline—her node is literally "off"—then your communications to her will hit a dead end and the circuit will be broken. Not only has your direct communication failed, your friend's dead link is of no use to the rest of the network and, however slightly, she slows the flow of information for all.

Networks work best when they are reciprocal, open, and big. The bigger, the better. Why? The more nodes that make up a network, the shorter the distance information must travel between individual nodes. More nodes make the transmission of information to all nodes more efficient. Thus, growth is the natural state of a network—the more people to interact with, the better. That is why the arrival of the next billion members to the network will make such a big difference in our lives. In essence, the bigger the network gets, the closer we all get to one another. That is the fundamental paradox of our times. As our world gets bigger, it also grows smaller.

The Way of the Virus

The Star Ferry linking Kowloon to Hong Kong's Central District crosses Victoria Harbor about every 10 minutes. On its choppy crossing, the small green and white ferryboat perilously negotiates one of the busiest shipping channels in the world, host to every conceivable form of floating apparatus, from gleaming tankers to floating sampans.

This unrelenting ship traffic is a testament to China's new role as an economic superpower. Hong Kong's shimmering skyline and its teeming streets are an enduring testament to human ingenuity. With nearly seven million people packed onto its relatively small geography, the island is one of the most densely populated places on earth.

But it is precisely that density, and the crowded farms and fowl markets within the city, that makes epidemiologists fear that Hong Kong could be the hot zone for H5N1—the bird flu—and the world's next deadly pandemic. For that reason, several times each week, mask-clad researchers in biohazard suits descend into the shadowy warrens and bustling bird markets to test for the virus.

The worry is that the virus might appear in the bird population without detection and then leap to humans through contact, the way it did in 1997. That steamy summer, 18 people took ill and six died from the virulent strain. Luck and fast action kept the virus from radiating around the planet like wildfire. As one of the planet's busiest ports of call, Hong Kong could launch and spread a flu outbreak very quickly, efficiently, and lethally, and the scope could be global.

In a densely populated "place," like our networked economy, information also acts like a virus. In March 2001, Hong Kong was ground zero for another kind of global outbreak—the ILOVEYOU computer virus, one of the most disruptive outbreaks to date. The computer bug was launched in a morning e-mail, and spread rapidly through the city's financial, commercial, and governmental networks. From there, it traveled with the sun, through East Asia, the Middle East, Europe, and on to the United States, causing service disruptions and havoc along the way.

While IT departments around the globe quickly dispensed patches that eventually quelled the ILOVEYOU outbreak, the lesson was clear about the behavior and vulnerabilities of a networked world. Hong Kong, like every major city, minor hamlet, and everything in between, is today part of a vast enmeshed network. What happens in Hong Kong doesn't stay in Hong Kong.

Viruses—whether flu bugs or computer bugs—are frightening because they are fast-moving, efficient, and relentless. They spread so quickly because they operate best in crowded, connected places—like big cities and the global network. But information viruses can be a positive force as well, rapidly disseminating early warnings, new ideas, and best practices to millions of recipients.

Viruses need help to spread. They need the cooperation of many hosts and many connectors. In order to understand how to tap the power of the network for your business—to make your message sticky and your company "contagious"—you need to appreciate why some information gets passed along and why other messages simply peter out.

Memes and Shared Culture

Ideas, products, and messages spread in ways that resemble the transmission of viruses. Biological analogies to the human network have been explored for decades, particularly on the subject of information passing and collective memory. Among the most cogent thinking has come from British biologist Richard Dawkins, who in 1976, published *The Selfish Gene*, which introduced his concept of the "meme."

Dawkins defined a meme as a cultural artifact, a shared idea passed along from person to person eventually worming its way into the collective consciousness. Catch phrases, commercial jingles, and jokes are examples of memes. Memes are potent because they "replicate," Dawkins held. That means they behave like viruses do, replicating themselves upon everyone they touch. It is that tune your friend whistled that you can't get out of your head, or that cliché you repeat over and again.

What is important to note is that Dawkins and others have theorized that we humans are uniquely susceptible to persuasive artifacts. When we are exposed to certain ideas, they grab us, and are not easily forgotten.

Knowing how and why memes are replicated is particularly important in this world of information overload, when we are each bombarded with more than 4,000 messages, images, and ideas a day. It is exceedingly useful to know why some ideas break through the noise, while others fail and become part of the wallpaper. And, in a world where information moves through a network with viral speed, but not always viral resilience or stickiness, it will prove invaluable for marketers to understand which forms of communications work and which do not.

It was a lot easier for a meme to get started back when Dawkins coined the term in the 1970s. The limited choices of media, and the narrow range of family programming on prime-time television, created a perfect environment for the fast spreading of memes. Because we had so few choices, we all watched the same shows, laughed at the same jokes, and endured the same commercials. In a decade like the 1970s, phrases from better advertisements and popular TV shows, like Alka Seltzer's "I can't believe I ate the whole thing," and the "Sweat Hogs" from the sitcom *Welcome Back Kotter*, entered the collective lexicon virtually overnight. It was not long after they aired on TV that people repeated the phrases at school and work, even wore T-shirts emblazoned with them. Those were halcyon days for memes.

Fast-forward to the present and we see a much more complicated environment. Thirty years after Dawkins first conceived of memes, the world is a changed place. Consider how many fewer mechanisms there were in 1976 to propagate memes. There were three national television networks and a couple of oddball UHF channels, a small number of national general-interest magazines and newspapers, and commercial radio largely found only on the AM spectrum.

Today, there are hundreds of television stations, multiple magazines for every niche interest, and multichannel satellite networks and personal MP3 playlists that are eclipsing radio airplay. In 1976, a top-rated television show like *Happy Days* might have pulled in 60 million viewers. Today, a comparable hit show like *CSI Miami* is lucky to attract six million viewers. And that doesn't factor in the Internet, with its 171 billion daily e-mails, 149 million unique Web sites, and 60 million blogs.

We are assaulted today with more messages per day than we would see in a month in 1976. Each message is competing for our scarce attention and a place in our memories. In this context, a meme seems a quaint concept. As Marshall McLuhan taught us, each new medium shapes messages differently, changes our experience, and requires a new culture to form around it. Blogs, vlogs, text messages, and podcasts are all new forms of peer-to-peer media that express cultural artifacts differently than anything before them. As we all move from receivers to connectors, from consumers to producers, we need a new word to capture our cultural yearnings.

In a 2006 blog, I proposed the adoption of the word *beme* for the cultural expressions of these noisier times. An intentional homage to Dawkins's meme, a beme is the shared language of our chaotic lives, an active message we send to one another in the hopes of making a connection. When we compose a personal profile on a community page, send along a product recommendation to a friend, or write a blog to articulate our passions, we are releasing a beme. As each of us gains the power to transmit bemes, the cultural landscape is going to get even more crowded.

It turns out that while my suggestion was embraced by many in the academic and research communities, it also raised more questions than I am yet able to answer.

As Tim Finin, faculty member at the University of Maryland, wrote in his blog, "It's useful to have a short term that doesn't already have meanings to refer to the spread of mental objects via the Internet. There are several basic problems to attack: How can we recognize new bemes? Can we track them back to their source or sources, who are influential in their spread? Can the spread be controlled? Can we find relations between bemes? What happens when bemes compete or cooperate? How can we track their mutation and evolution? Can they reproduce sexually? Is there a 'natural selection' at work for bemes? Are they like selfish genes? What are good metrics to measure their strength? How do bemes expire?"

Threadless T-shirts is a beme factory of sorts. Housed in a cavernous warehouse in Chicago's Northwest side, the company smartly uses the Internet to revolutionize the causal clothing business. Through its Web site, Threadless gives individual graphic designers a creative outlet, creates a mechanism to tap the wisdom of crowds, and at the same time secures a shrewd, risk-mitigating business model.

Started in 2000 by a duo of teenage graphic design students, Jake Nickell and Jacob DeHart, the company soon exploded onto the cultural scene. The business works this way: graphic designers—anyone at all really—can submit designs for new T-shirts to be printed and sold through the Threadless.com site. The submissions are juried by the 400,000 members of the Threadless community, and each week, the top seven vote-getters are selected and printed in a limited run available through the online store. The winning designers get a $1,500 prize and credit toward Threadless merchandise.

The company accepts as many as 200 T-shirt designs a day, of which 90 are chosen for the weekly bake-off. The community gets a week to complete the vote. Every Monday, printed versions of the winning designs are made available for sale on Threadless.com for a flat $15.

This clever model works the Internet on several fronts. It is community-based, democratic, and open; it empowers individual creativity—the customers design the products themselves; it harnesses the wisdom of crowds, who provide the marketing research and pick the products most likely to sell well. For their part, designers are trying to make T-shirts that connect with the largest possible audience. Thus, each shirt is a beme meant to connect with the current sensibilities of the Threadless community.

While even the trendiest of mainstream retailers, such as Urban Outfitters, Kitson, and Shop Intuition, struggle with long lead times and hit-or-miss seasonal buys, Threadless weekly prints short runs of well-tested products suggested by the consumers themselves. Since the audience knows itself best, more often than not the winning designs turn out to be winning sellers.

A different model, but one that also connects with a community vision, is Oddica. Oddica.com fast-prints T-shirts for fans of bands and retailers, and has begun to make shirts for fans of blogs and Web communities. The idea is simple: if you subscribe to a community or blog feed, why not express yourself in the offline world with a T-shirt?

For all of their success, the Threadless and Oddica examples also illustrate just how difficult it is to cement Dawkins' memes in our mass-customized world. With so many individual visions, so much personalized media, so many opportunities to be a producer and a consumer, a collective experience is much more elusive today than ever before. With so many empowered consumers on the Net, with so much noise from so many competing voices, just how do ideas get spread in the networked age? For the answer, we turn to the little-known science of rumors.

"An Irresistible Urge"

The most effective form of communication is word of mouth—when one person shares information directly with another. A particularly potent form of word-of-mouth communication is rumor-mongering. A rumor, it seems, is the sociological equivalent of a virus. That is, rumors spread from person to person quickly and efficiently under the right conditions.

When epidemiologists look at the transmission of a virus, they categorize a population into three groups: "infectives," "susceptibles," and "removed." Similarly, when modeling the epidemic spread of rumors, sociologists classify individuals as "spreaders," "susceptibles," and "stiflers." Spreaders have information to share, susceptibles have not yet received the information, and stiflers have received the information but do not want to share it further. In essence, those are the three types of nodes in any network—nodes that move information to those who await it, slowed by those who represent a dead end—and the three types of consumers you will encounter in the networked economy.

What explains the three types of people? Why do some people pass along information, why do people accept information from others, and why do some people opt out? In order to understand the motivations of today's networked consumer, we need to look at how and why rumors work.

It turns out that rumor-mongering—the passing along of provocative, often speculative information—may be the reason humans developed language in the first place (a form of social "grooming"). It is certainly as old as language and as deep-rooted in the human experience. As such, there have been quite a few studies on why people spread rumors and what they get out of the practice.

The most famous of these studies on rumor transmission were conducted by Gordon Allport and Leo Postman and summarized in their book *The Psychology of Rumor*, published in 1948. The most far-reaching assertion by the pair was "the basic law of rumor." Their "law" states that rumor strength will vary with the importance of the subject to the individual, times the ambiguity of the evidence pertaining to the topic at hand, expressed as $R \approx i \times a$. This formula is not intended to be scientific, but it does get us to consider the idea of "importance" to the spread of a rumor. In effect, we need to know why someone might think certain information was worth the time and effort to pass along.

Follow-on research based on Allport and Postman's work has explored patterns of rumor-mongering in groups of people. A prevailing, if not unanimous view, is that rumor-mongering may be a form of collective problem solving. In other words, people spread rumors in the hopes the group will take action on an underlying matter. For those people who place the norms of the group above all, this makes rumor spreading a beneficial, even noble, effort in service of the group interest.

Others think the opposite, and see personal gain motivating the rumor monger. In their view, at minimum the rumor spreader is deriving power or other satisfaction from his actions. This appears particularly true when one is either an expert on the subject or "first on the block" to learn something new. As to the impulse to spread rumors, researchers say that spreaders have "an irresistible urge" to pass along information. By contrast, stiflers are not so inclined, and like a Boolean "off" switch, these nodes can significantly impede the flow of a rumor.

Truemors.com, a new company from marketing maestro Guy Kawasaki, plugs directly into this vital impulse. With a call to "tell the world," Truemors provides users a fast and easy platform to post rumors, news, and sightings. As promised, the information is raw, unverified, and immediate: the fun is in teasing out the veracity for oneself.

So why is it important to understand rumors in order to be successful in the post–Jump Point economy? The simple answer is that one positive form of a rumor is a referral, and peer-to-peer referrals will be a big part of how shopping in the future will be conducted. Consumers are always more likely to buy based on the recommendation of a friend or colleague. The network makes that easier and quicker than ever. Just as important, the means of transmitting customer-to-customer buzz have gone mobile and multimodal; people today can seek consultation about a purchase via mobile phone while they are in the store aisle, or work with numerous friends on and offline to arrange a volume purchase, or text each other reviews in real time. Shopping and sharing—shopcasting—is destined to be a big part of the coming economy.

Shopping Gossip

Want to know where to get the best deal on a KitchenAid professional grade mixer, or verify the durability of a Hartman suitcase? Looking for a hard-to-find pair of Manolo Blahnik shoes or an offbeat gift for a colleague? What better way to get help than to ask people in the know—your fellow consumers? That's the premise behind social shopping sites such as Kaboodle, Wists, DealBundle, Whatsbuzzing, and StyleHive.

One company that adds a social community dimension to shopping is ThisNext. A private Los Angeles-based company, ThisNext allows users to discover new products and recommend them to each other, while at the same time cultivating new friendships with like-minded consumers. By simply adding a ThisNext button to your toolbar, you can tag and recommend any product you discover while cruising the Internet. The company emphasizes that it offers "real recommendations from real people."

Company founder Gordon Gould calls people who use ThisNext "curators," because they capture and share the new and novel with their friends: "I think the biggest growth area in the expanding definition of a socially networked friend is in what I call the *curatorial layer*. ThisNext focuses on [this] curatorial layer: we want you to friend/recommend people because they are socially proximate to you based on your interests, not just geography or happenstance. The curator layer is also where the greatest opportunity to leverage the collective wisdom of crowds resides."

As we will explore in the next chapter, we are likely to build communities of interest just as emotionally appealing as any other in our lives.

Ever since Silicon Valley venture capitalist Tim Draper asked the founders of start-up Hotmail to put a promotional link on the bottom of its e-mail form, there has been an obsession with "viral marketing." But, what does the term really mean? As we have seen, viral marketing taps the strengths of the network—the viral nature of the network—to spread information around. In a viral motion, communication is not broadcast; rather, it is passed along by the members themselves. As with the Foneros or the ThisNext communities, members of the network are full participants in the viral process. Information is shared willingly; its diffusion is seen as a virtue.

Therefore, in order to be viral, a marketing message needs to be propelled by people to other people. This necessity creates huge challenges to traditional marketing methods. Consumers today don't take marketing devices on faith; most will no longer even suffer advertisements gladly. And there is nothing worse than trying to manipulate this empowered public with its own tools.

The Astroturf Is Not Always Greener

By early August 2006 the little homemade movie had caused quite a stir with nearly 60,000 viewings on YouTube, and the world wanted to know more about the purported 29-year-old named "Toutsmith" who had created the film.

Entitled *Al Gore's Penguin Army*, the two-minute video was a send-up of the documentary *An Inconvenient Truth* featuring the proenvironment work of former U.S. vice president Al Gore. In the mini-"mockumentary," Gore is depicted as a sinister character who brainwashes penguins to do his bidding and blames global warming for everything from Middle East conflicts to starlet Lindsay Lohan's weight fluctuations.

The film appeared to be just another among the homemade spoof movies that made YouTube the runaway success it is. That, after all, is the appeal of YouTube: it is a platform for raw, unpolished authenticity. Home to thousands of amateur films of lip-synching students and wedding cake bloopers, all manner of music videos, feature film promos, outtakes, and even dull talking heads, YouTube can be a screening room for budding filmmakers. So it was not unusual that a higher-quality spoof like *Al Gore's Penguin Army* might be submitted by an amateur filmmaker. Except that it wasn't.

Journalists doing routine research on the man named Toutsmith tracked his Yahoo! e-mail address to a computer belonging to the DCI Group, a powerful Washington, D.C., public relations and lobbying firm that has clients that include oil companies like ExxonMobil Corporation. The DCI Group declined to say whether it made the film and refused to comment on its work for clients or even confirm its client list. ExxonMobil also denied having anything to do with the film. It was, however, obvious to all that the DCI Group had made the film in an attempt to discredit Gore, global warming, and *An Inconvenient Truth*.

Manipulations like *Al Gore's Penguin Army* are examples of *astroturfing*—attempting to manufacture grassroots support by deceptive means. Astroturfing in the networked world is anathema because it violates the code and spirit of peer-to-peer communications. As we will see in Chapter 8, in the networked age, nothing is more precious than authenticity and trust. Nevertheless, many companies and organizations already employ public relations tactics that boarder on astroturfing. Setting up fake "friends" in online communities and waging chat campaigns are examples of practices frowned upon by citizens of the network.

So, how do you get people talking about your company and sharing your product with others without the potential backlash of a high-risk game like astroturfing? How do you become contagious, your message viral, your growth pandemic? How can you be promotional and remain authentic at the same time? Those questions are answered in coming chapters.

Memes, Bemes, and Viral Machines

What should be clear by now is that the networked economy is not about servers and switches and routers; it is about people and organizations connecting directly with each other and making new things happen. As is the nature of networks, growth is an imperative. The more populated a network gets, the more efficient it gets, and the more useful it gets to everyone on the network.

Since communications are direct among network participants, information moves with the speed and fluidity of a virus. For cues on how and why information moves through a network, we look to the sociological counterpart of the virus, the rumor. Rumors spread through networks because participants willingly share the information with others—in fact, they have an urge to share what they know. People who share information are motivated to do so, but like all of us, they have limited attention and therefore limited capacity to share. I have suggested that information passed through a network should be given a name, beme. In an attention-starved age, only the most compelling beme will get through and be retained by the community. Creating a compelling message (or product or service), rising above the noise, winning a share of scarce attention, and then riding the "rumor express" is the essential challenge of doing business in the age of networks.

Theory is now about to become necessity. No company has the resources today to communicate to three billion or more people without support from the network. People must be willing and active participants in the transmission of the message, or the communication must be socialized within a community of interest. As we have seen, word-of-mouth communication works best among people who have established connections, who know each other. As members of a network are free to communicate with each other, so too are they free to associate with each other in useful ways.

Put all of this together and it is apparent that a key force in the next economy will be the formation of new and powerful affinity groups and special interest networks. Unbounded by geography, nationality, or demographic limitations, these social, professional, political, and consumer groupings will reshape the competitive landscape for all. In the next chapter we look at why and how people form subnetworks and what this means for managers and marketers everywhere.

Download This

- In the Jump Point economy, three billion producers and consumers will be connected directly in an unmediated global network.
- The fastest, most effective way to communicate in a network is virally—messages endorsed and propelled by the network members themselves.
- Information overload makes memorable, enduring communications—memes—exceedingly rare.
- New fast-moving mental objects—bemes—now populate the network.
- Network members need a motivation to pass on information to others.
- People-driven networks reject manipulation and attempts at fabricated buzz.

The Next Market Spaces

There are no masses, there are only ways of seeing people as masses.

—Raymond Williams

As we cross the Banpo Bridge over the Han River, the city of Seoul shimmers like a mirage in the heat.

It's early July and the temperatures have been soaring into the 100s; the grey-tinged air is windless. Exceptionally hot and muggy days like this one place extra demands on South Korea's already-challenged electrical grid.

As we make our way back to our hotel we hear rumors a government ordered a brownout tonight to conserve daytime energy. It's an inconvenience for visitors, to be sure. But the planned outage creates real anxiety for the locals.

You see, without electricity, their time spent on Cyworld that evening will be cut short.

Cyworld is a Web phenomenon in South Korea that is catching on around the world. Created by SK Communications, a subsidiary of SK Telecom, the Cyworld online community is a virtual megalopolis. In Cyworld, users create virtual personal spaces, called *minihompy* (literally "a small room"), that include a profile, blog, photo gallery, message board, and guestbook. A minihompy can further be decorated with furniture, wallpaper, and other items.

Citizens of Cyworld meet new friends and build relationships with like-minded people by linking their rooms to one another. Instant messaging is included in the service, so you can chat with visitors in real time, and members can enter Cyworld from a mobile phone.

Much like MySpace, Facebook, or Orkut, Cyworld is a platform for personal expression and social group forming, but in a more compelling three-dimensional environment. Indeed, with 19 million South Koreans using Cyworld on any given summer evening, it is easy to wonder which is more real: the hot, shimmering and chaotic world of Seoul, or the cool, ordered spaces of Cyworld?

Certainly the empty streets and sidewalks of Seoul on a busy Cyworld night argue for the latter . . . as does the amount of time users devote to their virtual existence versus their real-life one.

For example, since members appear as avatars, and avatars visit one another, the idea is to make one's room as hip and appealing as possible. Users typically decorate their spaces with digital furniture, TVs, and music features. Even one's avatar, or minime, can be adorned with new clothes, hair styles, and facial expressions. All of these items must be paid for in Cyworld's digital currency, *dotori* (Korean for "acorn"), which have a basic unit value of 10 cents each.

As we shall see, those acorns add up.

As *BusinessWeek Asia* points out, Cyworld has a viral construct to it:

One feature that has helped Cyworld take off is "wave riding." It works like this: When you're reading posts on bulletin boards or looking at photo files, you can click on the name of someone who has added a remark or photo you find interesting and you'll be transported to that person's digital room. If you like their art or music, you can introduce yourself and put in a request to become a "cybuddy." If accepted, you can use your buddy's goodies—from art to photos—on your own page. The [resulting] chain of wave-riding visits creates communities on the Net, which often develop into clubs of common interest in the real world: clubs for fishing, bike riding, and going to jazz performances, among others.

As a result of its welcoming premise and sticky features, Cyworld by 2007 engaged *90 percent* of South Korea's teenagers, and an astonishing *50 percent* of the nation's total population. Those little acorns? According to Gamestudy.org, they added up to $80 million in 2006.

This profit dynamic has not been lost on other enterprises, as some 30,000 businesses have opened shop on Cyworld, offering more than a half million digital products and content packages for sale. With 200,000 songs sold daily, Cyworld is also now South Korea's biggest music outlet.

Cyworld and online communities like it are reshaping the global landscape. They are helping to create new economic geographies, or "marketspaces," made up of like-minded, similarly disposed people who, given the right opportunity and message, may well buy what you sell in big numbers.

The rise, and ultimate dominance, of these marketspaces will be the most visible feature of the Jump Point and the transformed culture that follows.

The Power of Association

People are by nature social. We like crowds. That's one important reason why, today, most people on earth live in urban rather than rural settings. Even when we complain about the ill effects of congestion—crime, pollution, and traffic—more often than not, we choose to live in cities, instead of the countryside, in densely populated neighborhoods rather than sparsely populated ones.

Why? Because more people mean more options, choices, combinations, and possibilities.

As it is on the street, so it is online.

Social Web sites such as MySpace, Facebook, Bebo, Xanga, and hi5 attract people who want to communicate, collaborate, and share with others with whom they have or may develop an affinity. Online virtual communities have existed on the Internet for more than a quarter of a century. The Well started in 1985, and before that, Usenet newsgroups began popping up in 1979. As in the real world, people create or join communities wherein they can exercise social, professional, romantic, and familial connections. And, as it was at Catal Huyuk 9,000 years ago, we are building new online "cities" to contain our ambitions, aspirations, and pride. But even more than the value derived from a variety of contacts, there are psychic rewards to community. In these information-saturated times, it is becoming harder and harder to create a shared sense of culture.

Memes are harder than ever to create, and common frames of reference are more difficult to achieve. That explains the wild growth of all manner of social media, from blogs, vlogs, photo and video sharing, and particularly communities. In fact, the Internet's great twenty-first century surprise has been the rise—indeed, the growing primacy—of *affinity groups*.

Even in the early days of the DARPANET and ARPANET, the ancestors of the modern Internet, forward thinkers were already predicting that the Web would be a powerful tool for research, information access, and even retailing. But almost no one saw the coming of gigantic online assemblages of millions of people playing computer games together, business networking, or sharing some of the most private information imaginable.

Howard Rheingold, writing about "virtual communities" in the early 1990s, was an exception. He was prescient enough to predict that people would use the Internet to link up in loose communities through common interests, attitudes, and beliefs. A good guess, but he still made the classic mistake of most futurists in the digital age of seeing technology merely as a way of supercharging existing trends.

What actually happened was a small Jump Point, an early glimpse of the big one to come. The Web enabled people to reach down into their most elemental needs and create new, almost infinitely scalable, social institutions that leveraged the unique power of the technology. MySpace, Facebook, Twitter, YouTube, LinkedIn, Bebo; none of these enterprises existed in 2000. By 2007, MySpace had more than 200 million accounts. If it were a nation, it would rank fifth, larger than Russia and Japan. And it reached this size with no advertising, almost no marketing, and a staff equal in size to that of a suburban post office.

And MySpace wasn't alone. By 2007, Facebook had 28 million visitors per month. YouTube was sharing well more than 100 million videos per day. And Twitter, begun in mid-2006 and offering the most elemental experience imaginable—posting a real-time up-to-the-minute diary on one's activities on a cell phone or laptop computer—jumped from zero to 9 million users in less than a year.

Meanwhile, the computer gaming world, as it moved online, discovered the same phenomenon. Games like Counter-Strike, an online group gaming modification of Half-Life, found itself on any given evening in 2006 with 65 thousand kids from around the world playing one another in the virtual arena. Some particularly adept young players even found sponsors and turned their game into careers. Another virtual environment, Second Life, which offers users the chance to create a separate online existence in three dimensions, not only attracted two million residents, but also created the Web's first virtual land baron when Anshe Chung sold more than a $1 million in land (actually pixilated representations of land). By mid-2007, companies such as IBM were even holding "off-site" meetings of their employees' avatars on Second Life.

And those were just the most visible manifestations of the sudden rise of online affinity groups. Around the world on the Web, thousands of other, smaller groups were founded as well, coalescing around everything from photo sharing to home schooling to social activism to deviant sex.

Clearly this activity was not merely an extension of an existing cultural trend. Something more profound was taking place. Just as the shift from analog to digital, as described by Moore's law, had supercharged the last two decades of the twentieth century, now, as described by the laws of networks, centralized and structured social institutions were rapidly being replaced by self-proliferating affinity groups. Moreover, those laws also suggested, as with the exponential improvements in the computer chip over the previous 30 years, that this process of self-proliferation would skyrocket in the decade, subsuming one traditional institution after another.

And that is precisely what is now happening around us. Human beings, as we appreciate now more than ever, have a primal need to get together, to share their thoughts, swap ideas, and to feel a part of something bigger than themselves. But historically, that impulse has been circumscribed by a host of factors: lack of mobility, difference in language, limited resources, and, ultimately, limited choices.

The Web already has swept most of those obstacles away, and it will soon take care of the rest. And with that, affinity groups will quickly become the dominant social force in the emerging world economy, changing how we think about markets, fads, social movements, and, ultimately, power. According to Online Media Daily, by 2011, nearly half of adult users and 84 percent of teens will be members of social sites.

Who would have guessed that the template of our future would turn out to be the Rotary Club?

Let's Be "Friending"

Turning again to Howard Rheingold, he also observed that online affinities form "when people carry on public discussions long enough, with sufficient human feeling, to form webs of personal relationships." Moreover, he claimed, "Every cooperative group of people exists in the face of a competitive world because that group of people recognizes there is something valuable that they can gain only by banding together."

That virtual public works project, Wikipedia, defines endeavors like its own as "a social aggregation with a common interest, idea, task or goal that interacts in a virtual society across time, geographical and organizational boundaries." In that sense, Wikipedia draws people with a desire to build something bigger than themselves. These are modern-day cathedral builders, since Wikipedia, and efforts like it, will never be completed in anyone's lifetime.

But, even if we accept that people want to cluster together, why are they drawn to one particular community over another?

In a pioneering study, Cornell researchers led by Lars Backstrom asked: "What are the structural features that influence whether individuals will join communities, which communities will grow rapidly, and how do the overlaps among pairs of communities change over time?"

Their conclusion: "We find that the propensity of individuals to join communities, and of communities to grow rapidly, depends in subtle ways on the underlying network structure. For example, the tendency of an individual to join a community is influenced not just by the number of friends he or she has within the community, but also crucially by how those friends are connected to one another."

In other words, knowing someone already in the group is a big reason to join, but not knowing everyone in the group is equally important. Beyond the feelings of affiliation and belonging that come from joining a group where preexisting friendships exist, people want to be introduced to their friends' friends and beyond. These relationships with people we are not close to—those a few degrees away—are what sociologist Mark Granovetter calls "weak ties," and are what makes a network truly dynamic and useful.

The dawning influence of weak ties has changed for many the simple practice of befriending someone new. Today many people have turned meeting new people into an active campaign called "friending."

Like riding that wave in Cyworld, friending means turning everyone your network touches into a "friend." Part of this is related to status: many community sites publicly recognize how many friends or associates you have—a straw poll of sorts on one's popularity. In these situations, there is an impetus to show as many friends as possible.

But there is much more going on here. In her studies on how college students used communities like MySpace, Facebook, and Friendster, Danah Boyd has found some interesting responses to the friending practice. A fellow at the Annenberg Center for Communication at the University of Southern California, Boyd says her study subjects gave many reasons for accepting friending overtures from others:

1. You can make actual friends.
2. You can increase the number of acquaintances, family members, and colleagues.
3. It would be socially inappropriate to say no because you know them.
4. Having lots of friends makes you look popular.
5. It's a way of indicating that you are a fan (of that person, band, product, etc.).
6. Your list of friends reveals who you are.
7. Their profile is cool, so being friends makes you look cool.
8. Collecting friends lets you see more people (Friendster).
9. It's the only way to see a private profile (MySpace).
10. Being friends lets you see someone's bulletins and their friends-only blog posts (MySpace).
11. You want them to see your bulletins, private profile, and private blog (MySpace).
12. You can use your friends list to find someone later.
13. It's easier to say yes than no.

Clearly, a big factor is *process accordance*—befriending people on some sites results in more network privileges. Other responses show the power of tribal etiquette.

But perhaps the real conclusion is that something more primal is going on. People on a network are nodes, and as we have seen, nodes are driven to connect with other nodes; networks want to grow. People like to be connected; they like to see how far their network can be stretched. This objective has always been true; the Internet simply makes the machinery more transparent. In that sense, active friending may be a natural, even vital, part of being in a network.

So, what explains the wide popularity of a few giant communities? Simply put: people are attracted to what other people are attracted to. Economists call this drive *preferential attachment*—the more popular a site becomes, the more people are drawn to it . . . or as we have all observed at some point, "the rich get richer." As with the celebrities who are famous for being famous and for that fact alone gain even more fame, sites that suddenly become popular draw out the conformers and the curious and continue to gain popularity.

But preferential attachment can also have unexpected consequences—especially if it takes off on a tangential path during its creation. Take the example of Orkut. Launched as a social networking site by Google, shortly after the site went live, it inexplicably became popular with a large contingent of Portuguese speakers. This attracted more Portuguese speakers, to the point where those who did not understand the language became alienated and went elsewhere. The Orkut community today consists mostly of Brazilians.

Though we are just four years into this new online affinity group phenomenon, it is already becoming obsolete, supplanted by something even newer. In particular, we are already seeing a shift away from the one-size-fits-all community to more tailored offerings. This trend is going to continue through the Jump Point.

Cities of Our Own Making

As an undergraduate at Boston University, I studied urban dynamics as part of my major. I wanted to know what made cities and communities tick. I read Jane Jacobs and Lewis Mumford, and I knew that cities thrived on the density and diversity of people. But, given a choice, what draws us to a particular city?

By midcareer, as a marketing executive in Silicon Valley, I began to apply the same curiosity to online communities. With the power to form communities of interest at will, why, I wondered, do people join the communities they do? What keeps them in a particular community? How likely are these communities to endure over time?

In the 1930s, sociologist Emile Durkheim considered how people organize themselves in a modern society. He observed that groups tended to fall into two organizing models he termed *mechanical solidarity* and *organic solidarity*.

Mechanical solidarity occurs when people feel connected through similar upbringing, work, educational and religious training, or lifestyle. Such groups tend to be very homogenous, even rigid in their beliefs. They may include professional associations and church groups.

Organic solidarity, on the other hand, derives from choice; people with differing skills or "complementarities," band together because they believe there is strength in their diversity. In these types of groups, people associate not because they see the world identically, but because they have just enough in common to make their differences an asset.

Additionally, groups brought together organically tend to be the "wisest" type of crowd and make the best collective decisions. As James Surowiecki points out in *The Wisdom of Crowds*, "groups that are too much alike find it harder to keep learning, because each member is bringing less and less new information to the table. Homogenous groups are great at doing what they do well, but they become progressively less able to investigate alternatives."

In essence, mechanically organized groups are one-trick ponies, while organically composed groups bring enough variety and disparity to decision making that they typically achieve better outcomes.

There is of course a third way communities come together; *happenstance*. By accident of birth we all arrive at a location decided by others and that geography can define and sometimes confine us. One reason the Internet has proven to be so extraordinarily important is that it mitigates happenstance, making it possible to live outside the confines of geography and to associate with people we might never meet in our real-world neighborhoods.

The mass adoption of the Internet is allowing the post–Jump Point economy to revolve around cross-cultural, cross-national, cross-demographic communities of interest. These "cities of affinity" will provide a rich ground for marketers.

Passion-Centric Communities and Audiences of One

In some ways, the big, generic communities like MySpace, Facebook, Gaia Online, Friendster, Multiply, Xanga, Netlog, Piczo, hi5, and Bebo are all "starter" communities—extended schoolyards (complete with preening and posturing) where we get to experience a new world and learn the new social rules before graduating to better things. The communities of the future will look very different from these prototypes.

As we approach the Jump Point, new vertical and passion-centric communities are sprouting up all over the world. These sites reflect the future of social media. Beyond the general-purpose social communities, themed sites allow people to organize themselves according to their specific needs or interests. These sites are more useful, manageable, and engaging. These will be the true marketspaces of the future.

Communities are also developing for every age group and season of life. Eons, for example, is a social networking site for baby boomers over the age of 50; college kids swarm to MyCollegeDaily, Pick-A-Prof, and RateMyProfessors.com; Sconex is aimed at high school students, and dayZLoop.com at teen girls; and "tween"-targeted sites offering greater parental controls and oversight include Club Penguin and Whyville. After graduation, you can keep in touch through Classmates.com, myYearbook.com, and Reunion.com, or build new professional networks through the likes of LinkedIn, Ryze, and Ecademy.

Religious affiliations are among the deepest in life, and they will be represented online as well. Koolanoo is a social networking site attracting and focusing on Jewish people, Muslims can find community at MuslimSpace, and Christians gather at eBible.com and MyChurch.org.

There are self-help communities like inpowr, traineo, SparkPeople, 43 Things, Tools To Life, Sawlogs, and ObesityHelp, a site for severely overweight people looking to network and develop strategies to lose weight. Gay, lesbian, bisexual, and transgender sites include GLEE.com, FabFemme, OurChart, Olivia.com, and SocialButter. Ethnic sites include BlackPlanet.com, MiGente.com, ElHood, and AsianAve.com.

Mothers and mothers-to-be can find answers and share stories in communities like CafeMom, Maya's Mom, MothersClick, MommyBuzz, ParentsConnect, Famster, and Minti. Sports fans can trash talk, debate, and chest beat within the safe confines of communities like FanPage, FanNation, FanSpot, Tired and Tested, NHL Connect, Takkle, SportsMates, FastBreakClub, Bikespace, Sportsvite, Gimme20, MyTeamCaptain, YourSportsFan, FitLink, and UltraFan.

Do-It-Yourselfers, or DIYers, can share techniques and get answers in communities that serve both the handy and the tool-challenged, such as Answerbag, eHow, SoYouWanna, and ExpertVillage, a YouTube for self-help videos.

Besides the rapidly growing Cyworld, global virtual communities are also flexing their muscles. Mixi, Japan's largest social networking site (SNS), has nearly eight million members. In Taiwan, Wretch has become wildly popular because so many celebrities, musicians, actors, top models, and politicians host home pages there. New neighborhoods in India, like Froppy and Minglebox.com, are gaining momentum. In China, Wealink calls itself a "social capital bank" and connects the growing business community there. Zhanzou, a Facebook-like community, had seven million members by 2007. Australians are congregating at StudentFace, 3eep, and Babbello.

Music-related communities offer something for virtually every musical taste: Last.fm, ProjectOpus, Jamglue, Imeem, PureVolume, ReverbNation, MOG, YourSpins, Qloud, iLike, Bandwagon.co.uk, Jamendo, Pandora, Rapspace.tv, uPlayMe, FineTune, MP3.com, MusicHawk, Splice, and FIQL.

As these new spaces emerge to replace older social forms, it is important to note that these communities hinge on a vital ethic: reciprocal knowledge sharing. As Henry Jenkins observed in *Convergence Culture: Where Old and New Media Collide*:

> New forms of community are emerging, however; these new communities are defined through voluntary, temporary, and tactical affiliations, reaffirmed through common intellectual enterprise and emotional investments. Members may shift from one group to another as their interests and needs change, and they may belong to more than one community at the same time. These communities, however, are held together through mutual production and reciprocal exchange of knowledge.

All of this suggests the Internet is already self-organizing into a network of networks, a broad universe of "small worlds" defined by affinities. For every interest, there will be a community. Why is this organizing important? How people—your customers—organize themselves in communities of interest means everything when it comes to doing business. While markets, as always, are conversations between buyers and sellers, soon those conversations will happen in new places.

A March 2007 survey by online developer Communispace bears out this trend. The survey of 26,539 online social community members showed that the more intimate the community, the more people participated. The results indicated that 86 percent of the people who logged on to communities with fewer than 500 members made contributions: they posted comments, started dialogues, participated in chats, brainstormed ideas, shared photos, and more. Only 14 percent merely logged in to observe, or "lurk."

By contrast, on large, public sites, blogs, and message boards, the ratio was reversed, as the vast majority of visitors did not contribute. In a typical online forum, for example, just 1 percent of visitors contributed, while the other 99 percent lurked.

"Big public communities may attract more eyeballs, but they may not be the answer for marketers who are looking for deep engagement with customers," concludes Julie Wittes Schlack, Communispace vice president of innovation and research.

Motivate, Mobilize, and Monetize

It was a beautiful fog-free day in San Francisco and I was enjoying a late lunch with the charismatic Lee Smith, West Coast president for music juggernaut Live Nation, and our friend and music impresario, Ted Cady.

Live Nation is the largest producer of concerts in the United States, so the conversation naturally came around to the major changes taking place in the music business. The animated conversation was like trading field notes about a newfound asteroid hurtling toward Earth.

Always a tough way to make a buck, the rock music industry is being challenged today at all levels. Concert sales are down, music stores are vanishing, and new acts can't command an audience the way the classic rockers once could. Besides all that, bands can now afford to do a lot of the recording work themselves, using readily available, professional-strength software like Pro Tools, Frooty Loops, and ACID. In fact, albums today can be cut and produced, labels printed, and products sold through online stores—even directly through iTunes—all without the involvement of traditional record labels.

Everybody in the vast interconnected web of the music industry, from recording studio executives to videographers to booking agents, is feeling the heat of the Jump Point. Naturally, the lunch conversation eventually zeroed in on the direct and Web-enabled business models being adopted by today's musicians. No longer willing to be passively managed or insulated from their fans, artists have taken to opening lines of direct contact and communication—and commerce—with their fan bases. That means a whole new world of direct-via-Internet sales of compact discs, concert tickets, and merchandise that is dramatically shaking up the hidebound music biz. These days, bands have far greater control of their total businesses, from ticket sales to T-shirts and tube socks.

I asked my companions what would happen if bands sold tickets for some shows exclusively through their fan sites. They thought about it for a moment, and then acknowledged that it could change everything. After the costs of talent and venue, the next biggest cost to produce a concert is promotion. And, even with a big promotion budget, you can never be sure how well a show will sell. Many a concert seat has been left empty because a show was promoted well but to the wrong people (or more precisely, not promoted to enough of the right people).

But there are devoted fans out there eager to see their favorite bands. Top new acts like The Killers, Fall Out Boy, Jimmy Eat World, and AFI have large and enthusiastic fan bases. Megasites like Musictoday have fan "sitelets" for numerous new bands, as well as for established acts, such as the Rolling Stones and Dave Matthews Band. As these fan communities grow, it may be possible to sell out entire shows, even a tour, without ever enduring the costs or risks of traditional promotions. This development will put the squeeze on the intermediaries, but the consumers and the artists will win.

In reaction to high markups from vendors like Ticketmaster, rock renegades such as Pearl Jam are already using their fan site to circumvent the middlemen. And, as the benefits of belonging to the fan community become widely apparent, more people will join and a virtuous cycle will perpetuate.

Proof that social communities can be monetized is already on the rise. A May 2007 report from online commerce analysts Hitwise shows that community site MySpace has become second only to Google in driving traffic to shopping sites. That means more MySpace members went on to shop in online retail stores than did people who searched for products on Yahoo! or MSN. The collective impact of passion-centric, interest-driven sites will be profound after the Jump Point.

A Community for Everyone?

Blame it on our "new" brains—that grey matter atop our craniums called the *neocortex* that evolved last and made us uniquely human. It is this area of the brain that appears to determine the maximum size of the community with which we are able to conduct a meaningful relationship.

As British anthropologist Robin Dunbar has observed, there is a "cognitive limit to the number of individuals with whom only one person can maintain stable relationships. This limit is a direct function of the relative neocortex size and that this in turn limits group size."

Based on his study of primates—and validated by other natural populations such as a company of soldiers, a Neolithic settlement, a terrorist group like al-Qaeda, and a Pennsylvania Hutterite colony—Dunbar's number is 150 (147.8). That means we can hold a meaningful two-way relationship with about 150 people before things get too complicated and require hierarchies.

The Dunbar number is validated by the behavior of such self-organizing groups as guilds in online multiplayer games. In a study of behavior on multiuser dungeon game Ultima Online, members settled into groups of between 60 and 150 members. Players began to see diminishing returns—politics and positioning—after groups reached that 150-member plateau, and they started to peel off to form new groups.

What is the significance of the Dunbar number to the future of social media? It is one of the paradoxes of the Jump Point: while scale makes the value *in* the network greater to all, the value *of* the network to the individual grows as it gets smaller. In other words, individuals find it most useful to be part of narrower nodes within the wider network where they can congregate with like-minded people. That requires subdividing the vastness of the global network up into smaller, more manageable worlds. It is that impulse that helps explain the spectacular growth in friend-to-friend publishing, blogs, message boards, wikis, podcasts, and vlogs.

Does this mean we will see a world punctuated by thousands of smaller communities linking to larger ones? *Yes.* As we have seen, that is the very nature of nodes, concentric clusters and networks. After the Jump Point, we will all belong to communities defined by us, populated by an optimum number of material contacts, focused and diverse, guarded and open, at the same time.

Meanwhile, technology is cooperating. After all, we use our new tools to make our next tools. Self-organizing communities are getting easier to manage thanks to open source content management systems like Joomla!, Drupal, Plone, and PostNuke. These platforms, and others like them, will help us all to create the circle of friends that best defines our lives, values, hopes, and dreams.

What have we seen from the behavior of networks and the communities they create? The networked world is getting bigger and smaller at the same time. Even as people form and join subdivisions of their own design, there remains an ongoing tension between big and broad and small and specialized. That's because people behave online just as they do offline. Cities offer more variety, opportunities, and possibilities than do suburban and rural areas. And while there are distinct drawbacks to city life, most of us apparently don't mind them enough to go upcountry or disappear off the grid. While a city that gets too big can start to produce diminishing returns and could experience an exodus, most urbanites cope by picking a neighborhood that works for them and honing in on it. And so it goes.

One thing is clear; a network of three billion people will be far different than a network one-half or one-third that size. The world after the Jump Point will be more dynamic, complicated, productive, and dangerous than the world today. As we consider the impact of the coming networked economy and its unprecedented three billion nodes, it will be fair to ask, "What have we wrought?"

Will this enormous new world divide itself into new guilds, or ghettos, or gulags? Will the next economy's new strengths create corresponding new weaknesses? Will we of the first billion have the capacity, the forethought, and the will to use the Jump Point moment to think anew about the current state of the world and the human condition and make a change?

Clearly, a major change is approaching. It will be at times exciting, at times jarring and disorienting. In the next section of this book, we will consider in turn five of the major discontinuities facing people, organizations, and society as they pass through the Jump Point.

- ▪ The first of these discontinuities will be the escalating battle for our attention. It will be an arms race being waged in the noisiest marketplace in human history. New battle lines are already being drawn between increasingly desperate marketers on one side and those who argue for sanity and balance on the other.

- The second new challenge will come as our relationship with time changes. "Internet time" used to refer to the speed at which things could get done online. But the real point of Internet time is that it perpetuates the *permanent now*. To borrow from computer-age sage Ted Nelson, we live in an "intertwinguled" time, when here and now and past and future can seem to be happening all at once.

- Third, mobility and online presence are redefining the landscape, making it easier to locate but harder to connect with moving targets.

- The fourth discontinuity will be the breakwater of cultures the Internet represents and what this means for business and society.

- Finally, with the fifth discontinuity, we will be forced to face the vulnerabilities of globalization. How life behind the online veil is turning "trust" into the world's most valuable currency of exchange.

Download This

- People are self-organizing online into new market spaces.
- There will be a community themed for virtually every interest and affinity.
- There is a practical limit to the size of themed communities—fewer than 500 people is optimal.
- People join communities for a host of reasons—networking with new people is a deciding factor.
- Marketers will not gain access to these communities except by invitation.

PART TWO

The Five Discontinuities

The future always arrives too fast . . . and in the wrong order.
— ALVIN TOFFLER

When economist Joseph Schumpeter, the patron saint of the digital era, coined the phrase "creative destruction," he was deliberate in his choice of words. It was his belief that *change*—the good kind of change, the kind that spawns new markets, fuels new growth, and kicks the doors down to the future—is by necessity a painful, sometimes combative, and often bloody process.

In *The Shock of the Old: Technology and Global History Since 1900,* British historian David Edgerton, challenges the big-bang "innovation-centric" account of technology adoption and observes that new and old technologies almost always coexist together. That is true partly because new technologies take time to assert themselves; despite cases of romantic revisionism, the moment of invention is rarely a world-changing event.

More importantly, technologies create cultures around them, and cultures quite frequently coexist in human history. But that doesn't mean people are fools. While it is true that we continue to find uses for horses and small arms in combat, for example, we don't continue to design war strategy entirely around them. No, technology adoption is a gradual process—until it isn't. That is the definition of a Jump Point; the moment when an emerging culture becomes the dominant culture and all of us move forward a little bit together. Today, the culture of the network is rapidly approaching its crossover as the world's dominant view.

When they do arrive, Jump Points are necessarily startling and disruptive periods. They upset the status quo, threaten existing leaders, and rattle the complacent. There is no question that the coming Jump Point will wreak havoc on many industries—and many lives. Most of our prevailing business assumptions will be challenged and a whole set of new ones will be born as businesses everywhere make the Jump.

This part looks inside the Jump itself—at five major discontinuities facing all businesses: attention value, time-shifting, abundant thinking, mashup culture, and the primacy of trust. Each disjunction will have a profound, often unforeseen impact on all companies, including yours.

4

The Attention Wars

What information consumes is rather obvious: it consumes the attention of its recipients. Hence a wealth of information creates a poverty of attention.

—HERBERT SIMON

The aphrodisiac of the future will be full attention.

—LINDA STONE

The house lights cut to black and the crowd roar echoes deep into the night. Instantly, beams of brilliant light scud along the stage, while showering pyrotechnics explode from the flanks. Symphonic surround sound wells up from the theater. Already the senses are owned by the pounding beat, the metallic smell of smoke, and the vibrant laser filaments cutting through the haze.

A giant video screen appears along the entire length of the stage, revealing a familiar digital landscape. The crowd roars again. Two lone figures with game controllers take downstage positions and soon begin battling each other—and alien life forms—on the giant screenscape. The orchestra accompanies their every move in real-time renditions of the original game soundtrack. Throughout the performance, the audience is enveloped in sound and lights, buffeted by waves of game-playing tension. After chanting knowingly to every song and being enraptured in their collective moment, the crowd streams out into the streets at the end of the night, thoroughly spent and totally exhilarated.

The extravaganza is *Video Games Live!*, a tour-de-force show featuring music from the most popular video games performed by leading orchestras and choirs, combining video game footage and music arrangements with synchronized lighting, special solo performers, electronic percussionists, and unique interactive segments.

Video Games Live!, you might think, has taken place in Trenton or Columbus or Canoga Park, or some other big suburban center in the United States—drawing gamers and geeks out of their dimly lit apartments and parents' basements from miles around. But you'd be wrong: this show was held in São Paolo, Brazil, in November 2006, at the acoustically perfect Via Funchal. The orchestra: the prestigious Petrobras Sinfônica, with a special appearance by "video game pianist" Martin Leung, who has performed favorite compositions from the *Final Fantasy* video game.

That this show has been held in Brazil (and repeated in cities around the developed and developing world) speaks volumes to the global cultural phenomenon that video games have become. That there are now enough consumers sufficiently well versed in video games to fill auditoriums and even stadiums to hear orchestral renditions of game soundtracks is yet another fascinating insight. But it is the intrinsic nature of the event that is most telling.

Video Games Live! calls itself an *immersive event*, because the combination of live music, video, game playing, and pyrotechnics consumes all your senses and your total attention. A traditional concert experience simply would not be enough for the *gamerati*—music without video, laser, and smoke machines would be, well, just music. Today's audiences are accustomed to having their attention overwhelmed; they want to be overwhelmed with experience. They are comfortable with a multiplicity of concurrent stimuli; at home and work they multitask easily between e-mails, virtual meetings, and Webcasts; and their social lives are a blur of texting, game playing, videos, and hours of unfettered kvetching with friends, all to the beat of their iPods.

Remember this image of *Video Games Live!* because it is the look of our common future. It is as if the new consumers already sense this, building a high tolerance for information overload, in preparation for the world after the Jump Point.

Attention: The New Crude Oil

The clinical term is "cognitive overload."

Our daily lives have become centered on what scientists call *information transfer*, and the rate of that transfer is accelerating, its volume increasing exponentially. Between the Internet, e-mail, SMS (short message service) messages, podcasts, TV, radio, print, outdoor advertising, cell phone calls, and plain old conversation, each of us now is flooded with 4,000 messages per day, one million per year. Today, we are subjected to more information in just 12 months than our great grandparents negotiated in a lifetime. The modern challenge is to make room for it all. As the late Neil Postman worried:

> What started out as a liberating stream has turned into a deluge of chaos. The tie between information and action has been severed. Information is now a commodity that can be bought and sold, or used as a form of entertainment, or worn like a garment to enhance one's status. It comes indiscriminately, directed at no one in particular, disconnected from usefulness; we are glutted with information, drowning in information, have no control over it, don't know what to do with it.

And we only have ourselves to blame. The truth is that we produce nearly as much information as we consume. Whether at work in increasingly information-intensive roles, or in the exchange of family photos on Flickr, home-made videos on YouTube, homespun opinions on a Typepad blog, or any of a dozen other citizen media outlets, we are each contributing to this information tsunami. Today, society produces an *exabyte* of information a year. Never heard of the term? An exabyte is one billion gigabytes, or 1,000,000,000,000,000,000 bytes of data. That's roughly 250 million bytes of data for every human on the planet.

To put that in perspective, consider that book this holds about one megabyte. That means we are producing 250 books like this one, of new content, every year for every man, woman, and child on earth. Warren Thorngate, a Canadian psychologist, observed:

> Because information has been proliferating at such an enormous rate, we have reached the point where attention is an extremely scarce resource, so scarce that extreme measures—from telemarketing to terrorism—have proliferated as fast as information just to capture a bit of it.

That is the great information paradox: because time is fixed, attention is a zero-sum game; we only have so much time in a day, a year, a lifetime. That makes attention—one's ability, capacity, and choice to focus one's cognition—far scarcer than knowledge. In fact, our whole economy has now come to revolve around attention. Indeed, attention has now become the most precious nonrenewable natural resource on earth.

The idea of placing a value on attention, of an "attention economy," has been around for some time now. No one has written more cogently about the value of attention to the new network construct than author Michael H. Goldhaber. In 1997 he wrote: "Attention is scarce because each of us has only so much of it to give and it can come only from us—not machines, computers or anywhere else." He added, "What people do demand as privacy now is freedom from having to pay attention, not from being seen but seeing what they don't want to."

Because attention is finite and easily consumed, it gets scarcer every day. And that means that the emerging post–Jump Point economy will be populated by the attention-poor/cash-rich and the attention-rich/cash-poor. In other words, the world soon will be divided into those people who can pay attention and those who cannot.

What does that imply for business? It means that your primary customers today can no longer afford to pay attention to you. Meanwhile, those who can pay attention to your pitch may not be your true customers.

To illustrate that point, consider a mass study, conducted in 2003, of Internet advertising click-through rates in the United States by region. As it turned out, the leaders were not the big populous states or the big media markets; they were states with relatively little attention competition. According to Advertising.com, the five states with the best click-through rates were New Mexico, West Virginia, Arkansas, Montana, and Wyoming.

Again, your strongest click-through rates may come from your weakest prospects. So, if your business model is still dependent on the same old tactics and the same tired metrics—and fails to recognize the primacy of attention—it could be a recipe for disaster.

Awash in "Cruft"

Ours is a complicated relationship with information.

We welcome ever-more of it with open arms (and eyes and ears) at the same time as we abhor it. We can't imagine living without our mobile phones, but decry their hold over us. We permit always-on technology to connect us, yet we bristle at the shackles it creates.

As we all have come to learn, information is a double-edged sword. As the crowd at *Video Games Live!* underscores, we clearly love our information tsunami even as it is drowning us.

Many of us would readily call ourselves information "junkies" thanks to our addiction to the media stream—and award ourselves that title proudly. In that sense, we are not unwitting victims of this onslaught; instead, we are willing participants and codependents, equal parts pushers and junkies.

The problem is not simply too much information, it is too much unwanted and irrelevant information. *Cruft* is the hacker word for bloated or redundant code. In that sense, our world is quite a crufty place, and consumers are becoming increasingly shell-shocked from it. The future of marketing will be about removing the cruft, eliminating the waste, and sharpening the delivery of the right message to the right consumer. Any extraneous communication will not only be wasted, it will alienate and offend the receiver.

How can we keep up? The answer is: we can't. At best, we are coping with information overload by skimming and skipping and by giving only partial attention to any particular demand made upon us. Former Microsoft executive Linda Stone calls this fugue state we now live in *continuous partial attention*.

Author Thomas Friedman explains, "Continuous partial attention is when you are on the Internet or cell phone or BlackBerry while also watching TV, typing on your computer and answering a question from your kid. That is, you are multitasking your way through the day, continuously devoting only partial attention to each act or person you encounter."

Stone claims that:

> Continuous partial attention, anytime, anywhere, any place technologies, the era of connect, connect, connect, is contributing to a feeling of overwhelm, over-stimulation and a sense of being unfulfilled. We are motivated by a desire to be a *live node on the network*. We want to connect, we want to effectively scan for opportunity and optimize for the best opportunities—activities or people—in any given moment.

This always on, anywhere, anytime, any place era has created an *artificial sense of constant crisis*. What happens to mammals in a state of constant crisis—the fight or flight mechanism kicks in. It's great when we're being chased by tigers. How many of those 500 e-mails a day is a tiger?

Professor Itiel Dror of the University of Southampton suggests an answer.

According to Dror, a cognitive neuroscientist, the human brain is capable of processing enormous quantities of information received by the senses—within limits. To protect itself, the brain makes attention extremely selective. Moreover, the brain relies on various short-cuts in order to cope effectively. Noise is a big factor. It is easier for a person to focus his or her attention on desired information if there is minimal noise (extraneous information) surrounding it.

Researchers like Dror split simultaneous media consumption into two zones: "foreground" and "background." For example, when we answer e-mails with the iPod on, e-mail is in the foreground and the iPod is the background media; answer a phone, and then e-mail takes the backseat.

Recent surveys conclude that half of us experience two or more media at once during a typical day. The most common, it seems, is watching TV and surfing the Web at the same time. Usually, the Web screen is front focus, while TV plays in the background. This cannibalization has not been lost on marketers, who have come to realize that a dollar spent on one medium may in fact only be generating a few cents' worth of divided attention.

Meanwhile, rather than becoming more productive through attention bending and multitasking, people may actually be experiencing diminishing returns, at least at work. Gloria Mark, professor at the University of California, Irvine, has been studying attention overload and multitasking among workers in office settings. Her results show that the average employee switches tasks every three minutes, is interrupted every two minutes, and has a maximum focus stretch of 12 minutes.

The net effect of course, is to create a conundrum of choice.

Author David R. Loy puts the quandary this way: "To be attentive to everything telepresent would spread one's awareness so thinly that it would amount to ignorance. In terms of my responsiveness to that infinity of information, doesn't infinite possibility likewise imply paralytic indecision? How do I decide what to do, what should have priority, when nothing is more present than anything else, physically or temporally?"

Part of the resulting coping response is to progressively shorten our attention spans. Today, neuroscientists believe that the human capacity to pay attention maxes out at about 15 minutes. That is too scant a hold to sit through the typical TV sitcom, never mind luxuriate over a Shakespearian sonnet, labor over a model ship with one's child, or take in the aesthetic measure of a redwood grove.

The problem is that our brains adjust to changing conditions. As University of Oslo professor Thomas Hylland Erikson smartly formulates: "When an ever-increasing amount of information has to be squeezed into the relatively constant amount of time each of us has at our disposal, the span of attention necessarily decreases."

As our range of attentiveness continues to narrow, new media formats will emerge to exploit this dynamic, thereby feeding the cycle further. A good example can be seen in the three-minute mobile TV "miniprograms" available from Ericsson, and the exceptionally well-produced show, *The Burg* (theburg.tv), an online situation comedy that puts *Friends* to shame. With high-quality, bite-sized programming set for the small screen, expect attention spans to adjust accordingly.

Managing the Deluge

As Howard Rheingold famously advised, *pay attention to where you pay attention*.

People retain abundant capacity for the information they care about, and diminishing capacity to entertain information they don't care about. According to Itiel Dror, one way we deal with information overload is by "chunking" or grouping information in useful ways. Today, most of us develop our own systems for categorizing and managing information, but when the flow becomes overwhelming, we increasingly look to automated solutions.

Managing attention is becoming a big business. From the companies that provide attention management software, like aggregators and readers, to the spam and spyware blockers, there are numerous new businesses aimed at helping us manage the information onslaught. Services like Akregator, Attensa, BlogBridge, Bloglines, FeedDemon, and FeedReader lead the growing area of syndication readers and filters. Bill Gates has called applications such as real simple syndication (RSS) "the start of the programmable Web," because they give individuals added power to tame the flow of Internet feeds they receive in a day. Yet, these too can quickly become unmanageable without discipline and policing. That's led many to work on algorithmic solutions.

A stone's throw from the mother ship in Redmond, Washington, Microsoft researcher Eric Horvitz leads a team working to solve some of the most vexing problems surrounding the management of attention. One approach is to help make the interface more personal, intuitive, and predictive of user interest and intention. By employing feedback loops and other intelligent agents, Horvitz is hoping to make your computer learn from you and save you time and attention. The rich models they employ are built not only from search-related information (what you have looked for in the past) but also from previously visited Web pages, stored documents, and e-mails, both read and written.

This convenience comes with its trade-offs and risks. Privacy, needless to say, is a very big issue. When you turn over your click history to others, you risk losing control over who will have access to your "click stream," and over what others do with that information. We may rightly ask: is coping with information over-load steering us toward an intrusive Orwellian society that knows our every action and anticipates our very next thought?

The question then becomes: to what extent are we willing to give up control of our privacy in order to gain control over our precious attention?

The Era of Antimarketing

As we observed in Chapter 2, the nature of the network makes mass node-to-node communications easier than ever. But it also makes it less desirable than ever. People want to choose their networks and, in the process, choose the information they want to receive. But the network's impulse is toward viral behavior, for fast-moving and pervasive communications spread to all open and available nodes.

Consider that bane of modern online life, spam. It is so pervasive because the network inherently encourages information to move freely. It demands it, actually. Despite our efforts to filter it out and governments' attempts to set legal limits, spam is a natural part of the network ecology. As long as we are online and open for business (Boolean logic again), information will find us.

Of course, getting that message in front of you at all costs has been the history of modern marketing. Since long before spam, marketers have interrupted your reading, listening, and viewing pleasure with their "push" messages. These same practitioners will become increasingly desperate in the post–Jump Point years as push marketing falls from grace with no obvious or imminent replace-ment. In that uneasy interregnum, the old mass-communication methods will continue, but increasingly they will be seen in a neg-ative light. In the extreme, push messaging will be seen as "atten-tion theft."

In the near future, attempts to horn in on your cognitive band-width will no longer be seen as a mere nuisance, but rather as a true misdemeanor. As people come to see "shotgun"—that is, untargeted—advertising as a hostile act, there will be a natural backlash against attention theft. Suffer your audience to experience incidents of interruption, or indulge in imposition or insult marketing, and the market will likely exact a price on your product or service, even erode your brand position and equity. One day, you may even go to jail.

Welcome to the era of antimarketing. It will profoundly shape the post–Jump Point world.

The backlash against traditional marketing will not be confined to the Web, either. São Paolo, the city that has made *Video Games Live!* such a phenomenon, last year passed an ordinance banning all outdoor advertising. Declaring its cacophony of commercial communiqués "visual pollution," the city has prohibited all advertising in public places. No megatrons, no billboards, busboards, or train ads; not even posters, flyers, or leaflets. Nada. If this movement catches on around the world, advertising itself may become an artifact.

What are the practical implications of antimarketing? Clearly those vested in the status quo will be challenged by post–Jump Point realities. Today, the market for attention turns on *inefficiency*. Broadcast media provides broad brush coverage to a largely undifferentiated swath of consumers in the hopes that at least some on the receiving end will prove to be right for the product. As a result, all of us receive messages each day that we can't use and don't want.

That may have worked in, say, the 1970s, when there were fewer media choices and more available attention. But it hardly works today. And, a decade from now, it will prove self-destructive to anyone who attempts it. One-size-fits-all media—making people endure advertisements they don't care about—wastes consumers' time and attention. Yet, billions of dollars still hinge on the friction-fraught system. Change is coming only slowly, and begrudgingly. Some in the media business continue to dream of the old days and past glories. In reality, the game has already played out, and we're just waiting for the dust to settle.

In this age of antimarketing, the advertising industry juggernaut, built on the inefficient cluster bombing of markets, is under attack from all sides. It is useful to consider that the same information flows that are reshaping the attention wars are themselves dismantling the advertising industry. Advertising is no longer a black art performed by the high priests of symbolic gestures. A virtual defrocking is restructuring the entire industry.

Anticipation Marketing

If I am giving you the impression that advertising has become the new tobacco, note that I am only referring to the status quo of the practice. It is not that we revile advertising per se; it is just that in these attention-scarce times we cannot tolerate unwanted communications of any sort.

Fortunately, smart advertisers and agencies are working to make things better.

In electronics, a transmission is divided into "signal" and "noise." Signal refers to useful information conveyed by a medium, and noise to anything else on that medium. If marketers are to have any chance of connecting with attention-deficient consumers, it will be by scrubbing the noise out of their pitches. Companies like TACODA are trying to do just that with a brand of advertising called "behavioral."

TACODA, acquired by America Online (AOL) in 2007, starts by capturing anonymous data on how people browse the net—they track more than 15 billion page views per day on 4,500 of the top news, entertainment, and information sites on the Web, from NYTimes.com to MSNBC.com to Orbitz to WSJ.com. Armed with this mountain of data, TACODA delivers targeted ads to consumers based on interests, not context. Rather than simply place a banner ad on a site hoping the right prospects will pass by,

TACODA drops ads of predetermined interest into the click stream of the consumer. The idea is that the consumer gets a more appropriate ad, and perhaps even welcomes the information.

Behavioral ads help reduce the noise on the Internet because consumers only see pitches that have been prequalified for their interests and that are worthy of their attention.

For example, when Pepsi-Cola launched its new low-calorie, vitamin-enriched water, Aquafina Alive, the beverage company turned to TACODA to help it design a national ad program. Pepsi didn't want to run ads just anywhere on the Internet. Instead, to great success, TACODA helped Pepsi run the ads only on sites it knew would be visited by people interested in healthy lifestyles.

Similarly, when rival soft drink maker Coca-Cola wanted to grow the membership ranks of its My Coke Rewards loyalty program, the company turned to TACODA and its behavioral targeting technology. According to Coke's senior interactive brand manager Karna Crawford, the company wanted a cost-effective way to reach a mass audience by appealing to people's passions. Instead of merely speaking to Coke fans, TACODA's campaign also addressed adjacent consumer interests; like their favorite movie (*Pirates of the Caribbean*), favorite car (Volvo), even their favorite American Idol contestants. According to Crawford, due to its relevance factor, the behavioral targeting component of the campaign outperformed the other tactics by more than 250 percent.

Attention Credits

As we cross the Jump Point, the average consumer will better understand the value of his or her own attention. So aware will they be of their own power that you can expect that customers will soon require compensation for their attention—value in exchange for value. Attention value creates a new coin of the realm. I call this currency *attention credits*.

While it may be some time before we see a global market for the trading of attention credits, consider the companies that are already rewarding consumers for their attentiveness.

A program underway in Israel, by telephone service provider Orange, allows customers to earn points by watching personal, interactive advertisements beamed to their handsets. In exchange they get a discount—up to 100 percent—off their monthly phone bill. Blyk, a teen-focused phone company in Europe, is offering similar free calling plans in exchange for customer attention. A 2007 Q Research survey of young mobile phone customers in Britain showed that 8 out of 10 subscribers would welcome in-phone advertising in exchange for credits toward their monthly phone bill.

And the attention credits are not just valuable online. European airline Ryanair has said in-flight advertising may *eliminate the need to charge for tickets*.

So valuable is attention, some are suggesting that advertisers be "bonded" in order to talk to us.

The idea of attention bonds has been floated by Boston University professor Marshall Van Alstyne. According to Thomas Claburn reporting in *Information Week*, "The idea is that people or companies sending e-mail can't reach the in-box of someone with whom they don't have an existing relationship unless they promise not to waste the recipient's time. Senders would put up small monetary bonds, held in escrow and seized if they break their promises. Senders who aren't willing to post bonds wouldn't get access to in-boxes."

"We're really trying to give you back what's a property right in your own attention," says Van Alstyne. "Since interruptions are costly, what you're basically doing is asking the sender to make these interruptions worth your time."

In recent years, Van Alstyne has been busily making his case before a diversity of interest, from the Federal Trade Commission to giant online entities like Google and Microsoft. Will you be required to prove that you are a bonded advertiser in the future? It is already becoming a reality for e-mail marketers.

Attention theft from spam is a huge problem. Antispam vendor Vanquish, working with the Email Accountability Initiative, has introduced a product called Personal Message Bond, a bond-sniffing application that lets Internet service providers check for and assign sender liability.

Here is how it works: marketers post a nominal bond for the privilege of sending e-mail to a recipient's inbox. Bonded e-mail gets a free ride past set challenges, spam filters, and blacklists. If, however, after opening the e-mail the recipient deems the message to be a waste of attention, he or she has the option to seize the bond, requiring some form of micropayment or Internet Service Provider-issued credit.

On a similar principle, Return Path uses financial bonds to deter spamming. In this case, seized bonds get paid, not to the recipient, but to the nonprofit Internet Education Foundation.

Anticipating a need for greater attention advocacy in general, the online group Attention Trust advocates another paradigm—the idea that each of us owns his or her attention assets, or at least our "click streams," the record of where and when we've been online. To that end, AttentionTrust.org has proposed an attention "bill of rights" to assert some semblance of consumer control over one's own attention property. Part privacy right, part attention management utility, the ability to manage your own interest fund would keep the cruft and flotsam to a minimum while keeping the door open for good, relevant data. Armed with this data, you are surely more aware of your own interests and can better manage the incoming deluge.

The Attention Trust Bill of Rights

- **Property:** I own my attention, and I can store it securely in private.

- Mobility: I can move my attention wherever I want, whenever I want.
- Economy: I can pay attention to whomever I wish, and be paid for it.
- Transparency: I can see how my attention is being used.

The "Attention Movement"

David Levy is distracted these days. But, he assures us, so are we all. What's got Levy's attention is the general lack of available attention. A professor in the University of Washington's School of Information, Levy believes the attention drain is a bigger problem than society yet acknowledges: "Without adequate time to think and reflect, time to listen, and time to cultivate our humanity, and without spaces that are protected from the constant intrusion of information and noise, I do not see how we can respond to the innumerable social and political challenges of the new millennium with the quality of attention they deserve."

In addition to spearheading the creation of a new center on Information and the Quality of Life, Levy teaches courses like Information and Contemplation and Information, Attention, and Experience—which according to their syllabi explore the "fragmentation of attention" and help students consider ways to combat a lifestyle that has become "unsustainable and counterproductive."

Considered by many to be a visionary, Levy believes the attention crisis warrants a movement behind it—not unlike the environmental movement—in order to restore balance in modern life. Like Rachel Carson in the 1960s, Levy is sounding the alarm for a new way to steward our precious resources: "Much as the modern-day environmental movement has worked to cultivate and preserve certain natural habitats, such as wetlands and old growth forests, for the health of the planet, so too should we now begin to cultivate and preserve certain human habitats for the sake of our own well-being."

A decade ago, columnist Barbara Ehrenreich, writing in the *Progressive*, offered a foreshadowing of the attention consumerist movement when she suggested a controversial remedy to attention theft. "Simply refuse to buy from any company that does not pay people to pay attention to its ads," she declared. "If we boycott advertised products long enough, the important, big money guys may even, eventually, notice. Yes, they'll be forced to pay attention to insignificant us."

Extreme? Perhaps, but it is during the dustup of a Jump Point when many one-time extreme notions start to look altogether reasonable.

Attention after the Jump Point

Al Qaeda wants your attention. So do Hezbollah, Harakat ul-Mujahidin, Abu Sayyaf, Nagaland Rebels, Khalistan Liberation Force, and dozens of other shadowy hate groups.

That's what terrorists do; they aim to seize our attention. And, they are willing to pay a high price in human life to get it. That is the horrific side of the attention wars. The voices from the bottom of the pyramid, the disenfranchised, the nefarious, and the fanatical are starving for our attention just as we are choked by competing claims to it. Often employing brutal and medieval tactics and practices, they know they have to raise the ante in order to get you to stop what you're doing and pay them heed. Despite their primitive means, they are often media sophisticates, able to both manipulate the mass media and narrowcast beneath the radar to a network of sympathetic followers. And they know the value and the price of attention as well as any marketer today.

It may be argued that terror escalates as the price of your attention goes up. The harder it becomes to provoke a response, the louder, more desperate, and more violent they will likely become. On the other hand, our anger also may grow as moral outrage is joined by attention fatigue and resentment. We will not only hate their deeds, we will hate that they have stolen our attention. In this sense, the heat of the battle for share of mind may take a more ominous, escalating form.

The addition of billions of new consumers will create a conundrum of sorts for global marketers. Many among the new marketplace will be starved for information, while many others will be overwhelmed, with filters on, and guards up. This bifurcated dynamic will require new strategies and business models. Simply measuring marketing success by attention penetration rates could produce a fool's gold effect.

Meanwhile, subject to a fraction of the information flood that their first billion counterparts face daily, the third billion consumers will be information hungry and attention wealthy. They will be open to new ideas and novelties, eager for exposure to new marketing messages. Whether they act upon them is another matter. However eager they may be to hear your pitch, the attention rich may not be your target customers. Enthusiastic, curious, but poor, they may prove a dangerous distraction.

After 2011, the world will be divided into those who can pay attention and those who cannot. The twist, of course, will be that those with the highest incomes will be attention poor, while those with the least incomes will be attention rich.

After the Jump Point, attention may not be the universal virtue it is today. When customers have more attention than disposable means, the old metrics may misread interest as opportunity. In that sense, a well-received e-mail blast, a high-traffic Web site, even a heavy click-through rate may not mean as much as it does now. As we have observed in earlier chapters, some nodes—and some eyeballs—are simply more valuable than others. In general, marketers should be cautious of any consumer they can easily reach.

The future attention wars are likely to get more heated as certain customers emerge as more strategic targets than others. In the beginning, the Internet economy was about the mad acquisition of "eyeballs"; the more, the merrier. Looking ahead, raw impressions are no longer an accurate measure of attention (if they ever were), as savvy consumers find clever ways to block and avoid unwanted distractions.

Ultimately attention is a form of loyalty—it must be earned and nurtured. The coming consumer will see information as a right, and attention as an asset. New business models are needed that offer a fair trade, value for attention. As we prepare for the Jump, innovative companies are beginning to reward consumer attention in new and creative ways.

Many questions for marketers remain:

How will your company compete in the intense battle for attention? How will you identify and distinguish your core customers from those who can give you attention but not give you business? As attention is a form of loyalty, how will you win fans and friends without alienating people through interruption or imposition advertising?

Closely related to our ability to attend to new information and stimuli is our sense of time. Next, we look at how our relationship with time is changing all around us.

Download This

- Information overload has made attention the world's most precious resource.
- Consumers will closely guard their limited attention, using it only for the things they really care about.
- Unwanted advertising will be seen as a hostile act.
- Consumers will expect to be rewarded for their attention with value for value.

5

The Permanent *Now*

The only reason for time is so that everything doesn't happen at once.

—Albert Einstein

Researchers at the National Institute of Standards and Technology (NIST) in Boulder, Colorado, are nothing if not serious about time. At the sweeping campus set in the ancient shadow of the Indian Peaks range, teams of scientists there have been working for decades to develop ever-more-sophisticated ways to slice, measure, and tell time.

Their latest breakthrough is an atomic clock in which atoms of the heavy metal ytterbium oscillate, or "tick," at never-before-seen optical frequencies. The clock, which ticks 518 trillion times per second, is the world's most accurate timepiece, much more precise than its cesium predecessors. By slicing time into its smallest units yet, the research sheds new light on just how complex the concept of time really is.

Keeping time is a crucial aspect of our modern society and economy. Timekeeping allows us to orchestrate individual and collective activity and shapes relations among individuals and organizations, among organizations, and within networks of individuals. As we saw earlier with the great public clocks of Europe, mastery over time had been a major contribution of the Middle Ages. A shared sense of absolute as opposed to "task" time led to numerous new economic advances and forms, and paved the way for the Industrial Revolution and all that followed.

Now, our collective understanding of time is changing again.

Regardless of how advanced, the ytterbium clock is still based on a straight-line view of events, the Newtonian idea of a clockwork universe set in absolute time, space, and motion. In this mathematical paradigm, time elapses in a linear progression; seconds (however fractional) tick off the days, years, and eventually millennia in a predictable forward march. This rationalization of time is a foundation of the modern economy and society.

However, not everyone in the world perceives time as a straight line of past, present, and future events. For example, the Amyra people of the Andes see things the other way around. For them, the future is behind us, the past ahead of us. What has happened is what is driving us; the future is still unknown. When the Chinese speak of time, it rolls downhill into the future. The Pirah, the Hopi Indians, and the Australian Aborigines, by contrast, have no concept or word for time whatsoever. For them, the persistent present is all there is.

So time has never been a truly universal concept, and in the world after the Jump Point, our relationship with time is going to get a whole lot more complicated.

There will be new business and personal challenges as we surge deeper into the always-on, on-demand, download-now culture. No organization will escape these new influences. There will be no holiday from competition, or day off from the battle for share of market or mind. For individuals, the lines will be further blurred between work and play, public and private, and here and there. In short, we have entered the era of the *permanent now*.

New Meanings of Time

Time is so fundamental to our lives that we experience it unconsciously; we accept time as a measurable state, the clock as its objectification. We first learn to tell time as schoolchildren, and we obey it every day after that. In their brilliant examination of our changing relationships with time, *24/7: Time and Temporality in the Networked Society*, Robert Hassan and Ronald E. Purser observe that since the Enlightenment a clock-time economy has been our dominant social force: "Work, everyday life, the running of the economy and the philosophical and political foundations of the era all rested increasingly on a specific and narrow perspective of what time was—and that was represented through the external and rigidly mathematical time expressed on a clock face."

The rise of networks and the Internet, of computational and informational technologies—of so-called machine time—have reshaped our concept of the temporal on many levels. Hassan and Purser assert: "The emergence of communicative networks that stretched across time and space revealed that clock time is not an absolute backdrop against which we synchronize and 'tell' the time, but a human construction that has very little to do with time other than as an inflexible way of measuring duration."

Moreover, the boundary-busting, always-on Internet has expanded our definition of time to include many other types of time. As Adrian Mackenzie of Lancaster University puts it, in the age of machines we have established numerous new interpretations of time, which include "seek time, run time, read time, access time, real time, polynomial time, time division, time slicing, time sharing, time complexity, write time, processor time, execution time, compilation time, and cycle time."

Many of these takes on time are contradictory and even competing "task" times. But these new ways to measure experience beg the question: are we reverting to a preindustrial concept of measuring time in terms of tasks—for example, download time, mean time before failure (MTBF), and zip rates?

Of particular interest to researchers is an understanding of our changing perceptions of time, and more significantly, our changing perception of *now*. With the arrival of the Internet, and a new human infrastructure which leverages space to overcome time, everything is happening in an expanding now.

World Time Revisited

Comedian Steven Wright tells a now-famous joke about visiting an all-night convenience store only to find it closed. Seeing the proprietor cleaning up behind locked doors, he confronts him. "Your sign says you're open 24 hours," Wright points out through the glass. "Yes," the owner replies looking at Wright as if he were daft, "but not in a row."

It is a very funny line, but also indicative of our wildly differing views of time. Before the Jump Point, our concept of a twenty-four-hours-a-day, seven-days-a-week (24/7) global economy has meant *something is happening somewhere* around the clock. After the Jump Point, our orientation will shift to *everything is happening everywhere*. There's a big difference.

We owe our current system or world time to the introduction of a new technology. The emergence in the late nineteenth century of the railroad and scheduled travel across great distances in the United States catalyzed the establishment of standard time zones. Before then, every city, town, and hamlet in the world set its own time.

While there were numerous competing ideas on how to divide the world into a standard clock, most of the world finally agreed to a system offered up by Canada's Sir Sanford Fleming, a prominent railroad builder and engineer. In 1878 Fleming recommended dividing the world into 24 time zones each spaced 15 degrees of longitude apart (earth's 360 degrees divided by 24 hours). On November 18, 1883—known as the "Day of Two Noons"—U.S. railroads switched over at midday to the new time zones. A few months later, in 1884, an International Meridian Conference was held in Washington, D.C., to set the starting point, the prime meridian (also known as the international meridian). The group selected Greenwich, England, as zero degrees longitude and established the 24 time zones standard. Today we call this system Coordinated Universal Time (UTC) or Z, for "zero meridian" or "Zulu" (which is the word for Z in the International Radio Alphabet). Local times are represented by a UTC zone plus or minus an hour for offsets and daylight savings, if appropriate. For example, the U.S. Eastern time is standardly stated as UTC -4, Pacific time is UTC-7.

The problem with this universally coordinated time is it's not very coordinated. First, there are two types of times, astronomical time and physical time. Astronomical time tracks with the rotation of the earth around the sun; physical time is measured with incredible accuracy by folks like those at the NIST in Boulder, Colorado, using atomic clocks. Because the earth doesn't rotate with exactitude, the two times differ slightly, at the rate of about 32 seconds per year. The solution to this divergence has been to adopt "leap seconds." By agreement, the world's timekeepers insert or delete a leap second whenever the two times drift apart by more than half a second.

And then, there are the human factors. When you account for offsets—those accepted local variations—the time picture gets really murky. For example, Israel starts its day at 6 p.m. instead of midnight, and many places in the world use time zones offset by a half hour or even 15 minutes off of the standard 24 time zones. Newfoundland, India, Iran, Afghanistan, Burma, the Marquesas, and parts of Australia use half-hour deviations from standard time. Some nations, such as Nepal and the Chatham Islands, use 15-minute deviations. Even though the prime meridian passes through Spain and France, those countries choose to apply the mean time of 15 degrees east (Central European Time) rather than zero degrees (Greenwich Mean Time). And, China, which should encompass five time zones by geography, only uses one nationwide.

And these deviations don't include daylight saving time, which is unevenly and idiosyncratically used throughout the world.

Given the local deviations and the offsets, there are actually 39 time zones (which can be represented in 59 ways) in the world. In practice, that can mean, in the extreme, that a "day" can take up to 50 hours to cycle through the time zones, not 24.

Obviously, in our nonstop global economy, it is important to know at what time things happen, when agreements are made and contracts are signed, when goods and services are delivered as promised, and when appointments are supposed to occur.

As you can imagine, these quirky variations in time and time articulation have the Internet world flummoxed. Computers and network devices operate on event-driven systems—they need to know exactly what time it is. In order to interact optimally, two or more devices need to agree on what time it is.

There are several efforts underway to develop a better time and calendaring system—everything from the adoption of metric time (a 25-hour day) to more elaborate new schemas. The International Organization for Standardization (ISO) considers time management a crucial factor for quality processes and has task forces working on solutions.

A well-organized effort employing leading software and telecommunications companies and universities is called CalConnect.org. This broad-based group—including representatives from companies like Apple, Boeing, and Yahoo!; academic institutions, like MIT, Princeton, and the University of California, Berkeley; and the wider scientific community—is working toward standard solutions to some hairy issues like calendar applications, task interoperability, and the reconciliation of changing time zones in recurring events. As the Internet creates its own time relationships spanning across all boundaries and zones, CalConnect.org knows that the resolution of these issues is important for the future of the global economy.

If a system of time more reflective of modern economic realities is not agreed upon, some tricky current situations will persist. For instance, it is becoming increasingly significant that North America sleeps through the prime of the world's workday. That's right, while the largest swath of the world lives and works in UTC +7 to UTC +9, those are overnight hours here in the United States. So, while major cities in major trading regions like Beijing, Tokyo, and Seoul—not to mention Bangkok, Saigon, Jakarta, Hong Kong, Shanghai, and Taipei—all can do business in the span of a reasonable business day, the United States and Canada are "off duty" at that time. And while the business day in the eastern and midwestern time zones of the United States overlaps meaningfully with part of the business day of Europe, doing business between the western United States and Europe (and other parts of the world) is challenging.

If you have ever attempted a global conference call involving people in offices from far-flung parts of the world, you know how difficult that effort can be at a human and practical level. Someone, somewhere, is always working the call with his or her pajamas on.

Can the global economy grow to its potential if we don't master time? Doing so will be tough. The answer lies in rethinking how we do business, how we staff organizations, and how we manage our enterprises.

And we should take care not to permit time to become another way to artificially divide the world economy. If one day trade alliances are favored for time convenience, we in North America might live in one of the most economically challenged time zones. Are we likely to see the emergence of time gulags? No, given that the overarching benefit of our always-on global network is connecting all economic players, such a subdivision doesn't make sense. On the other hand, stranger things have happened.

Lunchtime in Mumbai

In the parlance of the radio and television world, the division of the day into useful chunks of time when advertisers can predict that people will be doing certain things is called "dayparting."

Dayparts have been used for decades to slot and price ads, and include "drive time," or morning and afternoon commute hours for radio, and "prime time," or the family viewing hours for TV. There have traditionally been five dayparts for radio, nine for TV.

But the emergence of the Internet as a pop medium has thrown a curve ball at advertisers. For one thing, Internet use studies show that traffic spikes in the morning after 9 a.m. when people arrive in the office and check e-mails and Web sites, and rises again during lunchtime, when workers are afforded a more leisurely hour to surf. And with the average lunch "hour" in the United States dropping to below 25 minutes, it is more likely that the typical office worker will eat at his or her desk and spend that time online. So, midmorning and lunchtime have become the new dayparts for the Internet.

As an always-on global medium, the Internet is demanding a different system of dayparting. As just illustrated, the realities of differing time zones mean that it is almost always lunchtime somewhere. In that vein, the information worker in Mumbai or Delhi—or Chennai, Channdigarh, or Jaipur, for that matter—is just as likely to spend premium time online during his or her lunchtime, except that it happens to be midnight in San Francisco at that moment.

It would be a mistake to dismiss these emerging markets as "plus" regions. Today, North America only accounts for 20 percent of Internet users. Asia—the UTC+7 to +9 time zones—is twice as large. And, according to a PricewaterhouseCoopers June 2007 report, China will be the biggest Internet country user by the year 2011. Clearly, establishing new and useful time bands for the coming 24/7 business day will be increasingly important.

Any Time, Any Place

Reconciling global time will not be the only time-related discontinuity facing all businesses after the Jump Point. The time- and shape-shifting consumer has other ideas.

The history of the consumer age has been punctuated with time-saving inventions; appliances that make short work of the drudge and toil of modern life. Mostly these have been machines to automate manual labor and to free us to do other, more cerebral types of labor.

But today's devices do something more than save time, they help us to rearrange it. We know by now that technologies such as digital video recorders (DVRs) and personal video recorders (PVRs) have markedly changed television viewing habits. With the digital recording service TiVo and others like it, consumers now have the ability to watch TV and consume other media at their own pace, on their own clock. This ability makes dubious at best the concept of traditional dayparts like "prime time," or the family hour. Today, viewers are free to watch what they want, when they want, and where they want.

This challenge will not be confined to the media world. The wider issue is that technology changes culture. Freedom from the tyranny of time is already spreading like a virus through all our relationships with media. Look at the explosive growth in the "TV-on-DVD" boxed-set market. As the grip of the broadcast paradigm has been broken, consumers are proving that they would rather buy or rent their favorite TV shows on DVD (programs they could have watched for free other than the price of enduring commercials) at the end of the season rather than be slaves to a time schedule during the year.

Again, delinking content and time is not just an issue for the old broadcast media, it is a new mindset that will affect all industries and businesses. Nowhere is this more evident than on the Internet, where people shop and buy at any time of the day or night they choose. The realization that this freedom of choice is even possible is changing consumer attitudes. What is emerging is a pervasive "latency intolerance" that threatens the established order. Simply put, any situation perceived as too slow by the consumer will be punished. And any opportunity to accelerate the delivery of a product or service will be seen as an advantage. "The faster the better" is the new consumer motto.

That's why the iTunes experience has virtually killed the record store. The ability to search and discover, preview, and download music instantly has been more satisfying to many music lovers than anything the less-efficient material world can offer. Even though physical stores have responded with preview stations and wider selections, the time element has been too much to overcome; many consumers can no longer countenance waiting. It would be a mistake to assume that this idea will go away or is merely a problem for the media world. Latency intolerance, the New Impatience, not only will be permanent, it also will be pervasive.

For example, users of DVRs typically fast-forward through commercials. There are some attempts underway to prevent fast-forwarding. These endeavors will fail as consumers react unfavorably to the nuisance. On the other hand, we can expect commercials to be recrafted to deliver their payload messages at fast-forward speeds. This may generate better results as long as viewers can still watch a 30-minute show in about 22 minutes, freeing up more time to do other things.

When I have been asked by journalists what accounts for the demise of commercial TV and, to some extent, commercial radio, my answer is always the same: time. Time-based programming has been the undoing of television. As soon as consumers experience time-bending, going back to the arbitrariness of commercial formats is impossible.

Point, Click, Now!

Waiting is so yesterday.

The ability to time-shift and to move in a nonlinear way is rewiring our brains to think and act differently. We are becoming less patient. And the faster things start to come, the faster still we want them.

When you live in the permanent now, you don't want to be satisfied later. In fact, everything takes too long. With digital products—music, movies, photos, books, and articles—you can buy and download instantly. For many online retailers of physical goods, fulfillment now is overnight. Not fast enough? You can use an online service like LicketyShip, which will deliver to your door products you buy online in just four hours. Still not fast enough? Buy products online at major retailers, like Best Buy and Circuit City, and the products are ready for pickup in less time than it takes you to drive to the nearest store location. Lessons for the material world: the new consumers are being retrained by the Internet to get their needs and wants satisfied faster. This rapid gratification will color the way they approach all shopping.

24/7 Party People?

So, how will humans respond to the pressures of a 24/7 world? When will we sleep, recharge, and recreate? Some people think we may not have to.

Circadian rhythms in humans are controlled by a central clock within the brain structure known as the suprachiasmatic nucleus. The clock is synchronized to environmental cycles of light and dark. From the dawn of the human era we have slept with the night and awakened with the sun.

The age of the networked economy, of blurred time zones, puts enormous pressure on the individual. For businesspeople, it can be maddening that the world is chugging along without us. It becomes hard to shut off the day, recuperate, and relax when the day itself does not shut off. It should come as no surprise that scientists think they can solve that problem, too.

Take the case of Modafinil.

It doesn't have the libidinous appeal of Viagra or the public relations machinery of a hot new diet pill, but Modafinil may be the next wonder drug to reach your medicine cabinet. It doesn't improve your sex life or your appearance, but it will safely keep you working a 22-hour day.

Modafinil is in a class of drugs known as a eugeroic, meaning "good arousal" in Greek. It delivers natural-feeling alertness and wakefulness. In fact, drugs like Modafinil and the experimental CX717 have been found to be remarkable in their ability to promote wakefulness without the negative side effects of caffeine and amphetamines. Without jitters, or the euphoria followed by the inevitable crash, Modafinil will keep you alert and let you gently stave off sleep and defy your circadian rhythms. The U.S. Defense Department has been doing trials with both drugs to see if they can safely extend a productive day to 72 hours—a critical safety consideration in military scenarios, particularly for special operations soldiers.

Promoters of wakefulness believe we can safely abolish sleep for several days at a stretch, and then take a new class of sleeping pills, such as Merck's Gaboxadol, that deliver what feels like eight hours of sleep in half the time or less.

Is the 22-hour or even the 72-hour day the answer to the demands of the 24/7 global economy? Must we really turn to pharmacological solutions—or mass quantities of energy drinks—to capitalize on the Permanent Now?

And how far off can the backlash to all of this pharmaceutical engineering be? Perhaps the future will include the passage of new legislation to protect us from ourselves. Like no-smoking or seat belt laws, no-working laws will be passed to prevent us from working ourselves to death. The major breakthroughs in labor laws in the past 100 years were meant to keep employers from exploiting workers. Laws to set working conditions and hours, including the eight-hour workday and 40-hour work week, came from this impetus. But what happens when we are exploiting ourselves?

These are questions for all marketers. How will you compete in the Permanent Now when customers are impatient and demanding, and intolerant of slow processes, long waits, and noncustomized solutions? How will you change the business rules not just by bending time, but by using time as a competitive weapon? How will you give your customers a role in the design and delivery of products and services? How can you take your experience to new places in the life of the consumer?

Download This

- Our relationship with time is changing.
- Consumers want on-demand, time-bending experiences.
- Beware of time gulags.
- Time zones are an artifice; the global economy is always on.
- Consumers are experiencing time differently: they are less patient than they were before.
- Companies that change the time equation will win in every category.

6

The Augurs of Amplitude

The only way of discovering the limits of the possible is to venture a little way past them into the impossible.
—Arthur C. Clarke

It could be a story straight out of Hollywood; except it isn't. Here's the setup: two 20-something filmmakers eking out a living in New York scrape together enough money in savings and credit cards to make a feature film. Not finding ready distribution for their independent ("indie") film, they release parts of it over YouTube, and subsequently get invited to more than a dozen film festivals where their movie is greeted with critical acclaim—but still no distribution offers.

Next, the pair makes podcasts of the movie's trailers and use the Internet to sign up audiences and sell tickets in major U.S. cities. Finding willing screens in a half dozen major cities, they quickly sell out an evening in each city. Still not landing a deal with a distribution house, they get a break when the movie review Web site Spout.com offers to pay them a dollar for each fan of the film they sign up as members.

So, the intrepid pair offers the film for free download on numerous Web sites in exchange for the Spout sign-ups. Enough fans take them up on the offer that the struggling filmmakers recoup their money, pay down their credit cards, get a DVD distribution deal, and live to direct another day.

Were it a script pitch, it might be too improbable even for Hollywood, but that is the tale of Arin Crumley and Susan Buice and their movie, *Four Eyed Monsters*. When, in 2005, Crumley and Buice, two starving artists living in New York City, decided to make a movie loosely based on their own courtship, they knew little about the Byzantine world they were about to enter.

Focused solely on producing a powerful film—the first look at the world of dating in the age of MySpace—the pair was oblivious to the ancient ways and exigencies of the film business and its nearly 100-year-old customs and practices. But it didn't matter; they simply believed anything was possible and that the path forward would reveal itself eventually. When they hit a wall, they turned to the Internet, to the crowd, for help.

Their story is not an uncommon one. Everywhere you look, you can see entrepreneurs and true believers hurling themselves into the unknown, fortified only with a faith that the "net" will catch them, that small acts by many everyday people can be as useful as the influence of the connected and powerful. Call it Horatio Alger meets Andy Hardy. In a sense, that's the real power of the Internet and the networked economy—people empowered with choice, latitude, and control. I call this power *amplitude*, and it will affect the coming market in many important ways.

The Abundant Economy

Amplitude is a wide-ranging state of being that combines the elements of *abundance*, *nonlinearity*, *mobility*, and *extensibility*. Customers with amplitude see the world differently; they have different expectations and demands. They believe that anything is possible. They will continuously push the limits—your limits. Understanding these dynamics is the key to serving them and surviving them after the Jump Point.

Earlier we looked at some of the factors the networked economy eliminates, including middlemen, inventories, and time. But
perhaps the most important thing networking eliminates is
scarcity. In fact, some economists argue that the networked economy operates on an entirely new paradigm. They call it the Abundant Economy.

Historically, economics has dealt with the management of
scarcity and inefficiency. The bedrock concept of supply and
demand is based on the perpetual imbalance between what is available and what is wanted at any given moment.

But in the networked world of digital goods, the friction
between supply and demand is erased—or at least reduced to a
time function. Digital products cost next to nothing to reproduce
and can be made available any time of the day or night. Incredible advances in technology, paced by Moore's law, have driven the
cost of transistors, storage, and bandwidth to virtually zero. The
underlying attitude of the Abundant Economy is "do it all, offer
it all, utilize free resources with abandon, consider waste a factor
of production."

Needless business models in the age of abundance must break
from the traditional models built on scarcity.

For example, in the physical world of scarcity constraints, the
now-defunct Tower Records could only house a maximum of
50,000 titles on its shelves. By contrast, with bandwidth and storage approaching free, iTunes can offer more than three million dig-
itized songs on its site.

Customers accustomed to abundance want more, not fewer,
choices, and this ultimately impacts all businesses. Rightly or
wrongly, the customer has come to believe that everything is
always available . . . and all things are possible.

But, there is a downside to abundance. Not everyone is so enam-
ored with the postscarcity world. CNN's James Ledbetter argues
that the distinction between digital and physical goods needs to
be kept in mind:

First of all, Amazon by and large doesn't digitize books; it sells and ships physical books. Second, to focus on rental shelf scarcity is to miss more important scarce goods elsewhere. The fact that I can burn, say, a DVD of a movie onto my iPod in a matter of minutes does not change the fact the movie cost $150 million to make. Much of that money goes to pay actors, directors and technicians who, presumably, possess one of the scarcest goods that exist—talent; the digitization of the medium doesn't affect that at all.

According to this view, the postscarcity mindset may be more disruptive than expansive. The push to free digital content puts unrealistic, some say unsustainable, pressure up and down the traditional value chains. As we so painfully learned in the dot-com bubble years, the Internet is not the right medium for all goods and services. And Abundant Economics may likewise not be right for all scenarios. Applying abundant thinking inappropriately just creates turmoil. In the end, you may have a physical world retailer like Wal-Mart squeezing the hell out of the subsistence-level garment workers in Cambodia or putting enormous wage pressures on Chilean banana growers. That is not a workable long-term model.

But this age of near-magical thinking has produced its spillover benefits. For every case of a traditional business being run through the grist mill of painful change, you have a *Four Eyed Monsters* forging a new outlet. It is now fundamental that anyone with a good idea, a little gumption, and the willingness to let the network do its work has a legitimate shot at success. As a result, abundant thinking is producing the most explosive period of creativity in human history. Anything really is possible when you can connect with and make your case before the whole world. Google can happen. YouTube can happen. MySpace can happen.

Nonlinearity

The personal computer, mobile phone, and Internet make all the headlines, but I predict *hyperlinks* will be remembered as among the most culturally significant innovations of our time.

Hyperlinks, or simply links, are navigational elements within electronic documents that take the user from one reference or document to another. This journey from one point to another one can take us in an infinite number of directions in pursuit of a train of thought or the right information. There is an element of discovery and serendipity to the use of links. You never know where the process of exploration will take you: you may be but one click away from adventure.

What are the implications? People of the Western world learn to read left to right, up to down. People in the East are taught to read right to left, down to up. Either way, from our earliest days forward we have been trained to process information sequentially, from start to finish, rudimentary to complex, from point A to B to C, and so on. Essentially, we have all been taught to be linear thinkers.

Since the arrival of the hyperlinked Internet, people increasingly are becoming nonlinear thinkers. Our brains have been retrained to find information and process it differently than those of the hunt and peck, assembly-line, Dewey Decimal System past. Naturally, this reprogramming shapes and informs our communications, our work, and even our world view. Instead of drilling down a single path, Web users today are more likely to let the information trail lead where it will. And with an array of tools to mark or "tag" their paths, we are prone to set ourselves free to stumble upon new things, new ideas, and never-before-imagined places. And, we are more likely to share our findings with others, as well as take the counsel of our fellow travelers.

Hyperlinks make people less predictable, their behavior less formulaic and reckonable. And that reality is already shaking up the young Web world. Whereas great fortunes have been amassed by the Yahoo!s and Googles because they brought order to the linear world of Web search, the emphasis is now on *discovery*, not search.

Discovery is a decidedly nonlinear process. When consumers adopt a discovery mindset, contextual, see-and-say advertising strategies break down. The online shopper who follows a link to a jewelry offer may be just a few clicks away from buying a car. And as consumers realize the power of discovery, they are more likely to become more elusive and intractable in their behavior.

And there are broader cultural implications to this nonlinearity as well, such as a greater acceptance of ambiguity and a tolerance for failure. The social acceptance of experimentation and failure, as well as a belief in redemption after an entrepreneurial failure, have long been tenets of Silicon Valley culture. Indeed, it would be difficult to imagine any of the iconic brands we know today were it not for the freedom to fail in Silicon Valley and places like it.

That mindset comes from a core belief that trial and error—discovery—is important, and that trying is more important than dreaming. This is nonlinear thinking at work. The message: the coming market will not punish you for experimenting and failing; in fact, the opposite is true. Your new customers will reward your innovation and willingness to be nonlinear.

Mobility

The mobility imperative in humans is primal. Mobility—moving with the food supply, traveling to new sources of water, avoiding danger—predates civilization. The urge to widen the circle of opportunity to see what's beyond the next horizon runs deep in our species. It explains all forms of transportation and exploration. It accounts for the drives to miniaturization and portability in our products. It underscores the wanderlust that defines our history on the planet and in the cosmos.

The downside to mobility has always been dissociation—separation from others, at home or at work. Wayfarers, from the Argonauts to the astronauts, have had to untie from something or someone in order to be mobile. That reality always has been part of the trials and tribulations of exploration. And it has remained true until just recently, when the era of *tethered mobility* began.

Starting with smaller, more portable computers, accelerated by the arrival of the wireless cell phone, and reaching an inflection point now with the convergence of several technologies such as Bluetooth, WiFi, WiMAX, and GPS, people today are more mobile and yet better connected than anyone could have imagined just a decade ago.

Building, as it has, off of a very familiar, preexisting technology, and enjoying perhaps the fastest adoption rate in history, the mobile phone is something we tend to take for granted. It is amusing to recall that when mobile phones first appeared on the scene, they were considered by many an arrogant and vulgar technology used only by the wealthy. Needless to say, we have adjusted our viewpoint considerably; today a mobile phone is standard equipment for people of all incomes and demographics.

So rapid has been its ascension as the world's communications medium of choice that we hardly have had time to absorb the true significance of this revolution. All we know is that it is hard to remember a world without the mobile phone, and impossible to imagine life without it going forward. And as we learned in the opening chapter, the mobile phone is only becoming more capable and useful; our dependence upon it likely to only deepen in the years ahead. Indeed, the Web-enabled mobile phone is the triggering device of the next Jump Point in the human adventure.

So, what are the implications of this widespread tethered mobility?

When people can travel and stay connected at the same time, it changes behavior. People are now free to break old boundaries and limitations. Workers aren't shackled to desks, families are not separated by distance, people stay in touch while they travel. You can be productive on the morning bus to school, collaborative during the evening commute. Activities start to shift their locus; we can watch TV on the train and take a conference call from a beach blanket.

On the negative side, we are coming to see that pervasive connectedness has its social costs. There is a human toll to a 24/7, always-on lifestyle. It can seem sometimes as if the mobile phone is an imposition, a ball and chain, rather than a tool of freedom. Users of BlackBerry phones have come to refer to the device as a "crackberry" because it so addicting to stay in constant touch. This is the dark side of tethered mobility, and it cannot be ignored even as we celebrate the rewards of this revolution.

Nomadic Connectivity

The biggest challenge facing retailers is that the more mobile consumers get, the harder they are to reach and engage. The emergence of WiMAX technology and its deployment in a range of computing, portable multimedia, interactive devices, and other consumer electronic devices promises to change the equation yet again.

WiMAX (Worldwide Interoperability for Microwave Access) is a high-speed, broadband, point-to-point connection particularly useful for sending a wide range of interactive digital media—"rich media"—the "final mile." By comparison, the WiFi (wireless local area network) one gets at the local Starbucks, is a less robust interface only suitable for short distances (within hot spots). With WiMAX, you can be on the move and online at the same time— and be as much as 200 miles away from the nearest "hot spot."

WiMAX isn't just WiFi on steroids. Because it has both greater bandwidth and much greater range, it will be WiMAX that, within the next decade, finally covers every inch of the planet, from the bottom of Death Valley to the top of Mount Everest, with broadband Internet access. And that, in turn, means that the electronic "tether"

will finally be cut, and that we will literally be able to go *anywhere* and still be as connected as we are at the office or in our home.

"Where are you?" is the most asked question on a mobile phone, according to Sam Altman, the 20-something CEO and cofounder of Loopt. Says Altman: "We are excited that we answer that question."

Loopt, a friend-finding service for mobile phones, was started by Altman while he was still an undergraduate at Stanford University. The company leverages technology that originally was embedded into phones to comply with a Federal Communications Commission requirement to provide the location of people who have called 911 from cell phones. Loopt can automatically update the location of everyone in a user's private network of friends and display the information graphically directly on a mobile map. Loopt can also alert you to when a friend is nearby.

Mobile virtual network operator Helio offers a similar tracking service, and other providers, such as Disney Mobile and Verizon Wireless, provide tracking services for parents who want to keep tabs on their kids.

The big investor in WiMAX has been service provider Sprint, which is spending billions to develop a nationwide wireless broadband network designed to "mobilize the Internet, bring wireless innovation to devices and deliver new mobile multimedia applications." In addition to partnering with Loopt on the Friend Finder tracking service, Sprint is also developing for its users full mobile phone GPS navigation, a family locator, and, most promising of all, a service it calls GPShopper.

GPShopper provides an important early glimpse at the potential of location-based services combining WiMAX, GPS, and shopping applications. Sprint partners with an opt-in shopping service called Slifter.com, which works from a database of 85 million products (including images and descriptions) and promotions to help consumers find exactly what they want at the location nearest to them. Based upon that "mobile shopping list," consumers can even allow the products they want to *find* them. And, purchases can be made with a few button strokes using the mobile payment services of PayPal.

By way of illustration, here's a scenario that brings all of this technology together: Imagine you are walking down a busy city street, passing a Circuit City electronics store, when your mobile phone rings with a message offering $100 off a digital camera— not just any camera, but the one you have been mulling over for weeks—if you act in the next 30 minutes. Now, normally you would not welcome ads, even those bearing gifts, sent to your phone. But this particular camera is part of the shopping list you recently set up on Slifter.com. What could be more convenient than to step in and make the purchase?

In a hurry to get somewhere? Buy it now using mobile PayPal and come back and pick it up later. It's sure to be the new mantra in the advertising business: *location, location, location.*

Extensibility

Consider this story of a man on an existential journey:

> In January 2007, a man named Molotov Alva disappeared from his California home. Recently, a series of seven video dispatches by a Traveler of the same name have appeared within a popular online world called Second Life. In these dispatches Molotov Alva encounters everything from Furies to Cyberpunks to Neo-Luddites to Sex Slaves to the King of the Hobos, Orhalla Zander, who becomes Molotov's guide as he searches for the creator of their brave new world.

Thus begins the tale of a fictional character, Molotov Alva, a man who leaves his real-world home in Petaluma, California, to immerse himself inside the virtual world Second Life. The project, from filmmaker Douglas Gayeton, offers an extreme example of *extensibility*.

Second Life is a virtual world populated by avatars—representations of real people—operating within digital landscapes and places. In a sense, to join Second Life is to be born anew, to adopt a new identity and to enter the world naked and penniless. For some, Second Life is transformative, a way to act out life on a second stage. Others see it as a rudimentary version of the complex Multi-User Dungeons (MUDs) that geeks have been playing in for years. Still others dismiss it all as rather silly. The last viewpoint, however, would be wrong.

Psychologists have long observed that people behave differently online than they do in the real world. The pros call this phenomenon *dissociative behavior*, explaining that it satisfies an unconscious need for omnipotence and control over one's environment. While such control may be absent in the real world, for many it can be attained online.

In effect, the veil of the Internet produces a "psychosocial moratorium" within which people can take on different personae than those they assume in their real lives. Thus, the meek ones in real life can be the aggressors online. The quiet folks at the office can be loud and obnoxious in chat rooms, while conversely, the office know-it-all can listen and learn without the impulse to be heard. This identity shifting allows people to extend themselves in new ways online, and this power further feeds a belief that anything is possible.

Professor Paul Channing Adams at the University of Texas calls this state of mind the "boundless self." He writes, "Extensibility transcends the body, allowing a person to overcome social and physical limitations and to participate in distant social contexts which affect his or her personal situation and shape social processes."

Importantly, these digital realms—call them persistent worlds, multi-user virtual environments (MUVEs), or massively multiplayer online games (MMOs)—are changing the business environment. Today's typical MMORPG—massively multiplayer online role-playing game—involve thousands of people from around the world in simultaneous real-time game play. As they play, the gamers intuit new forms of collective and cooperative behavior. The teens who flock to the popular realms like Maple Story, City of Heroes, Dreamlords, Jumpgate, and Flyff, are doing more than playing games, they are forming new ways to work and even shop together. One such gaming environment, Entropia Universe, calls itself a "virtual universe for interactive entertainment and trade" and is developing a full-fledged economy unto itself where people will work and shop, create and exchange value.

Today's online game and virtual worlds are more than just child's play; they are teaching us new ways to behave, to solve problems, to create opportunities, and soon enough, to execute commerce. To gloss over the significance of extensibility—of multipresence and multipersonality—is to misread the source roots of our emerging culture . . . and the worldview of your next customers. Extensible consumers are optimistic but also very hard to please. Ultimately, their optimism stems from a certainty that *you* will satisfy their needs and wants—or someone else will. In short, these customers know they are in command.

So, ask yourself: How will you track and connect with the most elusive consumers in history? How will you determine which personae are customers, and which are filtering agents and decoys? How will you overlay virtual and physical presence to satisfy customer needs? How can you make presence a personal experience?

Abundance, nonlinearity, mobility, and extensibility—amplitude—will be a driving force in the post–Jump Point world. For those organizations that can adopt and adapt to the new culture, the rewards will be enormous. For those that resist, the world will offer nothing but misery and conflict.

Download This

- The coming world will be defined by consumer amplitude.
- The world is abundant, the opportunities unlimited.
- We need no longer be prisoners of linear thinking.
- We can be mobile and connected, here and there, at the same time.
- Technology will bring personal fulfillment and the full extension of ourselves.

7

Mashup Culture

It's better to be a pirate than to join the Navy.

—STEVE JOBS

"**G**rey Tuesday" turned out to be aptly named.

The Los Angeles skies remained gray and overcast all day, with the threat of the season's first hard rain in the wind. At the iconic offices of Capitol Records in Hollywood, the mood inside reflected the dour day; and the demeanor and weather were no sunnier at the London headquarters of its parent company, EMI. That Tuesday, February 24, 2004, had company brass in a foul mood. After all, it was a moment that signaled the arrival of a new cultural force. Everybody sensed that things would be different from then on. And they were right.

To understand Grey Tuesday we need to rewind six months to the tail end of 2003. It was then that a little-known DJ by the name of Brian Burton, also known as Danger Mouse, after working for months in his homemade music studio, issued his grand opus, *The Grey Album*. The work was a "mashup," blending the music from the Beatles' *The White Album* with the vocal tracks from hip-hop star Jay-Z's *The Black Album*.

That the remixing of the two albums had created a new and unique third work did not matter. Burton was in violation of several U.S. copyright laws aimed at protecting the works of artists.

That Burton was not selling the album, only giving it away within the music community, also didn't matter; versions quickly found their way online, and people were furiously downloading the musically inventive, critically acclaimed album.

It was not long before the folks at EMI and Capitol, owners of the Beatles' copyright, caught wind of the mashup, and Burton swiftly received a nasty "cease and desist" letter from a powerful Los Angeles law firm. As he was simply practicing his art, and wanted no trouble, Burton did just that and pulled his remaining CDs from circulation. But that wasn't the end of the matter.

Upon learning that Burton got bullied by the industry suits, the music activist group Downhill Battle took up the cause. Downhill-Battle.org is a guerilla organization "working to break the major label monopoly of the record industry." To protest the clampdown on Burton, and to raise awareness to the rising tide of what some called "info-fascism" in general, the group called for a day of protest on February 24—"Grey Tuesday."

On that day of digital disobedience, and in direct defiance of EMI's legal saber rattling, hundreds of Web sites and blogs joined in to make free downloads of *The Grey Album* available. Some 100,000 copies of the album were downloaded that day. Even though it was free, in the parlance of the record industry, *The Grey Album* turned out to be a gold record.

The significance of Grey Tuesday is that it loudly signaled the emergence of the mashup culture out from the underground and started a very public cultural battle. The act of civil disobedience garnered national media attention for the cause of the "copy-fighters," those who objected to the overly restrictive controls big media places on copyrights. The battle lines were drawn.

Mashup culture signifies that we are at a new crossroads in our understanding of free speech, freedom of expression, and the fair use of intellectual property. This situation has broad implications for all businesses.

Everything Is Mashable

The Grey Album didn't represent a new genre of music; mashups aren't, and they aren't a passing fancy. And while Burton/Danger Mouse and his renegade contemporaries, with aliases like Freelance Hellraiser, Osymyso, and DJ McSleazy, helped make mashups more popular, the truth is that "mashing" is integral to the Internet mindset and worldview.

To those people acculturated by the principles of the network, the job of technology is to liberate and democratize information, be it news, political views, or digital forms of music and art. To these true believers, information should be free. And, like it or not, increasingly it is.

In today's do-it-yourself society anybody equipped with a PC and some off-the-shelf software—like FL Studio, Cubase, and Pro Tools—can deconstruct, manipulate, and reconstruct two or more tunes to create something new. And, as the attitude goes, if they can, they should.

Says Roberta Cruger on Salon.com:

> In DIY culture, consumers are the producers, owning the tools of production—a laptop instead of guitar, bass and drums. The bedroom is the studio and factory machinery moves out of the nightclub onto the Internet for millions to access. The media monopolies are fighting back, but with the airwaves gobbled up by conglomerates, homespun mash-ups may be the people's digital antidote.

The questions raised by Grey Tuesday are significant. Groups like Downhill Battle, Hip-Hop Summit Action, and PunkVoter have become politicized and galvanized over the important "grey areas" in our definitions of intellectual property. Mashing is a private matter, they assert, and a "fair use" covered by traditional rules governing property ownership. Should it be illegal, they ask, to manipulate digital information one lawfully purchases if it is for noncommercial private use? Or, they wonder, what is the difference between a DJ mashing another act's songs and a "cover" band playing them on stage? And, ultimately: isn't all work derivative? Aren't mashups little different than the borrowings that have shaped music and every other art form throughout history?

And then there is the issue of peer-to-peer file sharing. How, the free-use advocates question, can limits be put on the use and disposition of property one legally owns? And surely, how can a company be held liable for the actions of its customers? After all, that matter had been settled two decades earlier.

Sony Corp. of America v. Universal City Studios, Inc., commonly known as "the Betamax case," is a landmark copyright case decided by the U.S. Supreme Court in 1984. In the Betamax case, the Supreme Court ruled that a company was not liable for creating a product that some customers may use for copyright-infringing purposes—as long as the technology is capable of substantial noninfringing uses. Today companies such as Apple, Cisco Systems, and Hewlett-Packard that makes photocopiers, cameras, routers, or music players safely operate under this doctrine.

But the application of this to file-sharing technology would be tested in the 2001 matter of *A&M Records, Inc. v. Napster, Inc.* This case pitted music industry giant A&M Records against a scruffy little Internet start-up called Napster that gave people a platform to share personal files with one another. Napster's software allowed users to load files—of content they had presumably purchased lawfully—onto their own computers and allow other Napster users to access and retrieve those files on demand. The service became wildly popular as a way for millions of kids and others to share freely their music collections. *Freely* was the operative word, and the music industry took immediate action to shutter this perceived threat to its profits.

Although Napster served only as an intermediary and never actually housed any files or copyrighted material, the Ninth Circuit Court of Appeals decided in February 2001 that the company was indeed aiding the illegal copying and transfer of copyright-protected works. The Napster injunction effectively shut down the operation . . . until it reemerged later as a legal music download-ing service.

A less-definitive precedent emerged from *MGM Studios, Inc. v. Grokster, Ltd.*, which, like the Betamax case, also went all the way to the Supreme Court. In this case, the matter turned on the "intention" of the peer-to-peer services Grokster, Kazaa, and Morpheus that were the defendants. The Court ruled against them on the grounds that they "induced" customers to use the service specifically for illegal purposes. That distinction made this case different than the Betamax case. The Internet community inter-preted this ruling to mean that you could go on facilitating file sharing as long as you did not appear to promote the sharing of copyrighted material.

But a less ambiguous, more ominous response came in May 2006 when the Motion Picture Association of America (MPAA) prevailed upon the Swedish government to close down torrent file-sharing service PirateBay.com based in Stockholm. Attired in full SWAT gear, the Swedish police raided the PirateBay offices, seized its servers, and briefly detained employees.

Questions about "fair use," "originality" and "ownership" of creative content are among the defining issues of a new generation of consumers, and to that extent *The Grey Album* and Grey Tues-day provide important insights into the new culture. Mashups aren't simply a music industry problem that can be dealt with or stopped by legal means. In the post–Jump Point culture, mashing is a cultural keystone. And with the right technology, everything is mashable. The ability to transform, reshape, and recreate infor-mation is a fundament of the Information Age.

What are the roots of this changing definition of property? Again, we look to the network itself. The network makes infor-mation more available and more transparent than ever before. This great leveling demystifies and flattens; it exposes the inner workings of many processes and industries and weakens the power of—and regard for—hierarchy and command and control.

The result appears as antipathy toward the establishment and authority, but the attitude is more nuanced than that. Today, consumers aren't wasting attention, time, or energy to actively oppose any system; they simply see themselves as wielding power and they choose to ignore the old shackles.

As we saw earlier in the discussion of its basic properties, the network wants to share information; node-to-node communication is part of the genetic makeup of the Net. Trying to impede peer-to-peer file swapping contradicts the very imperative of the network. And you can't stop the network from acting like a network.

The other big issue is the murky nature of authorship and ownership in a world of collectivism. As more people participate, in one form or fashion, in the consumption-production cycle, establishing clear lines of authorship and ownership of creative works will become increasingly difficult—at least in the minds of consumers. After all the futile attempts to forestall this emerging reality through legal and legislative means are exhausted, some sort of new market accommodation will be reached. This will likely mean new formal and informal mechanisms to co-own and share outcomes. As with attention credits discussed earlier, many consumers will expect a level of rights concomitant with their level of participation in the creative process.

These attitudes cannot be dismissed as the folly of youth. According to a 2003 *New York Times*/CBS News poll, the idea that file sharing is acceptable has spread across nearly every demographic group, with 27 percent of Internet users between the ages of 30 and 49 already involved in the practice. A survey released the same year by the Pew Internet and American Life Project found that even 12 percent of those over the age of 50 participate in file sharing.

From the *New York Times* coverage: "Pew also found that among the 35 million adults that its survey indicated download music, 23 million said they did not much care about the copyright on the files they copied onto their computers. Among the 26 million who made files available for others to copy, 17 million did not care much about whether they were copyrighted."

Since the consumer is also a producer and the user an active participant, the lines of ownership are blurred. Again, the new politics of information says that content has many owners. The new consumer sees appropriation everywhere, on television, in cinema, in literature, and in the advertising that engulfs us. Why not join in?

Predictably, and despite industry attempts to stem the tide, the practices of file sharing and mashing have only grown, spilling over to other arenas. Today, people can share photos, slide shows, and movies just as easily as music. Some of this may be clear-cut violations of copyright law, other cases are more complicated. And teasing out copyrighted materials embedded into otherwise amateur works may simply be a fool's errand.

And, while the major film studios have begun taking action against copyright infringements propagated via the wildly popular file-sharing service YouTube, the floodgates are already wide open. Succeed at putting YouTube in check and a dozen other companies will fill the void. Companies like Vimeo, Eyespot, Jumpcut, Ourmedia, Dailymotion, Blip.tv, vSocial, Grouper, Revver, VideoEgg, and Revo already make it easy for users to watch, share, edit, or post videos online—including works of suspect ownership. There is a growing sense that controlling the consumer by controlling the middlemen may be a losing battle now best won by a business accord.

For its part, however, the music industry has refused to give up the ghost, attempting instead to tighten its reins on content by adopting various forms of subscription and digital rights management (DRM) schemes. Encoding musical works with secret DRM software prevents consumers from changing or sharing the files.

This attempt, of course, has provoked international outrage. Anti-DRM organizations have sprouted up worldwide for consumers to combat this perceived clampdown on fair use. The organizations include DefectiveByDesign.org, a campaign of the Free Software Foundation, which aims to "make all manufacturers wary about bringing their DRM-enabled products to market," and Digital-Freedom.org, whose mission is protect "the rights of artists, innovators and consumers to use digital technology free of unreasonable government restrictions or punitive lawsuits."

A growing campus campaign with even wider aims is being led by FreeCulture.org, a student organization with chapters across the United States. FreeCulture takes the view that information democracy is the key to a better world and that objective starts with the basic right of ownership. From the organization's manifesto:

> We refuse to accept a future of digital feudalism where we do not actually own the products we buy, but we are merely granted limited uses of them as long as we pay the rent. We must halt and reverse the recent radical expansion of intellectual property rights, which threaten to reach the point where they trump any and all other rights of the individual and society.

The Open Source Roots

Well before mashups made the headlines, the battle lines were being drawn in the battle to rethink authorship and ownership of knowledge products.

Begun in the 1980s, the Open Source Initiative was founded on collectivist ideals in reaction to behemoth corporate software programs like the UNIX computer operating system. The goal was (and is) the proliferation of software with relaxed or no intellectual property restrictions.

More than that, open source is a philosophy which holds that knowledge should be shared, that creative works improve with collective effort. The ethos is simple: software should be free to use, study, modify, and redistribute as long as those who share it also improve it along the way.

The most famous and well-supported open source software was originally developed by Finnish engineer Linus Torvalds. His project, which we now know as Linux, started out as a UNIX-like operating system for PCs. It has since evolved to become one of the most influential platforms in the software world. Ironically, and despite its anticorporate and antiestablishment roots, Linux is increasingly the software of choice for corporate players who want to benefit from the cost and practical benefits of an open source product. At the same time, thousands of organizations have sprouted up around the world to facilitate and moderate Linux and other open source platforms.

Make no mistake: the open source movement is a cultural force. It says that information is best when collectively produced and it should be shared with all who contributed to it. This is different than "free." Yes, there are those who believe knowledge products generally should be free. For example, the aim of Free Software advocates is actually to replace proprietary software under restrictive licensing terms with free software available to everyone. These folks do not advocate stealing existing software; instead, they support making free alternatives available.

By contrast, open source presupposes an obligation to contribute to the "stone soup" of a better end product. Making a contribution earns you the access. A variant of this ethic can be found in the idea of the "commons"—the belief that some, if not all, aspects of creative works are meant to be free from oppressive restrictions. The leading proponent of the commons approach is CreativeCommons.org, which aims to provide free tools that allow authors, scientists, artists, and educators to make their work at least partially available to the public. The idea is to change copyright terms from "All Rights Reserved" to "Some Rights Reserved."

The Wealth of the Commons

Ask any Pakistani on the street and he or she probably has a favorite Junoon song.

By no means a household name in the West, Junoon is nonetheless one of the biggest selling bands in the world, with more than 25 million albums sold. Its name is Urdu for "obsession" and the title fits: since its founding in 1990, the band, based out of Karachi, has become a pop phenomenon throughout South Asia. The band plays a fusion of conventional rock forms and subcontinental Sufi music. The resulting mashup creates a new form called "Sufi rock."

Junoon's founder and creative force is Dr. Salman Ahmad, a Pakistani doctor, musician, and former actor. In July 2007, the multiplatinum recording artist Ahmad made his entire catalog of music available on the iTunes alternative, Magnatune. To mark the occasion, Ahmad also made one of his most popular songs, "Natchoongi," available under license. In partnership with mashup Web site ccMixter, Magnatune sponsored a month-long contest to allow fans to make their own remixes or mashups of "Natchoongi." The best submissions were signed to a record deal with Magnatune, and the winning entries were released on a remix album.

This example stands in stark contrast to the imbroglio over *The Grey Album* and illustrates the differing mindsets of the pre- and post-Jump Point worlds.

Imagining a world in which three billion people can directly interact, communicate, and create requires new ways to manage knowledge products. That's the idea behind CreativeCommons.org. In order to maximize the creative wealth of a diverse citizenry, Creative Commons allows content producers to license their work with varying degrees of control. As explained on its Web site: "Creative Commons licenses give you the ability to dictate how others may exercise your copyright rights—such as the right of others to copy your work, make derivative works or adaptations of your work, to distribute your work and/or make money from your work."

Founded in 2001 by Stanford professor Lawrence Lessig, Creative Commons is based on the belief that ideas are abundant and that collective works can be both powerful and empowering. The resulting environment is a win-win situation, Lessig has argued. Artists win by retaining ultimate control of their work, while keeping open a collaborative conversation with fans. Users win by gaining better access to content they can rework to express themselves and produce a unique outcome.

The alternative to a world of abundance and collaboration, the advocates of the commons warn, is a world of conflict and creative stalemates.

Take, for example, the increasingly heated interplay in the world of patent law. Years of rulings and interpretations have produced what many believe are overly restrictive and overly broad patent regulations. Some people have gone so far as to call these restrictions an "innovation tax" on inventors and entrepreneurs. At worst, these restrictions could impede the discovery and development process as inventors become discouraged or frightened off. Yes, I believe the works of artists and authors—including my own—should be protected from wholesale pilfering. But we also have to strive for balance. Inherently, the creative process is iterative, even at times derivative. As copyright scholar and University of Michigan Law School professor Jessica Litman puts it:

> All authorship is fertilized by the work of prior authors, and the echoes of old work in new work extend beyond ideas and concepts to a wealth of expressive details. Indeed, authorship *is* the transformation and recombination of expression into new molds, the recasting and revision of details into different shapes. What others have expressed, and the ways they have expressed it, are the essential building blocks of any creative medium. . . . The use of the work of other authors in one's own work inheres in the authorship process.

In short, we all stand on the shoulders of those who came before us, and we must permit some latitude in the creative process or we risk tamping down the creative genius that is humankind.

Internet Speakeasies

Ingenuity always finds a way, and some believe the heavy-handed tactics of the entertainment industry toward file sharing has accelerated the adoption of *darknets*. A darknet is a private network, a sort of gated online community. Access is limited and protected by password. Like a Prohibition era basement speakeasy, you need to know the secret knock to get in.

Writing in the *New York Times*, Tim Gnatek describes darknets this way:

> Darknets, like their peer-to-peer predecessors Napster, Kazaa and Gnutella, allow users to browse and download digital files like movies and music from other people's computers. But while Napster and its ilk have allowed unrestricted access to files on any of the millions of connected computers, darknets are more discriminating. In a darknet, users get access only through established relationships—and only when they have been invited to join. This selectivity promises greater privacy, regardless of whether the networks are used for sharing personal or pirated media.

For their part, hosting services work to stay out of the crosshairs of the entertainment industry by publicly (at least) prohibiting illegal file sharing. Many limit music downloads or allow listen-only modes. They also rely on self-policing by keeping group memberships small and adding a whistleblower to the mix. However, the more savvy users are familiar with the many ways to end-run file-sharing restrictions. Some entire groups, such as Krakk'd, Warez, and Xbox Games are dedicated to quietly circulating pirated and cracked code.

Darknets exist for just about every conceivable interest, from sports to religion, politics, and hobbies. Grouper, acquired in 2006 by Sony, is one of the largest of the darknet services, and hosts more than 100,000 private groups. Users can build their own darknets or request admission to thousands of publicly listed clubs.

For those who want to build their own darknets, a combination of free and fee-based companies offer darknet technology, including Freenet, Waste, DC, BadBlue, and Groove. Freenet, the brainchild of Irish programmer Ian Clarke, protects user anonymity through encryption technology, not trust. This makes it a favorite platform for political dissidents in places like China and Iran to communicate and organize and remain undetected by their governments.

Pirates at the Gates

The propaganda warring surrounding copyright law took to the playgrounds in 2006 when Canada's copyright licensing agency, Access Copyright, published a children's Web site centered on the adventures of "Captain Copyright," a superhero "dedicated to fighting for the rights of artists." The controversial—and short-lived—campaign was aimed at teaching school children about the sanctity of digital and copyrights. The campaign was quickly scuttled when public outcry mounted, but not before Canadian writer and programmer "MCM" published the children's storybook, *The Pig and the Box*. A modern fable about the perils of overly restrictive digital rights management, the pig in *The Pig and the Box* finds a magic box that can replicate anything you put into it. At first, the pig hoards the box and tries to control what his neighbors do with it—until he sees the light and starts to share and trust his fellow barnyard denizens. That the book has since been translated into a dozen languages speaks to the global nature of mashup culture.

The politics of information control is not kids' play, though; it is heating up around the world. For some, the idea of hiding out in an underground railroad of closeted darknets is anathema. Information, these copyright contras believe, is overregulated and overcontrolled by media monopolists. They are fighting mad and fighting back. At the vanguard is a global political movement called the Pirate Party.

Launched in January 2006 by Swedish entrepreneur Rickard Falkvinge, the party now has chapters in 20 nations, including the United States, the United Kingdom, Russia, South Africa, and Australia. The stated platform of the party is to "fundamentally reform copyright law, get rid of the patent system, and ensure that citizens' rights to privacy are respected." The latter issue responds to the emergence of what the party calls the "surveillance state" it believes has accompanied the war on terror in the United States and Europe.

The genesis of the party was the passing in 2005 of a restrictive Swedish law on Internet downloads. Much like the U.S. model, the law made it easier for content providers to prosecute downloaders. Sparked by the law, the party's platform came together and its status as a political organization was formalized in early 2006 as it positioned to run candidates in Sweden's general election that year.

Successfully making it onto the ballot, the Pirate Party officially captured 34,918 votes for that first outing. Well below the 4 percent threshold required to win a seat in the Swedish Parliament, the tally was still large enough to make the Pirates, after just nine months in existence, Sweden's tenth-largest political party. The Pirate Party plans to run candidates in the European Parliament election in 2009 and again in the Swedish general election in 2010.

Despite not winning a seat in the Swedish Parliament, the Pirate Party is widely credited with changing the political climate and the positions of the other parties. Candidates from the Green, Moderate, and Left parties all changed their platforms on Internet downloads to match that of the Pirate Party during the 2006 elections.

When Crowds Speak

The era of the "programmable Web" is making mashups of all sorts ever more possible. Today, users can mix, match, and manipulate many online applications to create a unique personal experience. Companies such as Google and Yahoo! have embraced the mashup mindset and are allowing their users access to select application programming interfaces (APIs).

One such API is for the maps function. Employing the Google Maps API, users can embed full map functionality onto their own Web sites. They can also mash up the maps by adding their own information points. This capability has proven popular among online real estate sites wanting to show house shoppers specific neighborhood features.

By and large, business leaders are rational and they know a good thing when they see it. That explains the growing appreciation for, and adoption of, a form of mashup called "crowdsourcing," or as Trendwatching.com calls it, "crowd clout." In its various forms, from group shopping to collective product design, crowdsourcing builds on the idea of the wisdom of crowds—that all individuals know something and that crowds of individuals know a lot. Companies breaking ground in this category include CrowdSpirit, CrowdStorm, TeamBuy, LetsBuyIt, and We-Match.

One company working to ease the tensions around creative licensing is LegalForce.com. LegalForce is a marketplace for intellectual property, populated by a professional network for inventors, patent attorneys, entrepreneurs, licensing professionals, and investors. LegalForce allows users to buy, sell, and license intellectual property (and perhaps stay out of court).

In a broader sense, so-called we media citizen journalism is also a phenomenon of both the wisdom of the crowds ethos and the open source movement. Since the Internet gives people the power to communicate directly with one another, and because the business of newsgathering benefits from diverse reporting and sources, many established media players are opening their doors to journalists. CNN has established its I-Reporter online desk to capture the citizen reports from the field, as has NewAssignment.net and Wired with its Assignment Zero project.

Not everyone, however, is bullish on the wisdom of crowds. Critics worry that we may forget that an ignorant crowd is a mob, and that a confederacy of dunces is of no value. And, some people argue, citizen media and the rise of the amateur are actually dumbing down our culture.

In his book, *The Cult of the Amateur*, author Andrew Keen takes on what he believes is misguided exuberance for amateurs and crowds. Critical of everything from Craigslist to Wikipedia to YouTube, Keen worries that in our eagerness to embrace the technology and worldview of the network, we are placing in peril hundreds of years of institutional knowledge and shared values. He writes that "instead of a dictatorship of experts we will have a dictatorship of idiots."

As with governments, we do seem to get the culture we deserve.

Life in Absurdia

If you have ever sung *Happy Birthday to You* at a child's birthday party or office gathering, and you didn't pay royalties for that privilege, you committed a crime. Likewise, if you sing in the shower, or air it out exuberantly in the car during your daily commute or even whistle while you work, you probably owe royalties to someone. And lest you think these are insignificant indiscretions, think again. The rights to *Happy Birthday to You*—a four line ditty written in 1893 by sisters Patty and Mildred J. Hill—are today owned by the Warner Music Group and they typically charge up to $10,000 for a public use of the familiar song.

As we consider the future of mashup culture, intellectual property rights, and copyright and patent laws, the one thing we can be sure of is that a societal showdown looms certain. As our expanding definitions of freedom of speech and personal liberty—encouraged by our use of information technology—continue to clash with the expanding rights of authors and artists, tensions will only grow. And, as traditional distributors of music, films and literature become marginalized by personal technology, they are more likely to see their future as nothing more than hardass copyright enforcers.

How Strange Could Things Get?

In a 2007 paper entitled *Infringement Nation: Copyright Reform and the Norm/Law Gap*, University of Utah professor John Tehranian paints a bleak picture of an absurd dystopia where nearly every creative endeavor by one is hemmed in by the property claims of another. In the paper, Tehranian points out how frequently—if innocently—each of us today violates one or another statute of the Copyright Act. He colorfully makes his point with the example of a day in the life of a hypothetical college professor (not unlike himself), who through the course of the day unwittingly commits myriad violations of current copyright law. From reading a poem aloud in class, to baring an unauthorized tattoo of a copyrighted cartoon character, to singing *Happy Birthday to You* to a colleague at a restaurant, the professor racks up some 83 violations in a day, with potential fees, fines, and damages totaling $12.45 million.

More troubling is Tehranian's observation that the tools that allow us to create and share in new ways—the backbone of mashup culture—may also be used to enforce an environment of copyright tyranny. "The very technologies that enhance our media experiences are rapidly bringing us closer to the Panopticon state in which a near-total enforcement of intellectual property rights becomes viable," he writes. He suggests, for example, the application of voice recognition technology built into our car stereos that might hear us sing along to the radio and then send us a bill in the mail for the privilege.

"One can readily imagine a future dystopian world where the record labels, long since irrelevant to the development and distribution of new music, become nothing more than copyright trolls, drawing their revenue entirely from collections (or litigation) of this kind," he writes.

The Coming Global Mashup

The Monserrat Bar in Havana looked like it hadn't changed since Hemingway drank there.

My friend Mark and I had just settled in with fresh mojitos when a pair of patrons burst through the front doors. Dressed in old school jerseys, baggy pants, Converse All-Stars, and Red Sox baseball caps, the duo could have been out of Bed Sty or East L.A. Taking the stage vacated when the traditional *son* band took a break, they placed a boom box in front of a downstage microphone and pushed the On button.

What came next was an energetic and mesmerizing hip-hop version of the classic Cuban folk song, "Chan Chan." The song, written by the legendary Compay Segundo, touches a chord deep in the Cuban psyche; it is a precious part of the musical culture.

On stage, the two rappers creatively wove the song's chorus to a familiar hip-hop back beat and cadence. These weren't ghetto-wannabes or caricatures. They were making a statement about Cuba's vitality and future. The resulting work was stunning; not just for its musicality, but also for its symbolism. If there were any doubts that this poor island country could bootstrap itself into the future, these two kids allayed them.

The duo concluded to enthusiastic applause from the audience, collected a few pesos en route to the door, and disappeared back into the Havana night as quickly as they arrived.

The cynical might see this event as another example of American cultural imperialism at work. But, one might rightly ask, did these young artists bastardize their culture or improve it—and ours? Were they seduced by the American myth of the urban hipster, or did they create something new and vital, meshing old Cuba with new?

It is easy to worry that American or Western culture will dominate the post–Jump Point world; but that is Broadcast Era thinking. The network, by its very nature, does not favor homogeneity or hegemony. Yes, in the age of big media, American culture had been a dominant force. But consider that America also had more content to feed into the broadcast infrastructure—movies, television, print. By comparison, the Internet empowers cultural conversations, and that empowerment will mean convergence and compromise. It will certainly make for a more interesting world. And there are few, if any, structural barriers to this cultural pluralism. America itself is one big mashup, a rich amalgam of cultures as diverse as those who contribute to it.

Similarly, don't expect the Network Era to produce a global, vanilla, "mall of the world" pop culture. Rather, we can expect a hybridized and complex culture as rich in diversity as the three billion people who occupy the networked world.

Economic historian Eric L. Jones, in *Cultures Merging*, says this is how culture has always been revitalized and renewed: "Throughout history the growing trend has been for societies, belief systems and languages to come into contact, borrow from each other, and at times merge."

In that sense, the culture behind the new economy will be a merger, not an acquisition.

The network moves culture faster than any previous technology ever could. But it is a continuous loop: instead of being cultural imperialism, an idea goes out, gets reshaped, and comes back new. In this new reality, "mass appeal" is not a lowest common denominator; it is the highest form of acceptance.

In a world informed by mashup culture, customers expect to have a hand in everything. Sales become interchanges, not transactions, and everything is negotiable. The new power-sharing arrangement is a marketer's dream: the customer helps design the product to his or her exact specifications. But, customers who coproduce also expect to be rewarded.

How will you accommodate the new mashup mindset? When customers expect to change the product or the value proposition, when they believe they are empowered to mix things up, how will you create an interactive experience? How will you adjust your marketing plans for a new, blended consumer culture, including differences in language, tastes, and wants?

Download This

- People are now simultaneously producers and consumers of content.
- Our ideas of creative process and creative ownership are changing.
- Open source, peer-to-peer file sharing, and remix media mashing are cultural pillars.
- There is a growing global backlash mounting against overly restrictive property rights.

8

Trust Is the New Money

Nothing influences a person more than a recommendation from a trusted friend.

— FACEBOOK CEO MARK ZUCKERBURG

With more than 300 rainy or overcast days a year, Seattle seems the perfect city from which to launch a coffee roasting and brewing empire.

That Seattle-based Starbucks has grown to be a blockbuster global brand, with more than 15,000 outlets in 36 countries and five new locations opening somewhere every day does not surprise the locals. From its original quirky store, which opened in Pikes Market in 1971, to every location that has followed, Starbucks has pursued a consistent vision of providing customers with a unique experience: an array of artisan-roasted coffees, a passion for predictable product quality, and the kind of "third places" people like to gather and socialize in.

Like all great brands, Starbucks has developed a distinctive corporate culture. Treating its people well is part of the corporate vision, and "partners"—or employees—are well trained, receive good pay and benefits, and seem to really enjoy their working conditions and environment. Few companies have worked harder to build an image as a company with integrity, ideals, and a real moral center than Starbucks.

That's what makes the events of August 2006 so baffling.

To promote a refreshing version of its coffees during the dog days of summer that year, Starbucks' marketing department sent out an e-mail coupon to employees in the Southeast region redeemable for a free iced latte. Although the coupon was intended for use only in that region between August 23 and September 30, the coupon mentioned nothing about location, and the date was easily changeable. The cover memo encouraged employees to share the coupon with friends and family. And so they did.

To no one's surprise (with the exception apparently of the Starbucks' marketing brass), the e-mail coupon spread like a virus across the Internet. The coupon began showing up in stores nationwide well beyond the Southeast region. Employees outside the region had not been forewarned of the coupon, and confusion ensued. Within a few weeks, the rate of redemption of the coupons was so high and the head scratching by baristas so deafening that the company took action to kill the promotion. A crude sign started to pop at counters nationwide:

> An email offering a free Starbucks iced coffee beverage was distributed by Starbucks partners (employees) with instructions to forward it to their group of friends and family. Unfortunately, it has been redistributed beyond the original intent and modified beyond Starbucks control. Regretfully this email offer will no longer be valid at any Starbucks location effective immediately.

Needless to say, the sign only made matters worse . . . and raised even more hackles as regulars who had not heard of the coupon wondered why they hadn't. Even more confusion reigned as the counter staff waged a losing battle to assuage customers who felt, one way or another, truly or vaguely cheated. Photos of the sign and bitchy blogs started popping up all over the Internet, further alerting devotees who never heard of the brouhaha.

The bad news continued when a New York City lawyer filed a $114 million class action lawsuit initiated by a young woman who was "let down" when she learned that the coupon would no longer be honored. The lawsuit alleged that Starbucks had not only breached a contract but also acted fraudulently because it knew people would continue to stop in with the irredeemable coupons and probably end up instead forking over their own money for the beverage.

In a final indignity, rival coffeehouse chain Caribou made headlines and new friends when it announced that it would be honoring the besmirched Starbucks' coupons during a one-day promotion.

One has to wonder how a company as media and Internet savvy as Starbucks got into this mess. Clearly, management should have anticipated the potential risk of a viralized coupon. Surely someone must have developed a contingency plan in case this happened. It was, after all, not the first such outbreak. The same thing had happened to the company five years earlier, when a faux coupon for free Crème Frappuccinos circulated around the Washington, D.C., area. In the end, Starbucks needlessly brewed up a lot of ill will for the way the matter was handled on the front lines.

It was a tempest in a chai cup, you might say—a minor indiscretion by a beloved brand with plenty of goodwill in the bank. And assuredly, it pales in comparison to the scandalous behavior of the Enrons and WorldComs of recent memory. But the dust-up illustrates two important points about the networked economy. First, the Internet will always behave like the Internet. So only use it to distribute information you want to be replicated, repeated, and otherwise spread to all corners of the globe. Secondly, trust is the irreducible bedrock of business today, and even small breaches can have major consequences. In fact, in a global network economy where billions of impersonal and anonymous interactions take place daily, trust is everything: every breach is a crisis.

The Reputation Economy

It's a breathtaking reality: three billion people buying from and selling to each other—directly. No middlemen, arbiters, or government agencies between them. On the other hand, can there be a more unnerving thought? Without mediators, who will enforce the rule of law, guarantee performance, and punish cheats? The answer is not so simple.

Our current world trading scheme was many hundreds of years in the making. Forged in ancient places, like Catal Huyak and Jericho and cities at the dawn of civilization, the system has evolved, in fits and starts, over the course of several millennia. The process has been slow and difficult, sometimes even violent, but it has produced a business culture that, despite otherwise profound regional differences, is surprisingly consistent and coherent. Rules and protocols regarding everything from contracts to competition are largely adhered to by all players—and as a result the overall business environment acts as a multiplier to the billions of individual business transactions that take place every day.

Over the last 250 years, since the rise of the Industrial Revolution, this combination has had a remarkable impact on human society, producing unprecedented leaps in per capita wealth, overall health, and life expectancy. During that time, these forces have enabled the developed world to escape centuries of stasis and adopt a pattern of continuous improvement.

This global economic system is not only powerful, but also resilient and adaptive, not only surviving wars and depressions, but also emerging each time even stronger. But this system has never faced a challenge quite like the networked era of the Jump Point. We are entering a vulnerable stage of history, a time when old institutions, organizations, and standing rules will be challenged and could even be undone by the properties of the network. The resulting state will be fraught with what economists call "environmental" and "behavioral" uncertainties. In short, we may not know whom or what to trust.

One problem is that in a world of direct, unfettered communication and trade, governments and corporate entities can only do so much. Despite the existence of world trading bodies and accords, global people-to-people exchanges will be hard to regulate. In the end, self-policing will be essential, as will mechanisms to encourage and reward the only truly global medium of exchange that matters: mutual trust and respect.

Is such a trust-centered, reputation-based system possible? Yes. But to see it in action, we have to look back a thousand years.

The Maghribi Traders

If you think Baghdad is chaotic today, you should have seen it in the 10th century. In the interregnum between the decline of the Abbasids and the rise of the Fatimid dynasty, chaos reigned more than anything else. At the same time, the region had been engaged in fruitful and expanding trade throughout the Mediterranean region, from Gibraltar to Asia Minor. Despite the unsettled political backdrop, private merchants did not want to see that trade imperiled. To set up a system that could exist largely outside government intervention, they formed an alliance, a social group, called the Maghribi Traders.

Stanford economist Avner Greif has spent a career studying the Maghribi, and in his book *Institutions and the Path to the Modern Economy: Lessons from Medieval Trade* he shows how the group set up a complicated international trading system backed only by trust. He calls their scheme a "multilateral reputational mechanism."

According to Greif, the Maghribi's medieval mutual benefit society worked on the principle that people are rational and will act in their own best interests. Spice and textile trade between the Middle East and Europe was proving to be very lucrative. The incentives for participation in the trading were great and the inducements to remain in the trading alliance abundantly clear. Remarkably, the system, even across many miles and cultures, operated basically on a handshake.

Given the cost and time of going to court over business disputes—not to mention the often corrupt and uneven disposition of justice from the Fatimidi judges—the Maghribi created their own stateless form of justice that worked very well. The key to ensuring performance and compliance: cheats and deadbeats were immediately humiliated and ostracized. In today's parlance, they were voted off the island. The fear of public reprisal and shunning proved to be an extraordinary self-enforcing mechanism.

The power of public embarrassment and the fear of shunning is a dynamic that works well for a finite group of traders, in small towns and among tightly knit communities like the Mennonites and the Amish, but can it be applied to the Internet age?

Defining Trust

Australian scholar Roger Clarke sums it up succinctly: "Trust is confident reliance by one party about the behavior of other parties."

In an era when photos easily can be fixed, documents forged, and video fudged, you can't always believe even your own eyes. For companies, the Starbucks dilemma is a cautionary tale. Even when you flub, you'd better keep the faith and honor the coupon.

For customers, it makes you wonder whom you can really trust. And that question—whom *can* you trust?—will be the elemental force behind the coming post–Jump Point marketplace. More than technology, convenience, or price, trust will be the differentiator and coin of the new realm. Smart companies will pursue the goal of becoming the "most trusted" source, expert, or problem solver in their industries. And because trust can be lost, companies will spend a lot of capital cultivating and protecting their trustworthiness.

Trust Is the Engine of Commerce

Trust matters, particularly in a networked economy of three billion people where interactions are never face to face and are rarely between people who know each other well. Trust greases the machinery of the network.

As University of Washington's Batya Friedman puts it, trust "allows us to reveal vulnerable parts of ourselves to others and to know others intimately in return. A climate of trust eases cooperation among people and fosters reciprocal care-taking. The resources—physical, emotional, economic—that would otherwise be consumed guarding against harm can be directed toward more constructive ends."

In other words, the existence of trust frees the human spirit to be creative, generous, and authentic instead of protective, cynical, and false.

More importantly, trust has been shown to be at the foundation of economic growth. In their landmark study of 37 regions, economists Paul Zak and Stephen Knack found a direct correlation between economic growth and trust levels in a region. Factors contributing to the level of trust included a country's legal and regulatory environment; social norms; diligence by those doing the transaction; per capita income; income inequality; and social, ethnic, and linguistic heterogeneity.

The study found trust high in places like Norway (65 percent believe their fellow citizens to be trustworthy) and very low in places like Brazil (only 3 percent see their compatriots as trustworthy). In all cases, the countries with the highest trust levels have the highest per capita incomes and GDPs. "Because trust reduces the cost of transactions, high trust societies exhibit better economic performance than low trust societies," Zak explains.

Writes economist Kenneth Arrow, "Almost every commercial transaction has within itself an element of trust, certainly any transaction conducted over a period of time. It can be plausibly argued that much of economic backwardness in the world can be explained by the lack of mutual confidence."

An important measure of trust is reputation. Reputation is a way to predict future behavior based on past actions. It is an essential measure of trustworthiness. We intuitively measure reputation in our daily lives: reputations of individuals, as when we choose a family doctor; of groups, as when we decide what social networks to join; and of brands, as when we decide which dishwasher to buy. In fact, for some businesses, reputation is the stock in trade.

To illustrate, consider eBay. Millions of anonymous people buy and sell to each other every day using the eBay marketplace. It is safe to assume that none of them would do so if they thought they would be cheated, yet there are no institutional protections in place. In fact, eBay is only the moderator in these transactions and does not guarantee the veracity of the product claims and descriptions or the trustworthiness of the sellers or buyers. Instead, not unlike the Maghribi Traders, eBay helps the community police itself with a reputation feedback system.

After every trade, eBay users are encouraged to post feedback about the experience and rate their trading partner. Trades in which the buyer and seller promptly exchange money for value, yield positive feedback for both parties. Trades in which one party fails to come through fairly or in a timely way, yield negative feedback. Then eBay collects all feedback and makes it transparent to anyone considering future trades with the listed parties. In this way, the consumers decide for themselves who is trustworthy and who is not.

Reputation systems like eBay's are powerful enforcers of behavior in committed communities where reasonable people fear the reprisals of untrustworthiness. In low-commitment communities, or in cases in which nefarious people hope to cash in on reputation for a quick gain before exiting the community, reputation systems aren't as effective. And, no system is foolproof. For example, there have been numerous examples over the past decade of individuals working eBay's reputation system. Some will shill for others to establish fake positive reputations, or they will actually earn a good reputation over time, only to set up a big-ticket scam and then disappear.

Trust as a Competitive Advantage

A couple of years ago I was sitting talking shop with Scott Cook, the bespectacled and intense cofounder and chairman of software maker Intuit, when he asked me what I thought his company's key differentiator was.

As the company behind such products as Quicken, QuickBooks, and TurboTax, Intuit was and is the number one name in personal and small business financial software. I think Cook expected to hear something about market share or switching costs, but instead I answered "trust."

Indeed, in a business where you are handling people's money and livelihoods, there can be no more critical quality than the earned trust of the customer. Furthermore, I told Cook that Intuit could do well to leverage the trust it had already earned to enter new financial submarkets and businesses. Happily, the company has done just that, expanding into areas such as online banking and health and medical records management, areas where absolute trust must be a given.

Looking back, even if Intuit was a leader in something less intimate than personal finance, my take would have been the same. In fact, in the age of the Internet, no matter what business you're in, trust makes all the difference.

Today's consumer no longer sees the Internet as mysterious or something just this side of magic. It is simply a utility that allows every computer (or information device or phone) to connect with every other computer in the world.

One side-effect of this great web of human interaction is that when we connect with such a big network we inevitably deal with strangers as well as friends. It is possible for people to hide behind their computers—create alter egos, screen names, even fake identities—in order to remain anonymous. But, this only works to a point. One of the reasons to join this network of humanity is to connect and relate at a human level. The Internet favors community building because that's what people favor. Communities are hard places to be anonymous in.

Community members and visitors who don't identify themselves and, worse, don't contribute to the community are called out as "lurkers," and "social freeloaders," and they are frowned upon, even ridiculed. A lurker is someone who can't be trusted. And, when you may never physically see the other person on the other side of a communication, or never know the seller you are buying from, all new rules of engagement are required. That's why the new consumer prefers transparency in all things—open systems, full disclosure, user-driven ratings, candor, and trust.

The Internet both allows and demands transparency at the same time. Given the open access to information it permits, regular people are now privy to the inner workings of more things. The new consumers believe that information is their birthright. That genie won't be put back in the bottle. At the same time, the Internet as a trading medium is not sustainable without a belief system based on trust.

As peer-to-peer computing expert Todd Sundsted has written, "It's easy to establish trust in small networks where every entity knows every other entity. In small networks entities are on a first-name basis, and trust can be maintained by the same social forces that operate in the real world. The difficulty establishing trust arises when a network application grows big enough that conventional social forces no longer fit the bill. The exact size of the network obviously depends on the application, but growing pains typically begin at the point at which any entity on the network no longer expects to interact only with known entities."

A business like eBay, for example, would not survive were it not for the trust users can confidently place in the system. When we buy something on eBay, we are buying from a complete stranger. If we believed that we would or might be cheated, few of us would be eager to transact on eBay. But we do trust, not only eBay as the intermediary, but also the user community itself. The eBay community is self-policing and self-correcting of cheats and fakes. Sellers and buyers earn their reputations. And reputation is one's calling card and bond on eBay. Sure, a cheater may get away with it once, but the system will brand and marginalize that person quickly.

Jamais Cascio, who advises companies, large and small, on emerging business issues, places a high value on trust and reputation management. By its nature, he observes, the networked economy makes it difficult to outrun a bad reputation:

> The traditional model of business communication has long been the broadcast, one-to-many, advertising approach, where the power disparity between company and consumer is clear. In that model, as it's relatively easy for a business to control its messages and image, trust could be built upon brand strength and loyalty. The ability of everyday citizens to push back against a corporate message was limited by the ability of citizens to access broadcast media of equivalent reach. Stories of businesses violating the trust of their customers certainly could spread, but because of the power disparity between people and companies, such stories tended to be only the most egregious examples.
>
> The Internet up-ends these power dynamics in ways that we're still slowly understanding. It's as easy for an individual to have a prominent place in the Internet culture and community as it is for a transnational corporation; arguably, the individuals can be *more* persuasive than a company, if only because people encountering a corporate Web site or message have been trained by decades of traditional advertising to be extremely skeptical. This effect is compounded by the emergent online behavior of social filtering, where people active on the web (especially in the blogging world) come to rely upon each other to sort through the overwhelming amount of information out there online.

Cascio argues that the new global economy is less like a metropolis and more like a small town:

An intensely social environment, where news of misdeeds can be spread overnight and will outlast any negative results from the misdeed. Sound familiar? It's the stereotype of small town life. And what's the worst thing you can do in a small town? Betray the trust of a neighbor by cheating or lying. That kind of behavior brings down an immediate and resounding response.

The advice is pretty simple: behave toward your stakeholders— your customers, partners, employees and shareholders—in a manner appropriate for small-town neighbors. Abusive or deceptive behavior will be caught and identified. Transparency—openness, honesty, and clarity of behavior—improves trustworthiness (you have nothing to hide), while opacity reduces the willingness of your "neighbors" (that is, anyone else online) to give you the benefit of the doubt."

A betrayal of trust can end a relationship immediately; a breach can erode it over time. A betrayal is usually final, a breach, however difficult, can sometimes be mended. A level of banked goodwill and trust doesn't make your company bulletproof, but it does give you the benefit of the doubt. Erode that trust, or draw down your bank account without replenishing it, and it can cost your bottom line.

Look what happened with Best Buy. In 2006, reports starting circulating around the Internet that the world's largest retailer was allegedly misleading customers with a dual pricing system. Apparently Best Buy maintained both a public Web site, accessible from the outside, and another site used to check pricing while in stores.

The problem was the two sites had different prices for the same items. So, if you researched a product online and found it well priced at Best Buy and then trekked down to the store to find it priced higher, naturally you'd ask a sales agent to recheck the Internet site. More often than not, the agent would pull up the internal site and verify the higher price. After a time, customers started to catch on, and the rumor mill went into high gear.

The truth was the chain did host two sites, one for the mainstream Internet, another serving as a portal for sales associates. The reasons for that, and the story behind the apparent pricing discrepancies, weren't all that nefarious. Best Buy, like many big retailers, maintained regional pricing variations depending on store performance or inventory issues. And, it also had different prices for online-only offers. Theoretically at least, any customer could ask for and, by company policy, get a price match of the best of those listed prices (if one knew that the better price existed).

So, apparently nothing intentionally unethical was going on at Best Buy. The real problem was that a too-long history of poor customer relations by Best Buy lingered on Web sites and blogs, making consumers predisposed to mistrusting the company. Every new incident only reinforced prevailing negatives.

A few years ago, a company like Best Buy could brand its way out of such a jam through the careful implementation of a public relations or advertising program. A catchy new campaign and a few deep discounts, and the public would forget, if not forgive.

By comparison, today's customer horror stories and tales of woe survive permanently and are even amplified on the Internet. Best Buy, like any company, can make a mistake, or be misinterpreted. But when trust is low—in this case, the goodwill bank account was in arrears—every new issue only feeds the flames of customer animosity.

Discussion groups and even entire blogs have been dedicated to publicly vilifying companies that consistently behave badly. Importantly, firms that provide, in Professor Greif's words, "multilateral reputation mechanisms" are on the rise. Companies like Epinions and TrustedOpinion give consumers ways to share stories about, publicly criticize, and perhaps even shun or boycott the worst offenders. And, there is no doubt, people are paying heed.

According to a survey by Edelman Public Relations, 80 percent of people stop buying products or services from companies when their trustworthiness comes into question. More than that, most people spread their distrust to friends and associates. Again, according to the survey, more than 33 percent of people who lose trust in a company openly campaign against that company on the Internet.

Smart companies know the value of trust and the power of reputation, particularly in networked times. So valuable is the concept of trust to his company's balance sheet that AOL vice chairman Ted Leonsis created the post of chief trust officer in 2003. Initially responsible for security and authentication issues, the job of CTO today is to oversee a wide range of performance integrity and customer satisfaction issues.

The bottom line: in the post–Jump Point economy the most trusted player in every industry will eventually beat out the competition.

As William Gibson warned in a seminal *New York Times* article, "The Road to Oceania":

> In the age of the leak and the blog, of evidence extraction and link discovery, truths will either out or be outed, later if not sooner. This is something I would bring to the attention of every diplomat, politician and corporate leader: the future, eventually, will find you out. The future, wielding unimaginable tools of transparency, will have its way with you. In the end, you will be seen to have done that which you did.
>
> I say "truths," however, and not "truth," as the other side of information's new ubiquity can look not so much transparent as outright crazy. Regardless of the number and power of the tools used to extract patterns from information, any sense of meaning depends on context, with interpretation coming along in support of one agenda or another. A world of informational transparency will necessarily be one of deliriously multiple viewpoints, shot through with misinformation, disinformation, conspiracy theories and a quotidian degree of madness. We may be able to see what's going on more quickly, but that doesn't mean we'll agree about it any more readily.

Whom Can You Trust?

The eighth annual survey on trust conducted by Edelman Public Relations revealed some interesting new realities about trust around the world.

The 2007 Trust Barometer has captured input from hundreds of global opinion leaders and shows that trust in traditional institutions, such as governments and the media, continues to decline. Trust in the developing world is actually higher for business and technology than for governments and media. But among the more interesting revelations is the decline in trust for experts as information sources. The most trusted category of information source is listed as "a person like yourself," demonstrating again the power of peer-to-peer communications in the networked age.

Filmmaker Jean-Luc Godard famously said that "photography is truth. And cinema is truth 24 times a second." Unfortunately, these days, neither statement is necessarily true.

In the summer of 2006, the country—and political tinderbox—Lebanon was again in flames. Covering the fighting there for news agency Reuters was a veteran photojournalist named Adrian Hajj. Hajj had many years' experience capturing breaking events on the front lines of dangerous places throughout the Middle East. Reuters was accustomed to posting his compelling shots almost as fast has he could upload them back to the newsroom.

Yet, there was something different about a photo he transmitted back from the scene of a bombing raid in Beirut. The shot showed two plumes of smoke marking where a bomb fell in the city. The problem was, only one plume was real. Other journalists who had also been on the scene noticed the discrepancy right away, and some speculated on various blogs about the bogus photo. Alerted to the suspicion, Reuters investigated and indeed found that Hajj had used PhotoShop to alter the image.

As part of the investigation, a second doctored photo emerged—this of an F-16 fighter jet with additional flares added. And still later, it was revealed that a third photograph—one beamed worldwide—of a "soldier" carrying a dead girl from a house allegedly destroyed during an Israeli air strike was actually a staged shot of a Hezbollah public relations professional. Reuters fired Hajj and removed his more than 900 photos from its library, but the damage to the agency's credibility was done.

In response to a declining trust in media institutions, we are seeing a rise in the popularity of citizen journalism, both through self-published media such as blogs and co-opted into the traditional media outlets themselves. One appeal of citizen journalism is its omnipresence: civilians closest to the action report news as it is happening.

The idea is compelling: not even the largest news organization can cover as much ground as we empowered citizens can. For once, the prospect is for news not biased by circumstance. We sense that the reportage by regular people will at least be authentic; that what it lacks in polish it will makes up in veracity.

But as we look at the rising popularity of citizen journalism and "we-TV," we have to confront the possibility that what is authentic may not always be credible. As we celebrate the elimination of intermediaries and gatekeepers, we need to acknowledge that so goes with them some rigor and scrutiny. Trust is essential in news gathering since there is a presumption of objectivity and unbiased reporting. But citizen journalists, at least to date, aren't held to the same standard as professionals; they are admittedly (and often proudly) unschooled and unpracticed in the principles and ethics of journalism. They have the tools—e-mail, cameras, and phones— but not the grounding or judgment of professional journalists. Yet, as we know from the Reuters example among others, even the best professionals can be duped, events can be staged, and digital information can be manipulated.

The dynamics that allow information to move freely through a network, the technology that allows us to easily shape and reshape information content, the ethic that individuals are powerful and crowds are knowing, are all forces that cut two ways. Empowering individuals doesn't guarantee virtuosity, and technology is a catalyst, not a compass. Stripped to its core, trust is all we have. When it is lost, so are we.

In the Network We Trust?

Given the unique properties of the network, the "horizontal" way information and value change hands, and accepting that government oversight on a worldwide basis is difficult at best, is it possible to build a "trust infrastructure"?

Pauline Ratnasingam thinks we can and we are. An outspoken authority on the question of trust and e-commerce, Professor Ratnasingam thinks that technology itself is part of the answer. She believes that "structural assurances," made possible by the application of technology, have added—and will continue to add—rigor that the net economy needs to instill trust. As the structural safety net has created environmental certainties, she reasons, our comfort zone has risen as well. With the addition of encryption, firewalls, and privacy measures; the application of password authentication and logs; and the protocols of transaction confirmation, acknowledgments, digital signatures, and backend accountability, people increasingly believe in the integrity of the system. And, as the system makes it harder for the dishonest to cheat others and evade detection, prosecution, and public scorn, new behaviors are learned. Gradually, we are laying the foundation for a new system of checks and balances, for a new era of global growth.

Radical Trust

When three billion people can buy and sell from one another directly, not even the most rigorous structural safeguards will anticipate, mediate, or resolve every problem. Something more will be required, and that something creates opportunities for smart companies. As with the Maghribi long-distance traders of the 10th century, a self-policing reputation-based system will need to be adopted to ensure that global trade doesn't collapse of its own weight. A phrase used a lot these days to describe the desired new business climate is *radical trust*. It is a state of trust where safeguards are in place, but parties on both sides of a transaction fully recognize the greater benefits of reciprocal good faith.

Customers want to trust; it removes doubt, complexity, and extra layers of decision making. For today's customers, a key to giving trust is getting it first. They want to be allowed behind the curtain, to see and even to participate in the inner workings. The more a brand lets customers into the inner circle, the more trust it earns. Again, it is a paradox of the Jump Point: less control means more trust. For too many producers and marketers, it remains a heretical proposition to implicitly trust your customers.

On his Web site Radicaltrust.ca, writer Collin Douma spells out a compelling new vision of trust in the marketplace. He writes:

In order to build a brand in the future, marketers must radically trust that consumers:

1. Are best equipped to determine their own needs, and left to their own devices, are best equipped to get those needs met.
2. Would rather be communicated with than spoken to.
3. Require freedom of expression, but often require guidelines to create expressions in.
4. Will self-regulate communities to a level that the guidelines suggest and that the collective group they comprise will accept.
5. Will disconnect with a brand that silences them, and will align with brands that give them a voice.
6. (this one is the hardest) Consumers are people and people are inherently good.

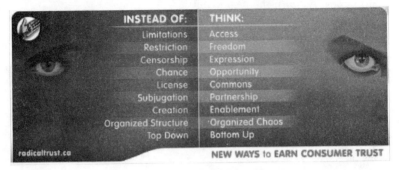

Figure 1

Are You the Trust Leader in Your Industry?

This is the only question that matters.

In a world of abundance and choice, where trillions of interactions are annually conducted by billions of strangers, trust has become the only measure that matters. How will you become the most-trusted name in your business? How will you leverage authenticity and transparency to give the consumer ultimate confidence in you? How will you harness the power of translucent and participative systems to deepen customer loyalty and long-term commitment?

Download This

- Trust is the real "currency" of the Jump Point economy.
- Stakeholders—consumers, investors, and employees—demand transparency and openness in all dealings.
- Multilateral reputation mechanisms will be very powerful.
- Leadership companies will elevate trust to new heights, transforming trustworthiness into a competitive weapon.
- High-trust economies will grow, low-trust economies will fall behind.

PART THREE

The Next Curve

The future is already here—it's just unevenly distributed.
—WILLIAM GIBSON

Jump Points throughout history have one good feature in common: they never arrive without warning. Technology transformations are messy, noisy, choppy processes—but at least they happen in plain sight. Unfortunately, they don't always reveal themselves evenhandedly. Initial acceptance is typically led by the intrepid few. In exchange for their courage, these early adopters get to use, kick about, and consider a new technology the longest. And what they discover shapes the way the rest of the market evolves.

On the other side of the equation are the early attackers; companies that see the trends first, respond quickly, and get to establish the rules of engagement. These companies are often hailed as visionaries or disruptors, but in reality they have simply read the changing landscape better than the rest of us. By moving early, they get to set the pace, the value propositions, and the profit points. As with the early adopters, we can learn a lot about the future from these early attackers.

The final part of this book looks at the world beyond the discontinuity of the Jump Point. It explores what we can learn about that future from the early adopters and early attackers of the coming Jump Point. What they do today, we all will do tomorrow.

First, we will try to get an advanced view of the post–Jump Point customer that will arise from the giant cohort of connected consumers called the Bubble Generation. These individuals, just now entering adulthood, offer a window on the future of all markets.

Next we look at the companies that have already embraced Jump Point discontinuities and are using them to create highly differentiated, high-growth businesses, from online communities to major consumer brands. Finally, we look at how all the pieces of the puzzle come together to set the stage for how we will all live, work, and play after the Jump Point.

The world after the Jump Point will in many ways resemble the one we live in now—and yet, it will be radically transformed. It will be a world of new and unfamiliar market spaces, where great varieties of niche and sometimes unusual products are bought and sold, and new and novel forms of value are exchanged—from attention credits to virtual dollars. It will offer more opportunities and greater dangers. It will create vast new wealth, but that wealth will be distributed differently than it is now. And it will be a world that will often seem to run at hyperspeeds, with trends, fads, and deals racing around the globe almost instantaneously.

But perhaps the one feature of the Jump Point—indeed, of all jump points in history—that we are least prepared for is that it will also change the way we think. *Time, space, geography and relationships will all be different after the Jump Point. And for a change like that, we can't start preparing ourselves soon enough.*

The Bubble Generation

The edge dissolves the center.

—STOWE BOYD

San Francisco's Hayes Valley neighborhood is an eclectic admixture of high-end boutiques, white linen restaurants, hip shops, new condominiums, and colorful Victorian homes intermingled with equally colorful street people, public housing, and the occasional remnant of what once was a rough neighborhood. It is a near-perfect boundary-busting blend of funky but chic—and, needless to say, it attracts the new generation of connected entrepreneurs and the people who work for them.

One such company that calls Hayes Valley home is a startup named Reactee, Inc. Reactee sees itself as a mobile communications company, although not in the classic sense. A true hybrid, Reactee mashes fashion and technology to create a new street-level medium: the response-driven T-shirt.

Here's how it works: customers visit the firm's Web site and design a T-shirt of their choice with a silk-screened slogan, also of their choice. Customer slogans range from favorite sports teams and bands, to presidential candidates and self-promotional tags.

After they choose their slogan, customers then select a keyword that gets printed on the shirt. They are also asked to prepare a text message that will reside in Reactee's database.

The purpose? So that when the customer wears the shirt in public, curious people who want to learn more about the person behind the shirt can simply send a text message (SMS) with the printed keyword to the Reactee short code (41411) emblazoned on the shirt. In response, they get that stored text message back from the owner. It is a new form of self-expression—and a new way to meet people—appropriate for a new, and remarkable, generation of consumers: the *Bubble Generation*.

Demographers give this cohort several names, including Millennials, Boomerangs, and Echoes. I prefer to call them the Bubble Generation, as they have come of age during the dot-com bubble and its aftermath. In fact, after the dot-com world imploded, the mania subsided, and interest among the press and financial markets retreated, this generation kept toiling away, playing with Internet technology, improving it, and making it their own. By the time the rest of the world caught on, so-called Web 2.0 was in full throttle and a new phase of the Internet era had begun.

Thanks to these BubbleGen'ers, we can now get a glimpse of how business will be done in the near future. This chapter will look at the major social, emotional, and cultural drivers behind this critical demographic, not only because it is an important wedge of the current market, but more importantly, because it is a harbinger of all markets to come after the Jump Point. My intention is to show how the big discontinuities of the Jump Point—attention value, time shifting, abundant thinking, mashup culture, and the primacy of trust—will figure into the markets of the post-Jump Point world, as seen through the eyes, actions, and behaviors of these early adopters.

A Trillion-Dollar Edge Field

The Bubble Generation is made up of people between the ages of 13 and 25. These are the sons and daughters of later boomers, the so-called yuppies, but more accurately, they are children of the Web.

The Bubble Generation has grown up with the Internet and can't remember a world without it. Theirs is a world of social media, third screens, peer-to-peer platforms, bit torrents, wikis, blogs, vlogs, podcasts, RSS, SMS, IMS, texting, GPS, video sharing, and photo swapping. Their culture, mores, tastes, and wants have been defined by their use of this technology. They have never taken a photograph they couldn't see instantly, or watched TV without a menu, or used a pay phone. Instead, they are comfortable finding anything on the Internet, they communicate via instant messaging, and they happily shop online and use collaborative tools that help them to keep in touch with friends and family as well as to work better and more productively with their colleagues.

Many will never hold a traditional corporate job.

By nature, members of the Bubble Generation are pragmatic, worldly, materialistic, driven by technology, and optimistic about the future. And they command wealth. According to the U.S. Census Bureau, BubbleGen consumers in the United States alone wield a pocketbook of about $1 trillion.

Importantly, the Bubble Generation is the first truly global generation. Linked by the easy and intuitive use of common technology, members of the Bubble Generation around the world are more like one another than they are like their neighbors in their native countries. They are of a technology class that easily exchanges information, is comfortable with rapid, discontinuous change, and possesses a deep and abiding belief that information ought to be free, open, and transparent.

And that in itself is a crucial differentiator: the Bubble Generation is more a "technographic" than a mere demographic label— a cohort united by culture more than just circumstance of birth.

As South African futurist Graeme Codrington has written, "Unconventional homes, increases in multicultural interaction, increased access to information in other countries and globalization, have bred a generation that is far more tolerant of difference than any generation before it. Instead of shying away from difference . . .

everyone has a right to his or her own opinion. No one has the right to impose personal beliefs on anyone, and anyone claiming to have a corner on the truth market will be ridiculed out of court."

Mottled hair, tattoos, piercings, and a liberal exposure to ethnic cultures and foods are representative of the diversity with which this generation has grown up. Progeny of the civil rights and gender-equity movements, these children of boomer parents reject prejudice and are incredibly accepting of other people—their looks, experiences, and personal preferences. According to political science professor Michael Kryzanek, "They have little problem with gay marriage or interracial relationships; they see nothing wrong with marijuana use; their sexual mores are driving their parents apoplectic. They are nonjudgmental about their friends' personal lives and don't see what all the fuss is about concerning some of the hot-button issues of the day, such as abortion."

In fairness, it should also be noted that this generation is also highly passive compared to its predecessors (a product of years of sitting in front of a computer screen), less cognizant of its place in history or the surrounding society, and increasingly less capable of extended commitment to anything—from social causes to relationships to institutions to attention itself. The Bubble Generation is quick, clever, almost superhumanly facile with technology . . . and often terrifyingly shallow.

Call them what you will, these new connected consumers form the vanguard of the Jump Point economy—the first wave of adopters that provides an early view of what the market mainstream will soon look like. Understand what drives and satisfies them today, and you have a head start on the future.

The Bubble Generation Worldview

The Bubble Generation is hard-wired to think differently than its predecessors. The Internet itself has reset this generation's thinking, teaching it that everything can be done faster, cheaper, better; that no one ever has to be alone, limited by time or place, or enslaved by the linear thinking of the TV, radio, and print ages.

The Internet has also impressed upon this cohort the utility of collective wisdom and the power of group action. And it has transferred to it an unprecedented level control; influence is now in the hands of the little guy, the individual is as powerful as the institution, and communities of individuals even more powerful still.

Some points to consider about members of the Bubble Generation:

- They don't watch a lot of TV or listen to commercial radio.
- They don't tolerate commercials—and they don't have to.
- They are very mobile.
- They rarely use e-mail—it is too slow.
- They are social and private at the same time.
- They reject overly slick, overly produced content and messages.

In short, they don't use the media the rest of use (at least in the same way), they don't want to be interrupted, they don't stay still long enough to engage, they don't want their space invaded, and they are turned off by highly packaged pitches.

What are some of the secrets to the way these new consumers *do* work?

1. Instead of search and buy, they prefer "discovery."
2. They rely on "alpha consumers" for their buying cues—people they admire, celebrities.
3. They want active engagement and interaction, not passive purchasing.
4. They have set boundaries outside of which your pitch is a violation.
5. All they hear is noise—so quiet down.

If you're General Motors, Procter & Gamble, or Nike, hawking your wares in the same old "interrupt and impose" model, the Bubble Generation won't buy from you. But if they discover you on their own terms, they may invite you into their lives. Consider these challenges:

1. **They won't hear you.** And, if you try to steal their attention, they will evade you. Young connected consumers don't watch much TV, don't listen to commercial radio, never read a newspaper (on paper anyway), and in order to cope with the barrage of ads they are confronted with in their lives, have learned to tune you out. They are decidedly online creatures: in a 2007 study by Grunwald Associates, when asked where their mindshare goes while they multitask between TV and online, by a margin of more than 4 to 1 this demographic says they focus mainly online. According to Saul Berman, IBM Media & Entertainment Strategy and change practice leader, "The Internet is becoming consumers' primary entertainment source. The TV is increasingly taking a back seat to the cell phone and the personal computer among consumers age 18 to 34. Just as mobile communications have replaced traditional land-lines, cable and satellite TV subscriptions risk a similar fate of being replaced as the primary source of content access." Moreover, years of intense marketing efforts aimed directly their way have taught the members of this group to assume the worst about companies trying to coax them into buying something. Ads intended to look hip and young often come off to them as contrived and opportunistic. Thus, trying to reach these consumers through traditional media is often a waste of money.

2. **They won't know you.** If you have not become a part of their trusted circles, they will consider you an interloper. BubbleGen consumers see shopping as a social experience and, for this reason, they are best influenced friend to friend.

Since they are less affected by traditional media, they rely on cues from one another. Chances are, your imposition or interruption ads won't come from a trusted or admired source, and they will ignore you.

3. **They won't be engaged.** With the overwhelming choices BubbleGen'ers have, and the scarcity of attention they must contend with, it is likely that you won't say the right things to motivate and mobilize them. BubbleGen'ers don't want to be bothered by ads in the first place; and ads that miss the mark are white noise. Few marketers understand the new science of behavioral ads, and most don't deploy the type of ads that break through the clutter.

4. **They won't trust you.** Trust is, must be, everything in the connected economy. Trust is the new money; it is the coin of the realm, the currency of social media. If you started today, you *might* be a trusted source for products and services by this time next year.

5. **They won't enlist.** Because you won't ask them. And that's the rub: the new consumer is a joiner of communities and networks and brands. You want a drive-by transaction; they want to be part of something bigger. So, you won't make a call to action, and they won't enlist with you. It's as simple as that.

Six Cultural Forces Behind the Bubble Generation

As the accompanying chart illustrates, the Bubble Generation is the first cohort shaped by Network Culture. More so than their Baby Boomer parents, their attitudes toward attention, time, personal power, private property, and trust have been shaped by their relationship to information technology and the Network. But, you might ask, what exactly makes them tick?

Through interviews, research, and surveys, I have reduced the cultural forces down to six drivers I see as the prime shapers of the Bubble Generation. These forces help explain the sometimes inscrutable attitudes, outlooks, and consumer behavior of BubbleGen'ers, and must be understood by anyone hoping to sell to them now or anticipate where they are taking us next. When combined in various permutations, these cultural drivers create the new rules of the era. Winning over the new connected consumer will depend on your ability to tap into these vital forces and understand the changing rules.

The six cultural forces driving the Bubble Generation are Immediacy, Angst, Affiliation, Authenticity, Individualism, and Prepotency.

Boomer vs. Bubble Generation

	Boomer	BubbleGen
Work	Career	Campaign
Politics	Polarized	Matrixed
Social	Hierarchies	Networks
Family	Nuclear	Postnuclear Nodes
Worldview	Nations	Communities
Media	Corporate	Citizen
Culture	Mono	Multi
Environment	Exploitative	Sustainable
Spirituality	Dogmatic	Enigmatic
Marriage	Lifelong Monogamy	Serial Monogamy
Time	Linear	Hypertextual

Immediacy

The Bubble Generation already lives in the Permanent Now. They believe that *instant* is normal: instant communications, instant answers, and instant gratification. The Internet is a tool of immediacy. So is the mobile phone. The Internet never sleeps, and a mobile phone is with you at all times. The new consumers want—no, demand—communications, interactions, and life in real time.

Want to talk to your friends? Shoot them a Bribble—a message popup. On the run? Text-message them. Lost them in a crowd? Jyngle them for their location.

The microblog Twitter embodies the idea of instant, persistent communications. As blog evangelist Anil Dash describes it, "Twitter is a simple service that lets you send simple status update messages to your friends via SMS, IM, or a very basic web interface. Those messages are then sent to everyone who follows your updates, using any of the communications methods available. Simply put, it's a buddy list or reply-to-all form of group communication for media which didn't really have them."

Importantly, in the postbroadcast world, when mass media no longer delivers a common experience, technology like that from Twitter, Bliin, Pownce, Jyngle, 3Jam, Loopt, Pinger, Dodgeball, and Moblabber enables constant, approximate presence with one's buddies.

The BubbleGen consumer is synched to a faster internal clock, a whole new circadian rhythm. The new connected consumer lives in the *now*, and the now is a speeding train that must be caught. While their parents and grandparents grew up in a time when patience was a virtue, this generation has come up in an age where you never have to wait for anything. To them, everything is too slow; all things can be done faster.

What are the implications of this immediacy mindset on your business? For one thing, it is likely that *everything* you do must be sped up. Latency and middlemen must be eliminated, the "air" taken out of every process. In practice, it means that all business processes need a radical rethinking to reduce transaction time by an order of magnitude. In order to satisfy the BubbleGen consumer, product development, manufacturing, distribution, and delivery need to be 10 times faster than yesterday.

Are you fast enough? Can you get faster? If not, someone else will. A recurring business theme at the Jump Point will be the reduction or shifting of time as consumers become more in tune with the permanent now.

Angst

Between mobile connectivity, instant messaging, texting, and microblogs, the new connected consumer is rarely, if ever, disconnected. But what explains this need to instantly—continually—connect, share, and express? Why is community so important, along with copresence and trust?

For the answer, consider the underlying mood of these times. A big factor is *collective angst*. The Bubble Generation lives at a constant threat level Orange.

Clearly, this is a generation coming of age in anxious times. Social scientist Jean M. Twenge has developed a map of three possible forces driving sociocultural anxiety. They are *overall threat* (anxiety increases as environmental threat increases), *economic conditions* (anxiety increases as economic conditions deteriorate), and *social connectedness* (anxiety increases as social bonds weaken).

By that measure, the Bubble Generation has hit the bad-luck trifecta.

Consider that this generation came of age as the nuclear family and community became a mashup of wildly different norms, just as the dot-com economic bubble burst and hurled much of the world into recession, and then hit its white-hot strike point with the events of 9/11 (the Kennedy Assassination and Pearl Harbor of their lives) and the War on Terror. From airport strip searches to the threat of extinction-level global warming, this by-the-book "angst cocktail" helps explain the need for *my space, my face, my place* and the impulse for instant outreach to friends and networks. It is self-expression to give one's life presence, connective filaments to give it meaning.

According to Hong Kong-based consultant Tomi T. Ahonen and his partner Alan Moore, "The single most visible change from entering the Connected Age is that we suddenly have permanent access to our peers, our friends, our colleagues and family members. We can start to live with a 'lifeline' to those we trust. Our communities, which previously only existed at given points in time, now become ever-present. We are no longer alone. In the Connected Age modern people are able to draw on the community for assistance, information and support. We learn to search, share and interact in a new way."

That helps explain why the top 25 online social communities now have a billion members, and why so much of Web 2.0 is about peer-to-peer and friend-to-friend sharing.

At the intersection of individualism and angst is the need to share the unfolding of life's events, even the most mundane and trivial, with friends and family. While MySpace, Facebook, hi5, and the myriad of specialty communities provide a center of gravity in a changing world ("know me, join me"), sharing photos on Flickr or videos on YouTube or poems on Moodle, is life affirming in another way: it says, "the events of my life matter."

This need to matter in an uncertain world has spawned dozens of media-sharing sites. Services like Flickr, Fotolog, ImageShack, Parazz, Photobucket, Pickle, Shutterfly, Tabblo, and Zooomr make photo sharing simple and easy. Videos of one's life are easily shared through dozens of services mentioned earlier, including Vimeo, Eyespot, Jumpcut, Ourmedia, DailyMotion, Blip.tv, vSocial, Grouper, Revver, VideoEgg, and Revo.

There are also many sites that provide a means to personally annotate, share, and navigate digital content and artifacts. Services like Ma.gnolia. Furl, del.icio.us, BlinkList, Clipmarks, Blummy, Listal, diigo, Blue Dot, 43 Places, Stylehive, and CiteULike allow individuals to share their knowledge among their social networks. Such people-produced "folksonomies" further advance the idea that every life matters.

Even after life, fading away into oblivion is not part of the plan. As Jamie Pietras, writing for Salon.com, describes it, MyDeathSpace.com is becoming the obituary of record and final reckoning of the social media era. "When a person dies, his or her MySpace page and its assortment of photos, blog entries, songs, videos and other digital ephemera becomes a de facto shrine to the deceased—teenage life's trivialities, dilemmas and existential crises packaged and displayed as a neat narrative."

Unfortunately, a by-product of this sense of imminent and ever-present peril is short-horizon thinking. Unsettlingly, there is among the BubbleGen'ers a "live today, for tomorrow we may die" ethic that helps explain its pragmatic, acquisitive, party-hardy, and short-term impulses. It is just such myopia that explains the racy photos and confessional entries that many BubbleGen'ers post to their community Web pages. It does not seem to register with posters that these postings may come back to haunt them in the future. They aren't altogether sure there will be one.

Affiliation

Clearly, generational anxieties have helped shaped the way the Bubble Generation uses technology. As the runaway success of social media sites illustrates, this generation copes with its angst through community building, human connection, and authenticity. In short, they long to belong.

That truth, however, tends to make BubbleGen'ers guarded and wary of people and things outside the protective cocoon. As a marketer, if you want to play, you'd better identify yourself: Do you represent one among a circle of friends? Are you willing to share? Will you be there when needed?

If you're an imposition marketer, you're not going to break into the circle. If you are phony, you won't get a second look. If you don't bring something to the party, you won't be invited back.

A decade ago, Robert Putnam's *Bowling Alone* painted a stark picture of a world made poorer by social isolation and withered community connections. Not so for this next wave of consumers. *The Bubble Generation does not bowl alone.* Instead, your new connected customer makes friends easily and readily; has many of them (all over the world); rolls with an entourage, real and virtual; likes to know where his or her buddies are at all times; and loves to share her or his little everyday moments (particularly shopping moments) with friends.

According to blog mogul Om Malik, this tendency to community is a deep-rooted trait. "Whether in Parisian cafes, Bombay chai stalls, or Manhattan singles' bars, humans have an overwhelming need to get together, talk, communicate and interact. Our genes are coded that way," he wrote in *Business 2.0* magazine. "It's no surprise that as we rush toward an always-on, ever more connected society, we want to mimic these offline interactions on the Net."

Multiplayer online game playing is a good example of group interaction migrating to the Net and then leading us somewhere new. Again, popular sites like Maple Story, City of Heroes, Dreamlords, Jumpgate, and Flyff (not to mention online versions of Nintendo, PlayStation, and Microsoft's Xbox Games) can at any time involve thousands of people from around the world in simultaneous game play—a collective experience on a scale we have never known before. It is important to understand that these collaborative game environments are also training the next generation how to work, solve problems, and even shop together.

Why is the Bubble Generation so adept at making friends? For one thing, as we have seen, the anxious times in which Bubble-Gen'ers have grown up encourage the seeking of affiliations. There is comfort in a circle of friends. But there is more to it than that. As discussed earlier, the openness and tolerance for diversity among this generation is unprecedented—a worldview that fosters the easy formation of friendship bonds.

And what's better than making new friends online? Meeting up with them offline. Numerous new Web services now help people meet online and hook up in the real world. And that is an important point to understand: the new connected consumer is not hiding behind technology but rather sees it as a natural part of the networking and socializing process.

Meetup.com is one of the most active of the offline community-building sites. The site offers people an easy way to find and connect with people of similar interests who live nearby. Topics of interest range from pets and hobbies to professional development, religion, parenting, and beyond. When a group of like-minded people forms, the group can then decide to meet in the real world at a local coffee shop, library, bar, or dog park. Such meet-ups represent the best spirit of the networked age; the Internet makes finding simpatico people online easier than ever, and it can also help schedule, communicate, and map the details of offline gatherings at the neighborhood level.

There is, of course, a flip side to this always-connected lifestyle. As they are rarely alone, today's young, connected consumers often have a hard time going "off the grid." As chilling as that may seem to many people, this, too, may be a survival strategy. When you consider the array of ways the new consumers will be tracked, trailed, followed, and found, their future will require a new tolerance for propinquity, or a new definition of personal privacy. Between GPS tags, the ubiquity of public cameras, the mobility of mail, and always-on phone services, it will soon be impossible to break away for an untethered, unmolested moment.

The new consumers are already learning to accept this new reality. They already know their every move, click, and download is tracked by someone—from the government to their favorite brand. Why should the rest of their lives be any different?

Persistent presence has created a belief system that anyone can be reached at any time. That means that each person—be it friend, family member, or colleague—becomes a continual presence in the connected consumer's life. Always-on connectivity is creating new forms of social behavior that blur the distinctions between work and play, public and private life, and online and real-world interactions.

Authenticity

The Bubble Generation expects transparency and abhors artifice. BubbleGen'ers have witnessed first hand the manipulations of mainstream media by advertisers, politicians, and hate groups, and they don't like what they have seen. As a result, this new generation of customers has a heightened sense of authenticity and intrinsic truth; what Hemingway called a "built-in [B.S.] detector." To that end, it has a hard-coded mistrust of major brands, resents obvious ad campaigns attempting to target its generational zeitgeist, and on the whole, would rather not be bothered with imposition marketing.

Authenticity is real, not perfect; it is that quality which breaks through the attention morass and invites trust. As Bill Breen in *Fast Company* magazine writes:

> Overloaded by sales pitches, consumers are gravitating toward brands that they sense are true and genuine. Hunger for the authentic is all around us. You can see it in the way millions are drawn to mission-driven products like organic foods. It's there in the sex-without-guilt way people respond to the footloose joy of BMW's Mini. You see it in the tribes of "i-centered" buyers who value individuality and independence—and whom Apple has so cleverly cultivated through its iMacs and iPods.

The new consumers don't trust the mainstream media to bring them authentic messages or the latest fashions. They do, however, trust "fake" news outlets like *The Daily Show* and *The Colbert Report*, because they are, in fact, authentic. And, they don't want some corporate fashionista telling them what's hot or not. Propelled by e-mail, IMS, texts, and shopcasts, the BubbleGen consumers are able to detect emerging trends at the speed of light. Moreover, their ability to viralize new trends among themselves means that fads will soon come, grow, and disappear in a highly time-compressed lifecycle.

This puts enormous pressure on even the fastest manufacturers and retailers. Where once a Gap could spin inventory in a leisurely eight or nine weeks, or Target could dabble in funky brands and mass niches, or Nokia could issue a new mobile phone a couple of times a year, the emerging reality calls for the acceleration of everything—weeks, not months; days, not weeks; now is not soon enough. Again, nothing is fast enough for the new connected consumer. And authenticity will be, among others things, deeply connected with responsiveness. As the next billion producers join the networked economy, expect to see the widespread adoption of fashions and music from these indigenous people precisely because they are authentic. The growing popularity of musical acts like Senegal's Orchestra Baobab and Sierra Leone's Refugee All-Stars is testament to the appeal of the real among the new consumers.

As blogger Stowe Boyd puts it, "Authenticity is strongly related to passion, openness and authority. In my own experience it derives from a passionate first-person involvement and persistence." In other words, real people and real life stories are what matter to the Bubble Generation.

The winning brands today connect on an authentic level. These brands don't ask consumers to drink the Kool-Aid; they invite them to make it. This trend of so-called citizen marketing is gaining steam, despite the obvious brand risks, because the new, connected consumer responds best to authentic endorsements from fellow consumers. Most often, polished, high-production spots, no matter how clever, are less effective. The new consumer simply doesn't trust the empty promises, exaggerated claims, artful agate type disclaimers, or the hype.

In response, smart companies, from Mercedes-Benz to Converse, are giving their brand fans opportunities to make their own advertisements. And, especially popular brands like the Mini Cooper and Starbucks have even spawned owner-run fan blogs.

Are there dangers? Sure, many brand communities openly discuss both the positives and the negatives of the product. Some of these discussions can be vicious and vocal. But for the smart marketers, all customer conversations net benefits. Good comments help sell the product; nasty comments (if authentic, and if listened to) improve the product.

Best of all, user-generated marketing is most likely to go viral. If you'll recall the connection made between viral behavior and rumor mongering in Chapter 3, people in a network need a personal motivation to pass information along to others. Authentic passion expressed through a homegrown advertisement is about as good as it gets.

Now users can even win money for their do-it-yourself (DIY) efforts. A recent entry to the video-sharing space is a company called Zooppa, which is taking user-generated advertising to the next level. At Zooppa, brands supply advertising briefs—information about the product, the target audience, any brand-specific features—and users create their own advertisements. When completed, the ads are uploaded to the Zooppa community and members vote on their favorites. After the votes are tallied, the winning video scores a cash prize.

Do viral video ads work? A 2007 study by The Pew Internet & American Life Project concluded that more than half of all online video viewers (57 percent) share links to videos they find with others, and three in four (75 percent) say they receive links to watch videos that others have sent to them.

At this point, it is important to emphasize that authenticity is difficult to fake, and trying to fool the audience will only break faith and breed mistrust—even resentment. Take the infamous example of Lonlelygirl15. Under the guise of being the true video diaries of a troubled teen named Bree, these blogcasts turned out to be a kind of fabricated soapy serial made by a couple of Creative

Artists rookies. When the truth about the project was revealed, many fans became angry and vilified the site.

The moral of the story: You can't fool people and expect to win. You can't conceal your foolery anymore, because customers are (eventually) all-knowing. And, you can't hope your customers will forgive you; they won't.

Individualism

The Bubble Generation is highly individualistic, but make no mistake; this is not another Me Generation. Its brand of individualism is decidedly more Emersonian.

BubbleGen'ers are self-assured and independent and very community-minded at the same time. They are natural team players, collaborate easily, and value group interaction and decision making. While they happily (and loudly) celebrate their individuality, they are not threatened by being one of many voices; in fact, they think crowds are smarter than individuals.

As might be expected of these graduates of "Montessori" self-esteem schools, BubbleGen'ers tend to believe everyone is special (the "Lake Woebegone Effect") and should be afforded products and services designed especially for them. They favor customized and personalized products and services—not to be petulant or difficult, but as Allison Muller of Accenture sees it, to cope with their world of abundance: "Personalization may be highly valued to these shoppers as it enables them to filter through an over-abundance of marketing messages, products and choices and only focus on what's most relevant to their own needs and preferences."

Pimp My Life

In the world of the Jump Point, not only is the customer right, the customer is in charge. Everything is not only available, it is negotiable, adjustable, and customizable. "One size fits all" won't work here.

At its extreme, this belief is driving new business models whereby the customer designs the product and then manages every aspect of production from development through delivery. And, buoyed by omnipotent thinking, the new consumer gladly accepts this mantle of power.

A generation ago, consumers would not have had the temerity to believe they could design a better laundry soap, never mind a superior automobile or computer. Today, the new generation of customers thinks nothing of weighing in on any decision available to them. And why not? The consumers of this generation have grown up designing their own TV stations with TiVo, and their own radio stations with iPod—why not their own sodas and candy, even cars?

Jones Soda uses digital technology to allow customers to upload a photo, write a label, select their flavor of soda, and ship themselves a case of custom-labeled pop. M&Ms allows them to do the same with special fashion colors and messages. Heinz will make personalized condiments for you. And you can send a picture and verbiage to Kleenex and it will make boxes of customized tissues for you. MyTwinn makes a doll that looks exactly like you—or your child. Vans will let you customize your own sneakers. And according to British Rover, 99 percent of all MINI Coopers are customer-designed.

Given the profound triangulation of technology, culture, and economics represented by the individualization ethic, we can expect BubbleGen consumers to drive this trend into every market they touch.

Prepotency

This generation is powerful, and knows it. Autonomy, choice, and freedom—"amplitude"—has produced within this cohort an expectation of power (though, ironically, one mixed with a sense of impotence about larger world events such as terrorism and global warming). BubbleGen consumers live in a scalable, abundant world where stores are always open, the lights are always on, everything is always available—and customized—and they are always free to move about the cabin. To them, anything is possible.

This grant of abundance, convenience, and latitude inevitably rearranges one's thinking and expectations. Amazon.com offers one million books; every song ever recorded can be found online as a downloadable file; and that Pokemon card you lost in fourth grade is available today on eBay. By comparison, "physical-world" stores offer fewer choices, fewer hours, and a lesser experience. When the benchmark is set at everything and now, it is hard to go back.

Mobility is another freedom of amplitude, and BubbleGen consumers are unconstrained by place and distance. The advent of mobile telephony, hand-held Internet, Global Positioning System, and radio frequency technology has given BubbleGen'ers the luxury of "space shifting," of roaming free and remaining connected at the same time. On one hand, this freedom produces a more elusive consumer; on the other hand, it makes location-based promotions extremely effective.

This generation doesn't obey the old laws of time; it doesn't even wear watches. Your new consumer doesn't want to be hemmed in by arbitrary schedules and doesn't have to be. With digital video recording, viewers can record and play back programming any time that suits them, making quaint notions like "prime time" and "drive time" meaningless. With the emergence of downloadable first-run films, moviegoing will change more dramatically than it has since the arrival of talkies.

For this generation, linear thinking is laughable. BubbleGen'ers are skeptical of old hierarchical systems, like government, and big hidebound institutions, like corporations, precisely because those organizations are governed by linear thinkers. The new connected consumer resists binary choices: things are rarely just black or white, wrong or right. They recognize that people and things in life are often ambiguous, varying, and complex.

For this group of contemporaries, the search for the right solution, product, or job is not a straight line or a solitary pursuit. This outlook reveals unique thought processes, logic flows, and decision trees. Ambiguity, unforeseen outcomes, and dualities are accepted. And, BubbleGen consumers not only welcome external input, they actively seek it.

Nonlinear thinking creates less predictable consumer behavior and puts traditional business models, value propositions, and delivery channels to the test. The sales cycle will never be the same again. And, moreover, there is an inherent mistrust by the new consumers in the tyranny of one-way thinking. They eschew the world of the "Old Corporates" and the control freaks, the heavy hand, and the hard sell.

And, for all its common views and values, the Bubble Generation is not a monolithic consumer base. BubbleGen'ers have come to embrace their own differences and others' diversity as a natural birthright. This attitude is reinforced by their generational media: television drove homogeneity, the Internet drives diversity.

There is, however, a downside to a munificent mindset. An unbounded world can create an experiential void: the attention beast must always be fed with new amusements. Easily bored and distracted, the new connected consumer hungrily desires variety and stimulation. As the reasoning goes, life is full of new experiences, why not sample them all? But, this insatiate vacuum can lead to dissatisfaction and free-floating spiritual want. And even when the bounty is unlimited, there is the problem of too many choices. This paralysis of plenty can have the same negative effects as information overload. There is a real danger that the 40-year-old BubbleGen'er of 2025 will be burned out on too many videos, too much porn, too many online games, too much conversation . . . and ultimately, just too damn many experiences.

BubbleGen consumers have high expectations of the world in which they live. Easy access to information has granted them much power and purview; theirs is a world of choice, range, and mastery. Experience is everything, and they want to try it all. But their optimistic headspace has a darker edge field. Attempts to fulfill unrealistic expectations can be a vicious, unsatisfying cycle. And having too many choices can be as debilitating as having too few. Marketers have to beware of getting caught in the breakwaters of these contradictory forces.

Time magazine ushered in 2007 by naming "You" as its Person of the Year in recognition of the growing online clout of the little guy. From the editorial:

> It's a story about community and collaboration on a scale never seen before. It's about the cosmic compendium of knowledge Wikipedia, and the million-channel people's network YouTube, and the online metropolis MySpace. It's about the many wresting power from the few and helping one another for nothing and how that will not only change the world, but also change the way the world changes.

The most adventurous and edgy of the "you" cohort, the group probing the boundaries and new frontiers of the technology, are those digital natives referred to here as the Bubble Generation. As we look ahead, the big themes of the coming Jump Point—attention value, time shifting, abundant thinking, mashup culture, and the primacy of trust—are being exercised right now in the attitudes, outlook, and behavior of the BubbleGen early adopters. Their ability to mesh and multitask, and their impatience with inauthentic, interruption-based marketing, shows a heightened self-awareness for the value of their attention. Their compulsion to always-on, immediate communications and instant gratification demonstrates their ability to bend time to suit their needs. Rejection of old models, middlemen, and taste makers in favor of group shopping, crowd sourcing, and new collaborative schemes reveals an abiding belief in the power of both individuals and groups of individuals acting in concert. Their mashup culture—an openness to nonlinear thinking, nontraditional views, and new extrapolations—is evident in the way they reset, remix, and reshuffle the world around them. And their ease with community building is paired with a guarded sense of whom to permit into that community, of whom to trust and whom not to trust.

Download This

- The vanguard of your new customers is here; listen to them carefully.
- BubbleGen'ers avoid traditional media whenever possible.
- They only know the abundant logic of the network.
- BubbleGen'ers' impatience and dissatisfaction with limits will soon be shared by all.
- Their friends are more important than your offer, except when their friends make your offer.
- Shopping is a social event; make it fun for groups.

Jump Point to Growth

*All truths are easy to understand once they are discovered—
the trick is to exploit them.*

—GUY KAWASAKI

N orrath is like no place you have ever been.

It is a multifarious and bewildering landscape composed of
six known continents and untold undiscovered regions; a fantas-
tical topography of arid plains, misty canyons, and ice-covered
mountains. Populated by all manner of creatures, beasts, and ban-
dits, Norrath can be a dangerous and unforgiving place.

Yet, it is estimated that some 60,000 people visit Norrath every
day, to work, explore, and to battle. Among the visitors are hard-
ened veterans, seasoned warriors who can claim great victories and
conquests. But there is also no shortage of ill-equipped "noob-
sticks," who frequently become sword fodder for the stronger
combatants (or food for wild bears).

Life in Norrath centers around survival: fighting monsters
called "mobs" (short for "mobile objects"), hunting for platinum
pieces (the currency of the land) and joining others to form guilds
for mutual benefit and protection.

As you've no doubt guessed by now, Norrath is a fictional planet,
a central locale in the EverQuest virtual universe—a synthetic

world for and by online gamers. Although it may be fictional, Nor-rath is not fake: in many ways it is a simulacrum of life on earth; complete with life, death, competition, and society building.

Like many online gaming worlds, Norrath suffers from wicked *mudflation,* a rapid devaluation of once-valuable turf, tools, and objects. Mudflation can strike in an instant; a change in the play-ing environment can wipe out overnight the value of a lucrative ore mine, strategic weapon, or sacred artifact. And what once made players rich and powerful becomes worthless in a blink.

The circumstances will not be quite as dramatic or the swings quite so visual, but the post–Jump Point world will have its own share of mudflation. Things will change, products and services will lose their value—often quickly—and some businesses will be blindsided. But the smart companies and astute executives will have seen the signs ahead of time, and have taken decisive moves to transfer the value somewhere else; and like an arbitrager, they will make more or capture market share in the process.

This "grasping the gap" is the real Jump Point opportunity. In discontinuous times, the trick is to identify subtle environmental changes earlier than everybody else and move first to attack.

Every Jump Point has its "buggy whip" clichés—stories of incumbents who resist the tide of change until it becomes too late. Looking back, you can always find the clipper ship builder who saw the steam engine as a passing fad, the vacuum tube builder who dismissed the transistor as irrelevant, or the broadcasters who called on Congress to legislate away satellite radio.

Today, our buggy whip makers are the nostalgic content providers who sue kids and grandmothers over alleged digital rights violations, and the inflexible manufacturers who still try to sell one-size-fits-all-products in a highly customized world.

Protecting the past during a Jump Point is almost always a futile enterprise. When momentum builds toward a point of inflection, it cannot be reversed. You can try to slow it down, but you can't stop it.

And that momentum is building fast. The next Jump Point is revealing itself in plain terms that can no longer be ignored. For example:

- The convergence of personal computing and communications has created a worldwide network that allows people to connect directly to each other without middlemen, brokers, or arbiters between them.

  This is a lousy time to be a middleman, broker, or arbiter.

- Consumers, overwhelmed by information overload, struggle to reconcile the many competing claims for their attention in daily life.

  This is a bad time to be an attention-stealing interruption advertiser.

- People don't want anyone dictating when they do something, buy something, or watch something.

  This is an unfortunate time to be in an inflexible or time-bound business.

- People don't want restrictions on how they use, enjoy, manipulate, store, or share their property.

  Trying to command and control information rights is a losing proposition.

- Consumers are acutely aware of their power to change the equations, flip the ratios, and obliterate the old market rules.

  Provide mechanisms for customer influence and expression . . . or go home.

- People don't trust their governments, large corporations, or political parties; they have an inherent trust in one another and in authenticity.

> *This is a dangerous time to be untrustworthy, shifty, or phony—especially if you are a large, established institution.*

Ten Truths of the Jump Point

Okay, that's what you *shouldn't do.*

But what we really need are some basic rules about what you *should* do to succeed in this new post–Jump Point world. And for that, we need to develop some understanding of the underlying truths of that new marketplace.

The best way to start is to consider what the technology that is already out there is telling us, how the early adopters are responding to it, and what some of the early attackers are doing to exploit these shifts.

First, a Jump Point gives us license to question everything, an opportunity to renegotiate current accords and accommodations, and the freedom to imagine new schemes. For example, does our respect for an artist's work really mean that he or she has an inherent right to amass vast wealth from it? We may like the rapper 50 Cent and respect his work product, but where is it written that he should be granted a license to print money in perpetuity?

On the other hand, if we do believe that 50 Cent is the sole and complete owner of his creations, shouldn't he also have a right to a piece of the revenues accruing from *every* use of his work, from ringtones to samplings to mashups?

In other words, the old rules are out the window, the tables are cleared, and we have the chance to rethink it all, to start again from scratch.

In music, television, publishing, radio, newspapers, and a hundred other industries, this radical restructuring has already begun. And that fact shouldn't be surprising: the old and established ways of doing things are often undermined by discontinuity long before the trends become clear. Over time, in small, imperceptible ways, our underlying beliefs and attitudes evolve, creating new and unmet needs and at the same time revealing new truths.

Here are some of those truths:

1. You Can't Fight the Network

As explored in the first section of this book, a network behaves in immutable, predictable ways. Use those properties and behaviors to move closer to your customers, win their trust, get them evangelizing for you, and grow your business.

Business leaders today must accept that it is futile and foolhardy to try to change the way the Net works. That means knowing, in the words of Stewart Brand, that "information wants to be free." It also means accepting that all content is public content—and that, in turn, means appreciating that information will be shared, modified, and bastardized the moment it leaves your hand.

Amazingly, even after nearly two decades of use, many businesses still try to resist the forces of the network, or worse, attempt to impose their will on its freewheeling nature.

Consider these two contrasting worldviews of content.

First, a February 2007 *Wired* magazine item on Joost, a newly launched free Internet TV company founded by Niklas Zennström and Janus Friis (founders of Skype and Kazaa):

> The vision: universal TV, running on a hybrid P2P platform—millions of exquisitely networked PCs fortified with traditional video servers. Free to viewers who download the player app. Friendly to content owners, thanks to industrial-strength encryption. Delightful to advertisers, adding pinpoint targeting to their all-time favorite medium. Everyone's a winner!

Now, compare that to this item three months earlier from the CNET news service:

An invention from Royal Philips Electronics prevents TV viewers from switching the channel during commercials or fast-forwarding past commercials when watching DVR content. Viewers would be released from the freeze only after paying a fee to the broadcaster. The freeze would be implemented on a program-by-program basis, giving viewers a choice at the start of each one.

Talk about opposing visions! Free and open TV versus command and control. Care to guess which one will win?

Between legal fees, research and development dollars, and software code costs, untold billions are still being spent by well-intentioned executives trying to rein in and manage the way networks work. Ultimately, these resources—and shareholder value—would be far better spent in gaining an understanding of how networks naturally behave and then capitalizing on those native properties.

For example, the companies Skype, Fon, and Threadless, which we learned about earlier, have grown rapidly around the world because they understand a basic viral property of the network: *a customer is the shortest line between two other customers.* When your customers have a vested interest in your product or message, the momentum is unstoppable.

So, what gets customers emotionally invested enough to freely promulgate—to viralize—your product or service message? Three things:

- When your product or service truly impresses them as remarkable.
- When it allows them to be the first finder among their peers.
- When its utility to them personally will be increased by the participation of others—the network effect.

Thus, the profile of an ideal viral download is an application that is unique, simple to use, and easy for people to pass along, and one that creates a mutual benefit or bond for all who download it together. Most often today, these viral downloads come in the form of spare, single-function, often whimsical apps called "widgets."

A widget is a portable block of code that can be loaded and launched on a Web site or blog without a lot of programming knowledge. A widget adds a capability to your Web site; popular widgets allow you to manage and manipulate content, "poke" (reach out to) friends in a fun way, or let your visitors play a game. Widgets are popular because they make sites "stickier" and visitors hang out longer.

Widget makers hope you will pass along their free apps to others because they have given you a value, because they have made it easy to pass along the item, and because they have created a conversation-worthy reason for people to reach out and connect. How do widget makers make money? They sell ads or sponsorships or promote premium, for-sale versions of their products. These are basic network truths and important lessons for anyone who wants to tap the network to grow a business.

2. Social Communities Are the New Marketplaces

The network allows people the freedom to connect and congregate with others of their choice. In the case of consumers, they are forming new communities around common interests and affinities.

This is a different dynamic than choosing a zip code to live in or a profession or assembling a brand profile. Group forming is a very powerful social exercise, and groups formed out of free will often display great unity and loyalty. And a community of like-minded people who have come together of their own accord is a marketer's dream.

According to a 2007 Fox Interactive Media study, 70 percent of Americans between the ages of 15 and 34 are active in online social communities. But that tendency is by no means limited to the Bubble Generation consumer: According to Web analytics firm comScore, the world's top 25 social communities already have one billion members, cutting across all demographics and age groups. And at the beginning of 2008, social sites have remained the fastest-growing online category.

Importantly, people are developing deep loyalties to their online communities. According to a 2007 study by the USC Annenberg Digital Future Project, an estimated 43 percent of Americans who belong to online communities say they feel "just as strongly about their virtual worlds as their real-world counterparts."

But a caveat: online communities are not new channels for *mass* marketing, a means to aggregate attention. You cannot broadcast to an online community. They operate on a code of behavior centered on respect and reciprocity, participation, and affiliation.

Smart marketers are patient and mind the code. They aren't too forward or polished or hungry; and those who are get quickly outed and ostracized. Rather, we see in the examples of Scion, Coca-Cola, and Helio brands that build a personal relationship with their fans by providing something of value—usually of "pass-around" value.

No place represents the market power of online communities more poignantly than the rapidly growing economy sprouting up around and within the social community site Facebook.

Started in 2004, Facebook began as a site to provide college students with a social center of gravity, a place to post profiles, upload photos, and share the latest news. In 2006, Facebook changed the game by opening its doors to people from all walks of life, and its membership swelled to more than 30 million people, placing it second only to MySpace in population.

Facebook founder Mark Zuckerberg decided to change the rules again in 2007 when he announced that the company would now allow outside programmers to write applications for use within the community. To widespread applause, the move turned Facebook into an open platform and gave birth to the Facebook Economy, perhaps the best view we have today of the future of global commerce.

Today dozens of designers are making and promulgating hundreds of widgets and small applications written expressly for use within the Facebook community. As a result, Facebook is now poised to become the first fully realized online metropolis, not in a virtual way, but in a way that best approximates why so many of us choose to live in cities in the first place: diversity, choice, and synergy.

In the post–Jump Point economy, the world will be divided into new, self-organized market spaces. These spaces will be built around affinity and affiliation, they will be focused and passion-centric, but they will not be small. Web philosopher Clay Shirky calls the new market spaces "meganiches," and asserts, "a meganiche is a thin slice of the Web that nonetheless represents roughly a million users. The meganiche is something new, and it will have a lasting impact on online business and culture. The basic math is simple: A tiny piece of an immense pie is huge." In other words, the new markets will be well defined, single minded, and gigantic at the same time.

3. Use the F-word

"Free is always good for the consumer," Jason Hirschhorn, MTV's chief digital officer, told an audience gathered at the 2006 3GSM Congress in Barcelona. At a panel where new business models for mobile content were explored, the idea that free content—cost free and restriction free—supported by advertising, was on everybody's mind.

At once heretical *and* paradoxical, the question is, how do you make money from "free"?

Venture capitalist and blogger nonpareil Fred Wilson calls it the "freemium" business model: "Give your service away for free, possibly ad supported but maybe not, acquire a lot of customers very efficiently through word of mouth, referral networks, organic search marketing, etc., then offer premium priced value added services or an enhanced version of your service to your customer base."

Wait a minute, you say, can you really make money by giving away your product? It's already being done. Look at the examples of companies like Adobe and its PDF Reader and Macromedia (now an Adobe company) with its Shockwave Player. These companies established deep, loyal customer bases (and turned their products into de facto standards) by handing out the software free to end users and then charging content producers for the authoring tools.

Six Apart, which offered its LiveJournal blogging platform for free, had more than two million of its customers go "pro" by buying a premium version that cost $20 per year. Flickr (photos) and FreshBooks (billing services) also offer free and premium versions.

The benefits of being free are numerous for the right products and services. Free is fast and removes the barrier to rapid mass adoption. Free can be first, which can establish defensible standards behind which more products can be driven. Free is friendly, it creates brand loyalty, and gets people generously passing the product or message around.

In other words, free works.

4. Reward Attention

As I've already noted, attention is the most precious of all human resources. In the post–Jump Point economy of information abundance, that attention will become even more rare and valuable.

Attention holders will demand their rights. Assaulting an audience with unwanted and irrelevant communications—in effect, stealing their attention—will be regarded with the seriousness of crime. Consumers will come to expect to be rewarded for their attention—it is, after all, too precious to give away for free. The message is clear: give prospective and existing customers value in exchange for their attention.

Still in its early stages, the business for what I term "attention rewards" is heating up. Look at Virgin Mobile's Sugar Mama program: under the banner of "earn airtime in your spare time," Sugar Mama establishes a hard value for the time a visitor spends with a sponsor's advertisement. In exchange for watching commercials from brands like Pepsi, Xbox, New Balance, and Subway, customers get prepay credits to their wireless account.

"The general value is 'one minute of your time for one minute of air time' credits," says Scott Kelliher, director of mobile advertising.

Nearly half a million Virgin Mobile customers currently subscribe to the program, with one thousand new users signing up daily. It seems that people like to be rewarded for their attention.

Many other companies are also looking to exchange attention for value. Qtrax, with the support of major music publishers like Universal, Sony/ATV, Warner Music Group, EMI Music Publishing, and BMI, is a peer-to-peer music-sharing service that gives customers unlimited music downloads in exchange for watching ads. GameTap is doing the same for game downloads and, like Virgin Mobile, Xero Mobile is allowing customers to earn minutes in exchange for their attention.

Big enterprises in particular are coming to understand the cost value of employee attention. One new company, Seriosity helps the employees of big corporations and collaborative organizations figure out what communications are worth paying attention to and which are not. Seriosity says it solves information overload in groups by "giving recipients the ability to prioritize messages and a reserve of currency that they can use to signal importance of their messages to others."

Interestingly, Seriosity does this by establishing an attention economy based on a unit of currency called "Serios." "Because Serios are in limited supply," says the company, "people can send meaningful signals about what's important by attaching them to messages."

In essence, Seriosity keeps employees from stealing one another's attention.

5. Break the Time Barrier

Here's what a poll of "knowledge workers" in the United States conducted in late 2006 by research group Ipsos found:

- 85 percent are available 24/7 by personal digital assistants (PDAs), cell phones, or e-mail.
- 92 percent read, send, make, or take work-related communications in nonwork situations.
- 73 percent have kept their communications device(s) on during the weekend.
- 45 percent still tune in to the office while on vacation.

Is this need for near-continuous connectivity a symptom peculiar to information-intensive industries, or is something more sociologically significant going on?

The survey respondents went on to explain that far from feeling shackled to their always-on devices, they see them as sources of professional and personal freedom. Even though ubiquitous mobile communication technologies are eroding the boundaries between their professional and personal lives, the people asked clearly see more benefits than drawbacks to a 24/7 life.

Why? More than 80 percent of those polled said always-on technology allows them to work more flexibly and to be more productive. Seventy percent said they think they are more successful *because* of their atypical lifestyles.

This data, added to growing list of examples of clock-voiding behavior, tells us that the new consumers want to decide "when" is right for them. We see evidence of this desire in the mass appeal of time-shifting technologies, such as TiVo, DVRs, and on-demand services. We also see this attitude resulting in the place-shifting propositions of Slingbox, Avennu, Orb, and WorldOnDemand.net.

And this imperative goes well beyond the online world; the desire to eliminate dead spots in life is spilling over to many other interactions. Look at what's happened with airline travel.

The launch in 2007 of Virgin America airlines was a smash success on several fronts. Yes, ticket prices were very competitive, and the white leather seats and playful pink and purple interior lighting (described as like being inside an iPod), in-flight movies, games, and Google maps were customer pleasers. But the top-rated features listed by inaugural flyers were the two 110-volt power sockets available for every three seats in coach, Ethernet and USB (Universal Serial Bus) ports for every seat, a pair of wireless access points for Net connectivity (pending Federal Aviation Administration approval), and seat-to-seat text chatting—all the things that allow passengers to stay connected and use their flying time in a more productive way.

Before the Virgin America launch, an airplane was the last disconnected place on Earth, the stratospheric equivalent of the dark side of the moon. Virgin rejected those old assumptions and realized that passengers didn't want to be incommunicado, cut off from home and office, during hours of flying.

Just as Virgin America allowed its passengers to repatriate what once were lost hours, every marketer today needs to see time— particularly world time—differently.

That's also the real lesson from the popularity of YouTube, TiVo, and other on-demand platforms. Side issues, like copyrights, bandwidth, and whether the box will be a TV or a PC, aren't important. The "on-demand revolution" is not about technology or law or form factor, it's about people's wants and expectations. Once consumers experience the on-demand paradigm, they immediately get it; there is no going back to prepackaged, laugh-tracked sitcoms set to a programming executive's schedule.

Television, commercial radio, and any other time-bound businesses take heed: people want control over the clock.

In order to satisfy the rapid metabolism of the post–Jump Point economy, marketers will have to marginalize time wherever possible. The real bonanza will come when we offer consumers new and novel ways to use, save, or shift time. All digital content should have a *download now* option. All physical products need premium, accelerated delivery options. All production cycle times need to be shortened to the nub. And since the world economy never sleeps, no truly global contender can ever afford to shut its doors. After all, the world is always open for business.

6. Make Everything Mashable

Digital rights management, or DRM, is how content owners today control and restrict the use of digital data—music, movies, literature, and software—by others.

DRM is why music on one platform won't play on another (why iTunes only play on iPod, for example). It is why people who purchase movies can't copy them any way they want. In short, DRM is a relic of a clumsier age, and it soon will be a thing of the past. Instead, we are entering the Era of Open: open source, open systems, open-ended growth.

As I have argued throughout this book, the open source and freeware movements are more than just business issues; they have social and political implications as well. The mashup culture is a growing global undercurrent. For companies today, the dividing line has become where one stands on the issue of copyrights and intellectual property rights. Professor Henry Jenkins, author of *Convergence Culture: Where Old and New Media Collide*, describes the cultural divide this way:

> One can trace two characteristic responses of media industries to this grassroots expression: Starting with the legal battles over Napster, the media industries have increasingly adopted a scorched earth policy towards their consumers, seeking to regulate and criminalize many forms of fan participation which once fell below their radar.

At the same time, on the fringes, new media companies (internet, games, and to a lesser degree, the mobile phone companies), are experimenting with new approaches which see fans as important collaborators in the production of content and as grassroots intermediaries helping to promote the franchise.

The anti-DRM advocates at the DefectiveByDesign.org campaign offer a more strident view of restricted use products: "These products have been intentionally crippled from the users' perspective, and are therefore 'defective by design.' This campaign will identify these 'defective' products and target them for elimination. We aim to make DRM an anti-social technology. We aim for the abolition of DRM as a social practice."

Recently, chinks have begun to show in the DRM armor. Announcements in 2007 were harbingers of changes in the music industry. Two behemoths of the recording industry, EMI Music and Universal Music Group, decided to offer DRM-free music. This, in turn, has caught the interest of the big retailers, like Wal-Mart, Best Buy, and Amazon, signaling that the end of the DRM era is closing in.

The bottom line is, in this mashable age, smart companies realize that restricting the customers' use of a product is ultimately unprofitable. Besides the costs to implement and enforce, which usually get passed along to the consumer, a restrictive stance only creates customer alienation and animosity in the market. The paradigm shift is taking us from what Jenkins terms the "prohibitionist model" to a more collaborationist model that actively seeks to engage the consumers by surrendering control and allowing them to generate their own content on the platforms of their choice.

The lesson? Regardless of industry, give customers the power to make your product or service their own.

For a good example of this ethic in practice, look at what Google has done with its maps. The company made headlines in

2007 when it opened up to the public the application programming interface (API) for Google maps. This gave nonemployees access to the source code, allowing them to manipulate and recast it for their own purposes.

Once considered a sacrilege in software circles, Google's exposure of the inner workings of its code displayed faith in its customers—and, indeed, the move won praise and loyalty from the community generally.

Today, anyone can mash a Google map for use on his or her own Web site. For example, real estate Web sites use the Google maps to overlay pop-up features and point out highlights in a prospective neighborhood such as schools, restaurants, and nearby services.

Google now supports more than 30 public APIs for functionality, ranging from calendars to mini-apps called "gadgets."

When it was introduced to the world, Linux was a subversive technology—an act of rebellion against the status quo. Today, versions of the code touch businesses from the consumer facing to the enterprise. "Hacktivism" has gone mainstream; mashup culture is no longer just about frustrated programmers wanting to play with code; it is an entire ethic, a social view that says innovation is best when it is democratic and open.

Every company must ask itself, "How can we open our source code—literally and figuratively—to our customers?" The key is to give customers a heightened sense of ownership and of loyalty to you. If you don't, someone else will.

7. Think Abundantly

When you think of the most powerful economic and social models of our day—blogs, message boards, forums, social networks, video sharing, picture sharing, podcasts, vidcasts, wikis, and virtual worlds—what do they all have in common?

They connect people, are participative and editable, and allow users to add content. That is the new customer paradigm, and all marketers must in one way or another adapt to it. Software pioneer Dan Bricklin calls it the "Cornucopia of the Commons: Use brings overflowing abundance."

There are two basic models available to exploit abundance in the market. The *commons model* allows for a large number of volunteers to contribute to the building of a common product as a public good. Examples include Firefox, CiteSeer, and parts of Linux. The community is largely self-governed and policing, although there is usually a nonprofit group, such as Mozilla or the Apache Software Foundation, to help with coordination. Sometimes, as in the case of GasBuddy.com, which helps consumers find the lowest-price gasoline in their areas, it is a totally grassroots effort. One of the most popular commons projects is Wikipedia. Since its founding in 2001, Wikipedia has engaged thousands of volunteers from around the world to create a massive encyclopedia of human knowledge. As of 2007, Wikipedia included eight million articles in 253 languages.

By comparison, the *crowdsourcing model* allows companies to tap the collective wisdom of their own customers. There are several approaches. InnoCentive matches top scientists around the world to relevant research and development challenges facing leading companies, like Procter & Gamble and Eli Lilly, for rewards up to $100,000.

Another example is Cambrian House, which is a user-owned co-op of sorts that designs software. Yet another path is taken by CrowdSpirit.com, which aims to revolutionize the consumer electronics industry by inviting consumers to design, invest in, produce, market, distribute, and support products that they collectively choose.

Several firms are using virtual communities to engage groups of customers. In advance of the 2008 opening of aloft, its new hotel concept property, the Starwood Group has made aggressive use of crowdsourced feedback, including hosting a simulation of its new hotel in Second Life.

The lessons? Human creativity is an inexhaustible resource; and never say no to a customer who believes anything is possible. Co-opt that customer instead.

8. Compete on Trust

The beauty of the network economy: three billion people are linked directly to each other. The peril of the network economy: three billion people are linked directly to each other.

In October 2007, the Internet Society (ISOC) held a special session in Toronto with just one thing on the agenda: trust.

Among the subtopics: the changing nature of trust, security, privacy, control and protection of personal data, methods for establishing authenticity and providing assurance, management of threats, and dealing with unwanted traffic.

A professional association with 20,000 members in 180 countries, the ISOC is the closest thing to a governing body that the Internet has. But it is decidedly not a government. And therein lays the rub: there is no United States of the Internet to oversee, and enforce, the free flow between three billion people linked in a single network of communications and commerce. And national governments, even working in cooperation, wouldn't be much help anyway—the network is by design ungovernable, at least by conventional means.

In order for the global networked economy not to devolve into a *Mad Max* commercial landscape, we, the users, must make trust the new medium of exchange, if not a high religion.

In the book *The World is Flat*, Thomas Friedman sums up America's key moral advantage in the world today: "If you wanted to summarize the net effect of all these institutions, cultural norms, business practices, and legal systems, it can be reduced to one word: trust." In other words: America has invested in trust and trust is in the doing.

Similarly, in a world of three billion independent actors, trust will also be in the doing. Many of the new consumers don't know your brand; they have no history with your company. Your next billion customers will give the default position and the benefit of the doubt to the most trusted players in the market. The winning companies in the Jump Point economy will be the most trusted on a grand global scale.

And trust will be reflected in actions. Does the company foster openness and create transparency? Does the company give it straight, or hide it in corporate-speak? Does the company deliver on its promise and potential? Most importantly, does the company extend trust to its customers and its employees?

The lesson: be the most-trusted name in your business.

The Speed of Trust author Steven Covey argues that benefits of being a high-trust company are clear:

> When the trust is high, you get the trust dividend. Investors invest in brands people trust. Consumers buy more from companies they trust, they spend more with companies they trust, they recommend companies they trust, and they give companies they trust the benefit of the doubt when things go wrong. The list goes on and on.
>
> On the Internet, a trusted brand versus an untrusted brand—the differences could not be clearer—you only give your credit card number to those you trust. And look what happens when a brand gets diluted or polluted or compromised, we see how fast consumers, and investors, turn away. They quit buying.

From an internal point of view, the networked economy will make it impossible to govern a company with a low-trust culture; there is simply too much information coming and going in real time to sustain a command-and-control decision bottleneck. As we learned earlier, radical trust means giving and getting trust in all interactions.

9. Become Contagious

"Friending is the next advertising," claims a 2007 Fox Interactive Media report. The report also finds that 40 percent of social network users claim to have "discovered brands and products that [they] really like" through their communities. Marketers have come to call it the "momentum affect." It is what happens when a brand becomes contagious and its product infectious.

We have already learned that networks are a latticework of nodes (see Chapter 2), that some nodes have more in- and outbound connections than others, and that these nodes have a weighted influence over others. Influential nodes—individuals—have what is known as a high Social Networking Potential (SNP); that is, a large number of ties to others and measurable influence. In group dynamics, these are the "influentials," individuals who shape the opinions of many others. In marketing terms, I call these the "alpha shoppers."

How do you motivate, mobilize, and monetize the alphas in your category to get the momentum effect started? It goes back to one of the basics of viral behavior: seeding the epidemic. And it can start with a small group of brand advocates.

Duncan Watts, a Columbia University sociology professor, describes the process this way: "It assumes that one starts with a seed of individuals who spread a message by infecting their friends, where the expected number of new infectious people generated by each existing one is called the "reproduction rate," or R. When R is greater than 1, each person who gets the message will, on average, spread it to more than one additional person, who then does the same thing, and so on, leading to exponential growth in the number of people who receive it—an epidemic."

In 2007, leading brands such as Adidas and Electronic Arts (EA) attributed more than 70 percent of their marketing return on investment to the "momentum effect." According to a Fox Interactive Media study, "Adidas directly influenced 1.2 million people to purchase its product and, after those people talked to their friends, influenced 4.2 million more. Similarly, EA directly influenced 1.8 million consumers and indirectly influenced 4.5 million consumers to say they intended to purchase its products."

In order to "ride the wave" in the parlance of CyWorld, you have to make it easy for your customers to share your story. Start with a core group of brand "friends," ask for their help, give them something to share with others, and repeat as needed.

What kind of widget—literal or figurative—can you offer your brand advocates?

10. Pandenomics—The Network Favors Blockbusters

It has been well documented that the Internet promotes long-tailing economics: its abundant "shelf space" means that even niche products have very long lives.

But the Internet is more than a giant remainder table. In fact, when you understand the physics of the Internet, it is easy to see that while it may accommodate long tails, it's really designed for Blockbusters. Besides, Blockbusters are better than Long Tails.

For one thing, these are fast times; speed—time to market—is at a premium. And Blockbusters get you in the money faster—and a quicker return on one's investment means less risk and more money to pour back into innovation. What's more, Blockbusters create new markets and stimulate innovation and competition

The lesson: All companies should make maximum use of network properties for Blockbuster results.

To consider this thesis, we need to recall from Chapter 2 that the networked economy is a viral medium built for pandemics; it is designed to move information quickly and completely to and among all nodes in the system. Epidemic dissemination of information is the natural state of the network.

Proof of this intrinsic preference for pandemic economics—what I call pandenomics—can be seen in the recent history of network behavior. According to Web analytics group Compete, in 2006 the Top 10 domains accounted for 40 percent of the total page views on the Internet—a 29 percent increase over five years earlier.

How else can the rapid, epidemic-like growth of a MySpace or Facebook be explained if not by the Blockbuster properties behind preferential attachment? The rich get richer, the bigger sellers sell more.

Again, I point to a basic law of networks: *bigger is better*. The network is a tense coil waiting to spring out the next big-selling, big-headed Blockbuster—when the conditions are right. A contagious company with a viral product in a well-articulated network is the perfect recipe for explosive pandemic growth.

Designing products and services with the belief—faith, really—that the Long Tail will bail you out is plain dumb. All the ingredients to build a Blockbuster are online and in place: cheap production, cheap distribution, cheap promotion, and markets of massive scale and fluidity. The mantra of Pandenomics: build a Blockbuster and ride it for all its worth.

In the jargon of the industry, the Internet is exiting "beta." The trial period is over, the concept has been proven, and critical adoption arrives during or about the year 2011 as the user community spikes past three billion people.

We've looked at the impact of the Jump Point on businesses, markets, and consumers. But the Jump Point will be far more sweeping than that. So, what can we expect for life to be like in this new era? What will we experience as the forces pick up and the network unleashes its true potential across the world's cultures?

In the final chapter we look ahead to life beyond this next turn in the great human adventure.

Download This

- Networks behave as they will: it is futile to fight the inherent properties of the network.
- Networks are composed of clusters of nodes; on the Internet, these clusters are called "social communities."
- Social communities are the new market spaces.
- Market spaces welcome peer-to-peer communications and resist broadcast.
- Free is good.
- Attention is a value; its use must be rewarded.
- Time is a device; use it to serve your customers now, not to delay their gratification.
- Mashing is an inalienable right.
- Abundance means never having to say "no."
- Friends are the new marketing medium.
- Offer widgets—conversation starters—to your love base.
- Be a Blockbuster.

Future–Perfect–Tense

Time present and time past
Are both perhaps in time future
And time future contained in time past.

—T. S. ELIOT, *Four Quartets*

The ferry that crosses the Strait of Gibraltar, from Algeciras on the Spanish side to Tangiers on the Moroccan, took less than an hour, but for some of my fellow passengers I'm sure it seemed like an eternity. The boat daily crosses the strait precisely where the headwaters of the Atlantic Ocean meet the breakwaters of the Mediterranean Sea, which makes for a tumultuous ride. More than a few passengers showed the ill effects of the rough crossing.

Upon landing at Tangiers's bustling port, my friend David and I worked our way through the labyrinth of the ancient medina, its narrow stone pathway lined with every manner of merchant, selling every imaginable good, from leather products and felt tarbooshes to pirated software and CDs. The bazaars were a sensory bombardment of color, noise, and smells.

Not far from the Grand Socco market square, we sat at an outdoor café for a typical Moroccan lunch of assorted salads and *mechoui*, lamb with preserved lemon. At a table across from us, a man dressed in a traditional *jalaba* sat with a plate of nougats enjoying mint tea. Every few minutes, his cell phone rang, and he would have a brief conversation with the caller. This activity went on for some time. As it turns, the man was a *hawaladar*, a banker of sorts, a conduit really, for a centuries' old financial system called *hawala*.

Dating back to at least the eighth century, and much like the principles of the Maghribi Traders, hawala is an honor-based system of money transfer. Operating on the equivalent of a handshake, usually today a phone call, the practice is estimated to move millions of dollars per day throughout the Middle East, Africa, and parts of Asia—all of it under the radar. No paper trail, no digital fingerprints, no record at all.

By the afternoon call for prayers, our hawaladar paid his check—with cash—and left. Soon after, I settled our bill with my American Express card.

In the world after the Jump Point, new and old, digital and analog, the ancient and the thoroughly modern will seek out a restive coexistence. Paradoxes and contradictions will abound, hybrid cultures will be the norm—a confusing farrago of old-world pictures and futurespeak captions. Even if ours were a perfect world of perfect information—a peaceable kingdom of comity and concord— it would take some time for the dust to settle after the Jump Point. And, ours, decidedly, is not a perfect world.

When one is pondering an imminent cultural and economic transformation, it's easy to be either apocalyptic or utopian, sometimes even both. The future, always unknown, is disturbing even at the best of times. And when the times are topsy-turvy, when events seem to be racing toward a great historical inflection, it is hard not to let the imagination run wild.

This will be particularly true with the Jump Point, as it is coincidentally timed with a number of other predictions about the years 2010 to 2025 as old as the Mayan date for the end of the world and Nostradamus' of the apocalypse, and as recent as Ray

Kurzweill's prediction for the Singularity, when human brains and computer intelligence will merge.

It would be easy to conflate the Jump Point with all of that Millenarianism, and no doubt many people will do just that in the years to come—indeed, the Jump Point may even be pointed to as evidence of these transcendent events—but that is not the place of this book. We will stick with the practical realities, with the here and now of commerce and the marketplace, and leave the mystical to others.

So far in this book we have looked at the technological, social, and demographic trends that are driving humankind toward its next Jump Point, notably the rise of a fast, powerful global commercial information web and a population of people comfortable in its use. We have also established the pivotal historic moment that the future will likely look back upon as the date when the Jump Point occurred: the instant, sometime in about 2011, when the 3 billionth user joins the information age . . . and in the process becomes the final working person on the planet to become part of the World Wide Web. This will be a moment without precedent, when every person in the global economy is not only working within the same medium, but also capable of near-instant contact.

Finally, here in this third section of the book, I have tried to consider what the post–Jump Point world will look like by searching out early indicators in everything from new companies to new cultural institutions, even to changing human relationships with space and time.

But what we have not addressed is the one issue that will be of greatest personal interest to all of us: What will the Jump Point *feel* like? What will it be like to live in this new world? And how will our relationship to each other, to our work, to the universe itself, change?

The answer may well be that we will hardly notice the change at all, at least at first. Eight thousand years ago, did the citizens of Catal Huyuk recognize that they were the pioneers of a whole new human reality? That the city they lived in was the harbinger of a whole new way of ordering society? That they were embarking on a massive experiment in establishing market commerce, representative government, hierarchies of labor and distribution, and the reordering of time and geography?

Probably not. No doubt the people of Catal Huyuk knew they were residing in the biggest aggregation of humanity any of them had ever seen—and that this unprecedented density was leading to some unexpected changes: larger marketplaces, busier wells, a sizable local constabulary, greater specialization of labor (such as the rise of protorestaurants, barbers, butchers), the appearance of the first individuals whose job was to help run the operations of the city (namely, the bureaucrats), and the conversion of traditional guards and village watchmen into full-time soldiers.

In retrospect, every one of these changes was of profound and worldwise historic importance. But at the time, they were likely seen as simply pragmatic solutions to immediate and pressing local needs. Human beings are extraordinarily adaptive creatures, and no doubt the citizens of Catal Huyuk quickly assimilated these changes and moved on. In the course of a generation what had been radical and new had become everyday—yet one more invisible thread in the fabric of daily life.

When we look ahead to the brave new world after the Jump Point it is easy to become disoriented by the prospect of vast, new global markets seemingly bursting out of nothing; fads racing about the globe in a matter of days, even hours; vast new empires and fortunes being created by the most unexpected people in the most unlikely places; even the language itself changing on our tongues. Our businesses under attack, our culture evolving at breakneck speed, our perspective on almost everything turned upside down and inside out—it's all quite terrifying.

In fact, crossing the Jump Point into the different world that lies beyond may not be as traumatic as we imagine. For one thing, there is that seemingly infinite capacity of human beings to adapt to even the most radical change.

Many of us have had the privilege of knowing, perhaps as our grandparents or great-grandparents, members of that extraordinary generation born between 1880 and 1905, that probably experienced more change than any generation in human history. My Yia Yia and Papou—my Greek grandparents, were born into a world of horses, gas lamps, and one-room schoolhouses, yet they lived long enough to watch, on television, a man walk on the moon, to ride in a Boeing 747, and even to use a computer. And they did it all with aplomb.

As immense as the changes will be beyond the Jump Point, it is unlikely they will be as great as that. Moreover, as the last few chapters have shown, in any of a number of ways, we are already rehearsing our Jump Point future. That is, everything from mashups to Web 2.0 community sites to global virtual workteams can be seen as "training wheels" for the post–Jump Point world, early test runs of new technologies and social structures to prepare us for what is to come. And it is precisely because of these test runs, some (such as MySpace and Facebook) already in use by tens of millions of people, that the Jump Point may seem less a major discontinuity in history than a universal flowering of experiences and activities most of us already know.

Just as we woke up one day in the late 1990s to realize that the personal computer and the Internet had become inextricable parts of our daily lives, so too may we look around in 2020 and realize that we live in an entirely different world from the one we knew two decades before . . . and not be able to put a finger on just when that metamorphosis occurred.

It is possible to imagine what the post–Jump Point world will feel like by extrapolating from the emerging trends we already see around us.

For example, most researchers and semiconductor executives believe that Moore's law is likely to continue to reign at least until 2015, and perhaps much longer, as always driven along by the incredible creativity of chip designers and builders. What this likelihood signifies is that the torrid pace of change that has characterized the developed world for the last three decades will probably continue for at least two decades more—with two important differences:

1. This explosive rate of change will now affect the entire planet.
2. As we are now on the nearly vertical path of the exponential, J-shaped, curve, the nature of this change will probably be even faster than before.

By the Jump Point, the average personal computer will be almost as powerful as today's supercomputers, thus enabling such activities as realistic 3-D modeling, artificial intelligence, and robotics to become commonplace, which today are taking place only in laboratories. At the high end, big computers will have more computational power than the human brain; at the low end, chip-level computer intelligence (and thus, Web access) will be so inexpensive that it will be embedded almost everywhere. It is likely that every appliance, wall switch, streetlight, wristwatch, and toy will offer easy access to the global information network. Undoubtedly, there will be Web access devices so cheap that even the poorest people on earth will be able to afford them.

Moore's law won't be alone in continuing to race up its current trajectory. Information storage, the real miracle of modern technology, will continue to keep pace with processors, meaning that cheap, hand-held terabyte memory will be as common as gigabyte memory on today's iPods. This computer processing power will mean that most of us will carry our life histories with us at all times. It will also mean that the iPod of 2015 will arrive already filled with every music recording, television show, and movie ever made. Both features will have enormous implications in terms of privacy, copyrights, and creativity.

So, too, will the various laws of networks continue to spin out at their current hyperpace. Instant transmission—to billions of nodes ranging from computers to cell phones to embedded chips—of video, first-run movies, and various 3-D experiences will be commonplace. And the combination of the three—processing power, memory, and networks—will make global online games and lifestyle experiences (such as Second Life and EverQuest) more realistic, more complex . . . and ultimately blur the line between virtual and natural reality.

In the process, it is very possible that television networks, movie theaters, record companies, and other durable institutions of the twentieth century will fade away in the same manner that video stores and game arcades are disappearing today—and in many places in the developing world, they will never appear in the first place.

It also appears inevitable that the growing number of Web 2.0 communities will evolve into "Web 3.0" enterprises that will consume ever-greater portions of the lives of billions of people with ever-richer experiences of participatory games, surrogate lives, and personal networking. They will also begin to monetize those experiences, adding services ranging from news to retail to travel to education. Ultimately, many are likely to become among the world's largest corporations, with an impact upon the daily lives of their members often as great as the countries in which those members live.

That much, at least, seems obvious. One of the great advantages of living in the digital age is that much of the future spreads out before us in a fairly predictable way. If we can assume that the underlying laws of tech will hold—and they have for a quarter-century now—we can pretty accurately guess the digital world's capabilities at any future date.

What we can't know, of course, is how those capabilities will be put to use—that is, beyond the superpowering of existing products and services. There is simply no way of predicting what new video game or personal computer, cell phone, or iPod will appear—that is, an unexpected breakthrough invention that reconfigures not only the electronics industry, but society itself. One thing of which we can be certain is thanks to market opportunity and human ingenuity, those inventions *will* appear and on a regular basis.

What is even more interesting is the possibility that, with the addition of two billion more participants in the global world of commerce, the intellectual capital available to search for and exploit those breakthroughs could also triple. That would mean new inventions, of iPod or Google magnitude, emerging not once or twice per decade, but every couple of years—with the resulting continuous uproar in the marketplace.

That said, it should also be pointed out that these inventions probably won't be born in Palo Alto, Seoul, or Munich, where a mainstream and trade press, an army of bloggers and early adopters, patent lawyers, and publicists, is ready and waiting to bring them out to the public. After the Jump Point, the Next Big Thing will be just as likely to appear anywhere in the world, and probably in a distant corner of the developing world, where few notice—until it suddenly bursts on the scene, sweeping away entire markets and the companies within them.

What this means is that smart companies (that is, those that want to survive) will need to remain vigilant on almost every corner of the planet, eternally searching for the first clues—a blog entry, a patent application, a comment on a community Web site—of something huge still running beneath the radar. Then they will have to buy it, fight it, or co-opt it *fast* because, as we also know, in the post–Jump Point networked world, once a new "beme" emerges it will proliferate around the Earth at breakneck speeds. The best companies will set up picket lines of early-warning systems stretching around the globe just to head off such an eventuality. And they will need cash, legal talent, and local expertise in reserve to respond in real time.

But Jump Points aren't really about technology. If history is any guide, most of the technological revolution that drives a major historical discontinuity has already occurred by the time the Jump Point is reached.

Indeed, if Moore's and Metcalfe's laws were to hit a wall right now, if there were no important new commercial or consumer inventions in the digital domain, and we were left to merely spin out all of the implications of our existing inventory of chips, instruments, and electronic systems, we would *still* pass through a major cultural transformation in the next decade. The die is cast; the third billion is still coming on board; and the world is about to become fully wired.

Unfortunately—or, perhaps fortunately—human beings aren't as predictable as transistors and silicon gates. And predicting their behavior, especially against the background of technological change and the vagaries of the natural world, is especially risky. Just as decisively, there are key decision points that lie beyond the Jump Point that, once made, will send humanity down one path or another. As it is all but impossible to guess which path humankind will take, the best we can do is to identify those decision points and describe the alternatives.

The reality is that many of these decisions will ultimately be made without our being conscious of them. The mass migration of English field hands to the mills of Birmingham in the late eighteenth century, and the movement of southern African Americans to the cities of the north-midwestern United States in the early twentieth century—and, for that matter, the billion people around the world who signed on to the Internet in the 1990s—were not planned feats of social engineering but private decisions made by vast numbers of individuals to take advantage of opportunities created by technological revolutions a few years before.

The Jump Point will present a wide range of opportunities to us three billion consumers, all against a background of incredible noise and change, of fads and fashions bursting on the scene and then disappearing just as quickly. Everything is going to come at us so fast and furiously that it is very possible that we won't have time to stop and take stock of the many profound changes taking place around us—in other words, a lot like today.

After all, who among us noticed, except in retrospect, the transition to our current world of BlackBerries, Twitter, and satellite radio? For most of us, it seemed like one day these technologies didn't exist, and the next they were everywhere—including in our own lives. It's likely that the many of the major features of the Jump Point will arrive the same way: suddenly they'll just be *there*.

We'll find ourselves listening to a new kind of dance music from Indonesia, using a new cell phone designed in Latvia to buy an item on eBay from someone in Paraguay, and take our office meetings through our surrogate on Second Life. Odd new slang words—strange hybrids of English and Afrikaans or Tagalog— will silently creep into our daily conversation; and our favorite blog will be written by a promising new writer in Malawi. Meanwhile, our days of working at home or at Starbucks will dilate as we find ourselves working full time for a multinational virtual corporation with its official headquarters in Bulgaria.

And then one day, a half-decade on, we'll look up and realize that the life we know has irrevocably changed, and the world we lived just a few years before now seems so alien and far away.

Jump Points are inherently risky times: with everything thrown into the air to be re-sorted on the ground, with power and wealth being transferred to the inexperienced from the increasingly resentful, there is a greater-than-usual potential for either a cultural breakthrough or a disaster.

Similarly, the impending Jump Point could lead to a flowering of civilization, and a time of peace and prosperity the likes of which we have never known. Or, it could cast us all into a dark world of labyrinths and gulags, darknets, and roaming bands of stateless free radicals—a *Blade Runner* world of lawless confusion and self-interest.

The odds, however, are against either scenario. Social collapse is usually the result of either an aged and contracting society or an external pathogen such as a plague. While the latter is always possible, the increased creativity of the three billion improves the likelihood of a successful remedy. As for the former, the post–Jump Point world will be anything but aged and shrinking.

As for the arrival of heaven on earth—we know too much about history to believe that that scenario will appear anytime soon.

What we are most likely to get is something in between. But that's a lot of ground, ranging from a world of greater fragmentation, poverty, and violence to one of improved universal living standards, prosperity, and comparative peace. And even if there are too many variables and unknowns to describe the world beyond the Jump Point in any precise detail, we must still try to capture, in some rough way, the likely trajectory of humanity in the years to come.

The good news is that it already is possible to make out features and forms in the mist. And if we can't come up with precise answers, it is already possible to frame the right questions.

Here, I believe, are the most important of those questions:

1. *Will the global Web make the world more homogeneous, or will it empower people to become more diverse?*

We are already rubbing up against this question. A quarter century ago, the fear, especially among Europeans, was that U.S. cultural hegemony was becoming so complete, that the reach of its corporations from McDonald's to Disney so extensive, that the world risked becoming Americanized. The same fear was expressed (especially by linguists) of the world's many and diverse languages shrinking to just one: English.

Thanks to the Web, that first fear has begun to fade; while predictions of the second are largely coming true—though the version of English that will ultimately emerge may be very different from the one we know today.

So that raises the question: Does a Web-linked world increasingly support common standards, products, and culture because the dominant forms of each eventually overwhelm everything else in cyberspace? Or does the ability to use the Web to reach out and connect with like-minded people, as well as enabling participation in the world's economy without having to leave one's cultural enclave, actually strengthen the power and durability of local cultures?

Does the post–Jump Point world look like one vast Wal-Mart, or a million cyberbazaars?

2. *Will the second and third billions rise to the social contract—that is, the rule of law—that defines the first billion? Or will they pull the first billion down to their current level of lawlessness?*

In some ways, this is everyone's greatest fear—and not just in the developed world. Wishful thinking, combined with a belief in the robust nature of Western institutions such as democratic republics, binding business contracts, and courts of law, leads us to hope that the rest of the world, given a chance, will adopt our standards.

Unfortunately, history—especially the story of European colonies after independence—doesn't give us much reason for optimism. And, one shouldn't forget, those next two billion are twice the size of the first—together they win every vote. What's more, many come from cultures defined by corruption, lawlessness, and fraud.

Will having those two billion connected to the Web give them access to higher standards of business behavior that they will choose to adopt—and can we teach them the rule of law in time? Or will we be fighting a rear-guard action against world that wants to play by *its* rules.

Will the post–Jump Point world look like the West or the Wild West, a place of law-abiding businesspeople or one endless landscape of e-mail scammers?

3. Will the global Web after the Jump Point be characterized by trust or mistrust?

In a tense August 2007 meeting between the leaders of the world's third- and fourth-largest economies, German chancellor Angela Merkel warned China's premier Wen Jiabao and president Hu Jintao that relations between their two countries hinged on the matter of "mutual respect." Earlier that day, the newsweekly *Der Spiegel* had reported that a group of Chinese hackers had penetrated Germany's government computers in Berlin. On what the press came to term the "China Threat Theory," Merkel flatly commented to reporters, "At present there are a great many large countries such as China that are developing fast and there is a need to respect the rules of the game."

This question of trust looms large after the Jump Point. It is what Malcolm Gladwell would characterize as a tipping-point scenario, a logical extension of question number two. Will bringing all three billion of the world's working people onto the Web ultimately produce a global economy in which transactions made by two geographically diverse parties that can almost always be trusted? Or will it result in a global economy in which most such transactions cannot be trusted?

As we all know, this notion of trust is a very complex one, traditionally based upon all sorts of cues, from past experiences to credentials to visual cues given off by the other party. In a network transaction, especially one made in a networked world with someone from any utterly alien society, most of those cues are missing.

Will we develop new cues? And will we find them in time? And how much does the Net itself, especially within communities, reinforce honesty and trust?

Will the post–Jump Point world more resemble a shopping mall or a carnival midway?

4. *Which will become more valuable: continued fragmentation or aggregation?*

Probably the most successful business strategy of the last one hundred years is to carve up your target market until you have created a submarket in which you hold a dominant position or monopoly. It is just this sort of market segmentation that has made possible the proliferation of hundreds of successful companies within markets that used to hold only one or two.

Similarly, the professions have fragmented as well into "specialists," from gerontologists to adult orthodontists to immigration lawyers and Sarbanes-Oxley audit accountants.

This technique has worked brilliantly precisely because it takes advantage of traditional information scarcity. You go to a cardiologist for your heart instead of internist, not because the latter is less of a doctor, but because the former has better access to the latest medical knowledge about your problem and tools to deal with them. Any lawyer can file the paperwork for a divorce, but the assumption is that a divorce lawyer knows the specific laws best and can thus get you a better judgment than another type of lawyer can.

Market fragmentation will undoubtedly continue after the Jump Point simply because the incredible increase in the customer pool will reward product and service providers who can customize their offerings for all of those new niche markets that will come onstream.

But at the same time, the Web itself is an immense sea of free-floating ideas, images, phrases, and stories—a giant, untapped ocean of opportunity for anyone interested in combining these fragments into brand-new creations. This is today's mashup sub-culture as a global force—and we will likely need it to remain as innovative as we are today. After all, truly brand new ideas are few and far between, while putting together existing ideas is so easy even a child can do it—and they already are.

"Zeitgeist" is the term used to describe the dominant spirit of an age. So, will the post–Jump Point zeitgeist continue to be that of ever-finer fragmentation? Or are we entering the age of the universal mashup?

5. Will the post–Jump Point world be older or younger?

One last question about the post–Jump Point world for which we as yet have no answer: Will this new reality, because it has universal access to humankind's entire history of lessons, positive examples, and best practices, behave in an older and wiser manner than it does now? Can it actually learn from experience?

Or, given that the next two billion is younger and less educated and has a much higher birthrate than the current one billion, will the post–Jump Point world be the sixties all over again—a youth culture, with all of the creativity, immaturity, impatience, and volatility that comes with it? If the latter, given that the West is *still* recovering from the sixties forty years later, what happens if the whole world is 1968 redux? How patient will these millions be waiting for prosperity to arrive when they can already see it on their cell phones and computer screens?

Historically, Jump Points have also brought with them inherent social contradictions. For example, the rise of nation-states after the Industrial Revolution brought with them not only greater democracy but also total war. The automobile tied together the many cities and towns scattered across the United States, but it also shattered many of those municipalities (and the families that lived in them) by putting Americans on the road to move to somewhere else.

The Jump Point we are currently approaching already is exhibiting some very strange and paradoxical characteristics. How these will play out probably cannot be predicted beforehand; no doubt they can be explained only in retrospect. We will have to *live* them, and let billions of individuals make their own choices, before we can understand their conclusion:

1. *As the pace of change accelerates, time itself will seem to slow down.*

If this sounds a bit like Einstein's Theory of Relativity, you shouldn't be surprised. After all, when we talk about nanotechnology and quantum effects, of billions of computation cycles occurring on a semiconductor chip in less than a second, and terabytes of data racing around the globe on the Internet, we are leaving the natural world we know and entering into the strange reality of relativistic space.

We aren't quite there—yet—but it is still both humbling and awe-inspiring to realize that the modern microprocessor conducts as many operations in a second as a human being has heartbeats in a lifetime—and that right now there are as many transistors on the world's billions of computer chips as there will be raindrops that fall on the earth this year.

What this means is that what seems like just an instant to us are eons for our modern digital machines. Indeed, our computers, while they wait for us to press the next key, can perform millions of operations each on hundreds of different tasks *at the same time*.

We change our tools, and then our tools change us. And this is a perfect example. All of that unspent capability represents an opportunity that cannot long be ignored—and it hasn't been. Watch a teenager using a computer these days: he or she is likely to be downloading an MP3 music file, replying to an instant message, playing an online game, cruising MySpace, watching a video on YouTube, and researching a school paper on Wikipedia— simultaneously. And that doesn't even including texting, talking, and Twittering on a cell phone.

Such multitasking is an inevitable consequence of having a banquet of information available before us and a powerful tool for capturing that information and manipulating it. Thus, each new generation gets better and stuffs more experiences into a single brief window of time.

When you begin to cram a lifetime of experiences into a single moment, the result, even though the clock beside you is still ticking forward, is the sensation of time beginning to slow. And this sensation will only be reinforced by the fact that, with almost unlimited access to information and records, as well as predictions and speculations, the past and future will seem to be part of the present as well.

The result will be a kind of eternal present, with an almost infinite sense of extension as the entire world will be essentially "next door." This sensation will create a weird sense of immortality and omniscience—as if we are the very center of space and time, able to see everything going all the time.

Just exactly how this will play out is hard to imagine today. But we can get a glimpse of what it will be like from stories about college students disappearing into their dorm rooms for days to play online games, only emerging occasionally for food. We also have those disturbing anecdotal stories from Japan and other gaming hot spots of young men actually dying from cerebral hemorrhages from staying on the computer too long.

Obviously, that's not going to be a general phenomenon (though it is likely to become much more common than it is today), but certainly all of us will regularly experience these moments, while on the Web, of frozen time. And it will certainly be jarring to return to the real world afterward.

2. *The Web will give us a sense of omnipotence in regard to knowledge and reach, even as it reminds us of our impotence in the face of events.*

You can think of this as a corollary to phenomenon number one. Anyone who spends a lot of time these days surfing Internet news sites or visiting the blogosphere already appreciates this paradox. Thanks to powerful search engines, wikis, and real-time news gathering by citizen journalists around the world, the Web has become a vehicle for everyday users to quickly race around the world watching news events as they break, or conversely, burrowing down into libraries of knowledge once only available to the most assiduous and dedicated academic.

Want to know about this morning's flood in Kuala Lumpur, complete with video, first-person diaries, weather data, and professional reporting? It's a few keystrokes away. The same is true if you want to see a graphic representation of Giordano Bruno's Sixteenth Century Memory Theater or listen to a recently discovered Mozart sonata.

One of the greatest miracles of the Internet age is that it has put into the hands of everyday people the kind of access to news and information that wasn't available to the richest man on earth a generation ago—or even to giant wire services like Associated Press (AP) or Reuters just a few years ago.

But access to information doesn't necessarily come with the ability to influence events. There is little we can do about a flood in Kuala Lumpur, except perhaps to donate money. But there will be another disaster somewhere else in the world tomorrow and the day after that. And when sociologists are already writing about widespread "sympathy fatigue," how much greater will it become—and how much more indifferent will we be—when that sympathy is appealed to several times each day?

Again, we don't know how this phenomenon will play out. Will the post–Jump Point world become more indifferent and steeled to human misery? Or will something profound occur at the intersection of online communities and 24/7 news where groups of people will quickly organize in "sympathy affinity" groups and quickly race to help? Will they do the same to fight tyranny? Perform acts of sedition?

3. *As the world gets smaller, the scope of our individual lives will grow vastly greater.*

Even if we resist the ever-present calls for help around the world that will come to us on our computer and cell phone screens, there is still no escaping the fact that every day we are becoming more linked to the larger world. Many people have experienced that moment of astonishment, after winning a bid on eBay, and preparing the payment check, when they discover that the seller is somewhere in Africa or a former Soviet state or some other location with which they have never had contact before.

This phenomenon is only going to accelerate, if only because the Law of the Network demands it. Remember, the more linked nodes, the more valuable the network.

Until recently, the popular notion was that improved transportation (better roads, faster planes, and so on), a better communications infrastructure (cheaper international phone calls, WiFi/WiMAX), and global cable news would make the world a "smaller" place—that is, we would be able to contact, or even physically reach, distant lands so quickly that it would seem as if the planet had shrunk.

That is still true for actual travel. But in the sphere of communications and information transfer, the process has become so fast, so ubiquitous, so inexpensive that this image no longer works—a planet shrunk to a single point has no meaning.

Rather, and perversely, for individuals this "shrinking" world is about to become much bigger. Fifty years ago, even for people who lived in developed nations, communications with individuals on the other side of the country was uncommon, and with folks on the other side of the world, exceedingly rare.

Today, most of us in the first billion talk to or e-mail people in other countries and on other continents so often that time zones have become one of our biggest productivity challenges. For the second and third billion, joining this global conversation will be even easier. Already today we scarcely give a second thought to where an e-mail correspondent lives; in the world beyond the Jump Point, place of origin will essentially become meaningless, supplanted by the larger question of trustworthiness.

4. *In a connected world, isolation may become the rarest and most valuable commodity.*

Scarcity equals value, as long as there is strong demand. And there seems little doubt that in a world in which every working person is connected to the giant global grid, when GPS satellites and pervasive charge-coupled device (CCD) cameras track our every move, we are going to feel an increasing desire to be alone, to get off the grid, and to hide.

The irony of this urge, of course, is that the last two hundred-fifty years of technological innovation have been devoted to *ending* our lonely and frustrating isolation. Factories drew people in from isolated farms to work in busy cities, trains carried passengers from the countryside to towns, the telegraph and telephone enabled conversation to vault continents, and so on.

It goes without saying that this process, like Moore's law, has only accelerated in recent years. When Silicon Valley engineers regularly spend parts of their days sitting in virtual meetings with work teammates on the other side of the world, when Londoners are filmed by an average of 20 security cameras on a given day, and big Web sites like AOL and Google can track your every move on the Internet, it can be said with certainty that our days of isolation are over.

No one believes the scope of this connectedness is going to do anything but increase in the years to come. And while most of us will grumble but accept this new order, it will also grate on all of our nerves. The desire to disconnect, if only temporarily, will be deep and universal.

How will the post–Jump Point world deal with that desire? No doubt through services, both legal and illegal, to take those willing to pay off the grid. Will this effort create an underground of network "wraiths"—criminals, terrorists, spies, and also everyday people who just want some peace and quiet? Will this be a minor, and temporary, phenomenon; or will it be the new version of bootlegging during Prohibition? Or will the legitimate business world respond by offering safe and legal forms of the same services?

5. *The world is becoming less entrepreneurial even as it becomes more so.*

In some ways, this is the oddest paradox of the Jump Point.

On the one hand, a networked world in which an additional two billion people have joined the Web, where new business ideas can get a global hearing, where venture capital can be invested anywhere, and in which incremental marketing and sales costs can approach zero would seem the perfect ground for an entrepreneurial explosion. After all, many of those new billions are already shopkeepers who merely need better access to capital to fulfill their dreams.

But on the other hand, existing companies already have the capital to invest. And the smart ones are beginning to appreciate that to compete in this new economy they must have on-the-ground presence in thousands of these new local markets—especially where the physical infrastructure is insufficient to support customer service and support. Moreover, in reaching that third billion, who will often be located in small villages off the main track, these companies will also need to employ people who know the local culture, speak the regional patois, and most of all, who understand the unique customs and mores of their potential customers. Finally, and not least, companies will need to monitor those global early-warning systems to defend themselves from nasty surprises.

In other words, even though we should expect much of the business expansion of the post–Jump Point world to be virtual, delivered via the Web and wireless, there will still be a vast number of companies that will need to rapidly expand through a wide range of innovative (and often Web-based) employment and benefit programs.

Thus, it is quite possible that even as some giant corporations shrink their employment rolls through the use of automation and other electronic productivity tools, other companies may see their employment explode. Indeed, it is entirely possible that the post–Jump Point world will see the first million-employee corporations—with all that could come with them, including producing their own virtual currency, culture, media, and lifestyles.

What all of this means is that the post–Jump Point years may see an unprecedented, and largely unreported, race between giant global corporations racing to hire millions of new local employees, while at the same time more millions of budding entrepreneurs are searching for the funding to make their dreams come true. Will the latter succeed quickly enough to produce an explosion of exciting new companies and the global market volatility that will come with it—or will they fall short and be snapped up by giant companies, resulting in a more stable but less innovative and less shock-resistant world economy?

The outcome of that race is impossible to predict. But what can be predicted with near certainty is that not only will the post–Jump Point world see the first million-employee corporations, but also the first companies with a $1 trillion valuation. And, no matter which way the race goes, it also seems inevitable that from the ranks of this next generation of post–Jump Point entrepreneurs, most likely from the developing world, will come history's first trillionaire.

Questions and paradoxes.

That's hardly what you want to hear when facing the imminent arrival of the largest social shock of your lifetime, and deciding what strategies you need to pursue for your professional and personal lives.

Here is what we do know.

In the years to come, but especially after the Jump Point, sudden bursts of innovation and invention will seem to sweep the planet in a matter of days, producing regular crises in specific industries, as well as wild market swings.

At the same time, we are likely to see unprecedented bursts of creativity in culture as well, with the rise of global, but short-lived, "movements" in music, art, film, and the like.

So, too, will fads, fears, and "facts" (real or intentionally faked) also race around the world at extraordinary speeds, seemingly instantaneously popping up at the same moment all over the planet.

The experience of all of this will be both exhilarating and frightening. We will gain a greater sense of the sheer energy of the world of humanity, and at the same time we will recognize our powerlessness within it. This awareness will, in turn, lead us to become ever-more-committed to our "communities" as a way to affect change—and this will, in turn, challenge traditional political structures, especially nationhood.

Economic and social power will shift to new institutions, organizations, and individuals—and in the process huge amounts of wealth will aggregate around these entities. Some of these new beneficiaries will be criminal or terrorist organizations, which will take advantage of this new order to wreak havoc unless they are identified and stopped in time.

Meanwhile, in business, the biggest challenge will be *simultaneity*. Because demand will appear everywhere at once, how can you meet that demand everywhere at once—especially if the solution also must take account of local differences in culture, language, and customs? Those companies that cannot find the answer—which will require radical new thinking about global distribution, regional microproduction, and similar matters—will be quickly extinguished by ones that can. And that is likely to lead to shift in wealth and power from established companies in the current so-called developed world to more innovative and adaptive new companies in today's so-called third world.

All of these developments represent a devastating potential threat to many individuals and enterprises that, until now, have enjoyed great prosperity. But the post–Jump Point world also represents a huge and historically almost unprecedented opportunity for success, fame, and prosperity.

I say "almost" because, in fact, there is one historic era that also features such an overturning of existing orders, a multiplying of active participants, an explosion of creativity, and an unprecedented linking together of the world's populations.

We call it the Renaissance, and it was the greatest flowering of human imagination and potential in history. It was also a time of destruction of the prevailing order, violence, organized crime, and widespread corruption.

Is the Jump Point the opening of a portal to a new Renaissance? That depends upon how those questions are answered and those paradoxes resolved. But as the trends described in this book suggest, it may be our best chance in a half-millennium.

Let's hope we—and the billions about to join us—have the courage and strength of character to embrace this extraordinary opportunity.

Notes

Chapter One

5   Carlota Perez, *Technological Revolutions and Financial Capital: The Dynamics of Bubbles and Golden Ages*, Northampton, MA: Edward Elgar Publishing, 2002. This is one of the best books I have seen on the relationship between technology diffusion, financial, and social change.

8   For more information about the "penny blacks," the first postage stamps, Associated Content has a nice starting point, http://www.associatedcontent.com/article/235933/englands_first_postage_stamp.html.

10   Chris Anderson's Long Tail blog has a nice item on "Free-conomics" that discusses the drop of a unit of computing, http://www.longtail.com/the_long_tail/2006/11/the_rise_of_fre.html.

11   Simon Yates, "Worldwide PC Adoption Forecast, 2007 to 2015," Forrester Research report, June 11, 2007, http://www. forrester. com/Research/Document/Excerpt/0,7211,42496,00.html.

11   The GSMA's Emerging Market Handset initiative (EMH) was launched at the 3GSM World Congress in February 2005. It is part of the Association's strategic effort to give 80 percent of the world's population access to mobile communications by 2010.

11   TechnoFusion has a good pithy blog on the Lehman Brothers research, http://blogs.ittefaq.com/tech/archives/2005/08/mobile_handset.html.

11   Ibid.

12   Leonard Waverman, Meloria Meschi, and Melvyn Fuss, "The Impact of Telecoms in Economic Growth in Developing Countries," http://web.si.umich.edu/tprc/papers/2005/450/L%20Waverman%20Telecoms%20Growth%20in%20Dev.%20Countries.pdf

12   George R. G. Clarke and Scott J. Wallsten, "Has the Internet Increased Trade? Evidence from Industrial and Developing Countries," Policy Research Working Paper Series 3215, February 1, 2004, http://ideas.repec.org/p/wbk/wbrwps/3215.html.

12   The members of the W3C Web Access Initiative (http://www.w3.org/WAI/) are working hard to ensure that people with disabilities gain and keep access to the Web.

13   Winnie Mangaliso's story can be found on the SharedPhone Web site, http://www.sharedphone.co.za/winnies_story.asp.

14   This review by the World Resources Institute provides good analysis of the World Bank findings: http://www.wri.org/business/pubs_content_text.cfm?ContentID=4320.

14   Nicholas P. Sullivan, *You Can Hear Me Now: How Microloans and Cell Phones Are Connecting the World's Poor to the Global Economy*, San Francisco: Jossey-Bass, 2007. Sullivan's work explores the very real impact being made by Muhammad Yunus and his Grameen Bank and telecommunications operation.

15   C. K. Prahalad, *The Fortune at the Bottom of the Pyramid: Eradicating Poverty Through Profits*, Upper Saddle River, NJ: Wharton School Publishing, 2006. This makes the best argument yet about the potential economic power of the developing world.

15   Matti Pohjola, *The Adoption and Diffusion of ICT Across Countries: Patterns and Determinants*, Helsinki School of Economics *The New Economy Handbook*, Helsinki: Academic Press, 2003

16 A good source of economic statistics on China can be found on the Abacus Web site, http://chinese-school.netfirms.com/China-economic-statistics.html.

18 Luís M. A. Bettancourt, José Lobo, Dirk Helbing, Christian Kühnert, and Geoffrey B. West, "Growth, Innovation, Scaling, and the Pace of Life in Cities," Santa Fe, NM: Santa Fe Institute, April 2007. This is a fascinating white paper on the link between population growth and innovation.

19 David Reed explains his own "law" best in the article "That Sneaky Exponential? Beyond Metcalfe's Law to the Power of Community Building," available at http://www.reed.com/Papers/ GFN/reedslaw.html.

20 Andrew Odlyzko and Benjamin Tilly, "A Refutation of Metcalfe's Law and a Better Estimate for the Value of Networks and Network Interconnections," Minneapolis: Digital Technology Center, University of Minnesota, 2005, http://www.dtc.umn.edu/ ~odlyzko/doc/metcalfe.pdf. This article created quite a stir in Silicon Valley when it first appeared. Quoted from an e-mail to author May 23, 2007.

22 Eric L. Jones, *Cultures Merging: A Historical and Economic Critique of Culture,* Princeton, NJ: Princeton University Press, 2006. This book offers an insightful look at rapid cultural change.

25 Thomas Friedman, *The World Is Flat: A Brief History of the Twenty-first Century,* New York: Farrar, Straus and Giroux, 2005. *Flat* has become the *Dark Side of the Moon* for the book world: it seems to be in everybody's collection.

Chapter Two

32 Netvalley.com has a sweeping look at the history of the Internet era going back to 1836, www.netvalley.com/archives/mirrors/davemarsh-timeline-1.htm.

35 " 'ILOVEYOU' Computer Bug Bites Hard, Spreads Fast," *CNN.com*, May 4, 2000, http://www.cnn.com.

36 Before he took on God, Richard Dawkins startled the world with his insightful look at how culture propagates in *The Selfish Gene,* Oxford/New York: Oxford University Press, 1976.

37 Seth Godin's rants on "permission marketing" are legendary; the Fast Company interview from March 1998 remains a classic on the subject of consumer overload, http://www.fastcompany.com/ magazine/14/permission.html.

37 *Happy Days* in Season 4 (1976–1977) was the number one ranked show in the United States with an audience share of 31.5.

38 "A Beme Is a Meme Spread by Blogs," Tim Finin blog, February 18, 2007, http://ebiquity.umbc.edu/blogger/author/tim-finin/?jal_add_user_answer=true&paged=17.

40 The susceptibles-infectives-removed (S-I-R) scheme is a standard way to study the nonlinear diffusion of epidemics.

41 Gordon Allport and Leo Postman, *The Psychology of Rumor,* New York: Russell & Russell, 1965. This remains the classic text on the promulgation of rumors.

43 Gordon Gould Weblog, Monday, September 25, 2006. You won't find a more visionary observer of how people shop than Gordon.

Chapter Three

50 "E-Society: My World Is Cyworld," *Business Week*, September 26, 2005, http://www.businessweek.com/magazine/content/05_39/b3952405.htm.

51 Ibid.

51 CyWorld revenues analyzed: "SK Communications Unveiled," *Game Study.Org,* June 26, 2007, http://gamestudy.org/eblog/2007/06/26/sk-communications-unveiled/.

51 "SK Comm Merges with Empas: Cyworld Sells $80M in Virtual Goods," *Virtual Worlds News*, July 2, 2007, http://www.virtual worldsnews.com/2007/07/sk-commun icatio.html.

52 Howard Rheingold, *The Virtual Community: Homesteading on the Electronic Frontier*, Cambridge, MA: MIT Press, 2000. Rheingold was way ahead of his time.

53 I was astonished to find that my MySpace network had more than 200 million connections. My "friend" Tom Anderson told me so.

53   World population comparison according to http://www. internetworldstats.com/stats8.htm.

53   "YouTube Serves 100m Videos Each Day," *TechCrunch Weblog*, July 17, 2006, http://www.techcrunch.com/2006/ 07/17/youtube-serves-100m-videos-each-day/.

53   "Facebook Users Up 89% Over Last Year; Demographic Shift," *TechCrunch Weblog*, July 6, 2007, http://www.tech crunch.com/2007/07/06/facebook-users-up-89-over-last-year-demographic-shift/.

53   Waxy.org, "Tracking Twitter's Message Growth," March 15, 2007, http://waxy.org/archive/2007/03/15/tracking.shtml.

53   Gotfrag.com, discussion of Counter-Strike, http://www.gotfrag. com/cs/forums/thread/293648/?cpage=1.

53   Kevin Dugan, "Why Second Life Numbers DO Matter," *CNN.com*, January 2, 2007, http://money.cnn.com/blogs/ browser/2007/01/why-second-life-numbers-do-matter.html.

53   "Anshe Chung Becomes First Virtual World Millionaire," press release, November 26, 2006, http://www.anshechung. com/include/press/press_release251106.html.

54   Mark Walsh "Ad Spending on Social Networks Will Continue to Grow in '08," Online Media Daily, December 17, 2007 http://publications.mediapost.com/index.cfm?fuseaction=Articl es.san&s=72830&Nid=37462&p=219745.

54   Howard Rheingold, *The Virtual Community: Homesteading on the Electronic Frontier*, Cambridge, MA: MIT Press, 2000.

55   Lars Backstrom, Dan Huttenlocher, Jon Kleinberg, and Xianvang Lan, "Group Formation In Large Social Networks: Membership, Growth, and Evolution," In *Proceedings of the 12th ACM SIGKDD International Conference on Knowledge Discovery and Data Mining* (Philadelphia, PA: ACM Press, 2006).

55   Mark Granovetter, "The Strength of Weak Ties: A Network Theory Revisited," in *Sociological Theory, Vol. 1* (1983), 201–233.

56   Danah Boyd, "Friends, Friendsters, and Top 8: Writing Community into Being on Social Network Sites," *First Monday*, December 2006, http://www.firstmonday.org/issues/issue11_ 12/boyd/.

58 The Emile Durkheim Archive is a good online source of work by this pioneer in sociology, http://durkheim.itgo.com/.

58 James Surowiecki, *The Wisdom of Crowds*, New York: Doubleday, 2004.

61 "MySpace Faces Stiff Competition in Japan," *USAToday*, February 16, 2007, http://www.usatoday.com/tech/products/services/2007-02-16-myspace-japan_x.htm.

61 Jane Macartney, "Facebook's Hopes to Enter the Tangled Web of China Gain Momentum," *China Digital Times*, November 19, 2007, http://chinadigitaltimes.net/2007/11/facebooks_hopes_to_enter_the_tangled_web_of_china_gain.php.

61 Henry Jenkins, *Convergence Culture: Where Old and New Media Collide*, New York: New York University Press, 2006.

62 "Higher Levels of Customer Engagement in Private Online Communities," press release, *Communispace*, March 20, 2007, http://www.communispace.com.

64 "Shopping, Search, and MySpace," *Hitwise*, June 5, 2007, http://weblogs.hitwise.com/leeann-prescott/2007/06/shopping_search_and_myspace.html.

64 R. I. M. Dunbar, "Co-Evolution of Neocortex size, Group Size and Language in Humans," *Behavioral and Brain Sciences* 16 (4): 681–735.

65 Christopher Allen's blog Life with Alacrity has a great piece on the Ultima Online study, http://www.lifewithalacrity.com/2004/03/the_dunbar_numb.html

67 Ted Nelson coined the term *intertwingularity* in a 1974 paper entitled "Computer Lib: You Can and Must Understand Computers Now/Dream Machines: New Freedoms Through Computer Screens—A Minority Report."

Chapter Four

72 *Video Games Live!* http://www.videogameslive.com/index.php?s=info.

73 Neil Postman, "Informing Ourselves to Death," speech to *German Informatics Society (Gesellschaft für Informatik)*, October 11, 1990, Stuttgart, Germany.

74   Warren Thorngate, "On Paying Attention," in: W. J. Baker, L.
P. Mos, H. V. Rappard, and H. J. Stam (eds.). *Recent Trends
in Theoretical Psychology: Proceedings of the Second
Biannual Conference of the International Society for
Theoretical Psychology,* April 20–25, 1987, Banff, Alberta,
Canada. New York: Springer-Verlag, 1988, 247–263.

74   M.H. Goldhaber, "Principles of the New Economy,"
http://www. well.com/user/mgoldh/principles.html.

76   Thomas Friedman, "The Age of Interruption," *New York
Times,* July 5, 2006.

76   Linda Stone, "Attention: The Real Aphrodisiac," ETech
keynote speech, March 7, 2006.

77   A compendium of articles by Professor Itiel Dror can be
found at http://www.immagic.com/eLibrary/ARCHIVES/
GENERAL/BLOGS/F070319S.pdf.

77   Victor M. González and Gloria Mark, "Constant, Constant,
Multi-tasking Craziness: Managing Multiple Working
Spheres," speech delivered at CHI2004, Conference on
Human Factors in Computing Systems, Vienna, Austria, April
24–29, 2004, found online at http://interruptions.net/
literature/Gonzalez-CHI04-p113-gonzalez.pdf.

78   Quoted in "CyberBabel," special issue on Information and the
Quality of Life, *Ethics and Information Technology* 8, no. 4
(2006).

78   University of Oslo professor Thomas Hylland Eriksen quoted
in John Pratt, David Brown, Mark Brown, Simon Hallsworth,
and Wayne Morrison, eds., *The New Punitiveness: Trends,
Theories, Perspectives,* Cullompton, UK: Willan Publishing,
2005.

82   Karna Crawford, "How Coke Was Rewarded for Its BT
Program," *iMedia Connection,* August 22, 2007,
http://www.imedia connection.com/content/16346.asp.

84   "Ryanair Plans Seat-Back Advertising," *Cheapflights Ltd.,*
September 26, 2006, http://news.cheapflights.co.uk/flights/
2006/09/ryanair_plans_s.html.

84   Thomas Claburn, "The War on Spam Takes a Novel Turn,"
InformationWeek, May 17, 2005, http://www.information
week.com/story/showArticle.jhtml?articleID=163104354.

86 David Levy, "More, Faster, Better: Governance in an Age of Overload, Busyness, and Speed," *First Monday*, November 9, 2007, http://www.firstmonday.org/issues/special11_9/levy/.

87 Barbara Ehrenreich, "Make the Ad Guys Pay: Advertising Is Too Pervasive," *The Progressive*, August 1999.

Chapter Five

93 Robert Hassan and Ronald E. Purser, eds., *24/7: Time and Temporality in the Network Society*, Stanford, CA: Stanford University Press, 2007.

93 Adrian Mackenzie, "Protocols and the Irreducible Traces of Embodiment: The Viterbi Algorithm and the Mosaic of Machine Time," Lancaster, LA, UK: Lancaster University, May 2005, http://www.lancs.ac.uk/staff/mackenza/papers/mackenzie-algorithmic-time.pdf.

98 "Global Media and Entertainment Industry, 2007–2011," report published by Price Waterhouse Coopers (PwC) on June 21, 2007.

101 For an insightful look at the Modafinil experience, I recommend David Plotz, "Can We Sleep Less?" *Slate.com*, March 7, 2003, http://www.slate.com/id/2079113/.

Chapter Six

107 James Ledbetter, "Debunking the 'Economics of Abundance,'" *CNN.com*, April 19, 2007, http://money.cnn. com/2007/04/19/commentary/ledbetter_scarcity/index.htm.

113 Loopt, "loopt Lets Sprint Customers Keep in Touch with Friends Using GPS on Select Sprint and Nextel Phones," press release, July 17, 2007.

114 *My Second Life: The Video Diaries of Molotov Alva*, *molotovalva.com*, http://www.molotovalva.com.

115 Paul Channing Adams, "A Reconsideration of Personal Boundaries in Space-Time," Annals of the Association of American Geographers, Vol. 85, No. 2 (June 1995), 267–285.

Chapter Seven

119 Bill Werde, "Defiant Downloads Rise from Underground," *New York Times*, February 25, 2004.

121 Roberta Cruger, "The Mash-Up Revolution," *Salon.com*, August 9, 2003, http://dir.salon.com/story/ent/music/feature/2003/08/09/ mashups_cruger/.

123 Quinn Norton, "Secrets of the Pirate Bay," *Wired.com*, August 16, 2006, http://www.wired.com/science/discoveries/news/2006/08/ 71543.

124 *New York Times*/CBS News Poll is based on telephone interviews conducted September 15 to 16, 2003, with 675 adults nationwide, http://www.nytimes.com/packages/html/politics/ 20030915_poll/20030915poll-results.html.

124 Mary Madden and Amanda Lenhart, "Music Downloading, File-sharing and Copyright: A Pew Internet Project Data Memo," *Pew Internet and American Life Project*, http://www.pew internet.org/PPF/r/96/report_display.asp.

126 The Campaign to Eliminate DRM, *DefectiveByDesign.org*, http:// defectivebydesign.org

126 FreeCulture.org, Students for Free Culture, http://free culture.org/.

130 Tim Gnatek, "Darknets: Virtual Parties with a Select Group of Invitees," *New York Times*, October 5, 2005.

131 For an interesting question-and-answer (Q&A) session with Freenet founder Ian Clarke, visit http://grep.law.harvard.edu/articles/03/09/02/0125236.shtml.

132 A mixed Swedish English site, but the best view of the Pirate Party mother ship is found at http://www.piratpartiet.se/international/ english.

134 Andrew Keen, *The Cult of the Amateur: How Today's Internet Is Killing Our Culture*, New York: Currency, 2007.

135 John Tehranian's paper is well worth reading in its entirety, available at http://www.turnergreen.com/publications/Tehranian_Infringement_Nation.pdf

137 Eric L. Jones, *Cultures Merging: A Historical and Economic Critique of Culture,* Princeton, NJ: Princeton University Press, 2006.

Chapter Eight

140 For a look at the offending Starbucks coupon, visit http://urbanlegends.about.com/library/bl_starbucks_coupon.htm.

140 Caroline McCarthy, "Ticked-Off Starbucks Customer Sues for $114 Million," *CNET News.com*, September 11, 2006, http://www.news.com/8301-10784_3-6114370-7.html.

141 Chris Thilik, "Caribou Accepting Starbucks Coupons," *AdJab*, September 5, 2006, http://www.adjab.com.

143 Avner Greif, *Institutions and the Path to the Modern Economy: Lessons from Medieval Trade*, New York: Cambridge University Press, 2006.

144 Roger Clarke, "Privacy as a Means of Engendering Trust in Cyberspace," *University of New South Wales Law Journal* 24, no. 1 (June 9, 2001), http://www.unswlawjournal.unsw.edu.au/lj2/issue.asp?id=24-1&fid=f7-1; article can be found at http://www.anu.edu.au/people/Roger.Clarke/DV/eTrust.html.

145 Batya Friedman, Peter H. Kahn, Jr., and Daniel C. Howe, "Trust Online," *Communications of the ACM* 43, no. 12 (December 2000), http://www.acm.org.

145 Paul Zak and Stephen Knack, "Trust and Growth," *The Economic Journal*, 111 (2001):295–321.

145 Nobel Prize-winning economist Kenneth Arrow quoted in Luigi Guiso, Paola Sapienza, and Luigi Zingales, "The Role of Social Capital in Financial Development," *American Economic Review* 94, no. 3 (June 2004): 526–556.

148 Todd Sundsted, "The Practice of Peer-to-Peer Computing: Trust and Security in Peer-to-Peer Networks," *IBM.com*, June 19, 2002, http://www.ibm.com/developerworks/java/library/j-p2ptrust/.

149 Jamais Cascio, from an e-mail to author, July 31, 2007.

150 Evan Schuman, "Connecticut Sues Best Buy for Deceiving Customers with Dual Web Sites," *StorefrontBacktalk.com*, May 24, 2007, http://storefrontbacktalk.com/story/052407best buy.php.

151 EdelmanTrust Barometer, 2006

152 William Gibson, "The Road to Oceania," *New York Times*, June 25, 2003

153 EdelmanTrust Barometer, 2007

155 Pauline Puvanasvari Ratnasingam, "Interorganizational Trust in Business to Business E-Commerce," *Erasmus Research Institute of Management*, November 22, 2001, http://www.erim.eur.nl/ERIM.

156 Collin Douma, "Are You Ready to Radically Trust Your Consumers?" *RadicalTrust* Blog, February 18, 2007, http://www. =radicaltrust.ca/ 2007/02/18/are-you-ready-to-radically-trust-your-customers.

Chapter Nine

164 London-based business consultant Umair Haque also uses the phrase "Bubble Generation," although his definition is different than mine.

165 Global Information, Inc. (GII), "Attitudes of 18-24s Towards Consumer Electronics – US," London/Chicago: Mintel Reports, November 2006. The 72 million consumers age 18 to 24 have an average per capita income of $12,000.

165 Graeme Codrington, "Generation Y: It's Life, Jim, But Not as We Know It," *TomorrowToday.biz*, August 10, 2007, http://www.tmtd.biz/2007/08/10/generation-y-its-life-jim-but-not-as-we-know-it/.

166 Michael Kryzanek, "Anxieties Define Generation Y," *Boston Globe*, December 8, 2005, http://www.boston.com/news/local/articles/2005/12/08/anxieties_define_generation_y/.

168 "Kids' Social Networking Study," Bethesda, MD: Grunwald Associates, July 2007, www.grunwald.com.

168 IBM, "IBM Consumer Survey Shows Decline of TV as Primary Media Device," press release, August 22, 2007, http://www-03.ibm.com/press/us/en/pressrelease/22206.wss.

170 For the Boomer vs. BubbleGen chart, I owe a debt of gratitude to Stowe Boyd's chart of edglings versus centroids.

171 Anil Dash, "Consider Twitter," *Dashes.com*, February 14, 2007, http://www.dashes.com/anil/2007/02/consider-twitte.html.

172 Jan Matthews, "Anxiety Rising: Younger People Are More Anxious Than Ever. What's Up?" *Mindful-Things*, January 2001, http://www.mindful-things.com/Features/features_4.html.

173 Tomi T. Ahonen and Alan Moore, *Communities Dominate Brands*, London: Futuretext, 2005.

174 Jamie Pietras, "The New American Way of Death," *Salon.com*, July 31, 2007, http://www.salon.com.

175 Om Malik, "Reach Out and Twitter Someone," *CNNMoney. com*, May 16, 2007, http://money.cnn.com/magazines/business 2/business2_archive/2007/05/01/8405660/index.htm.

177 Bill Breen, "Who Do You Love? The Appeal—and Risks—of Authenticity," *Fast Company*, Issue 115 (May 2007): 82.

178 Stowe Boyd in an e-mail to author, August 10, 2007.

179 "Technology and Media Use" (topic: Online Video), *Pew Internet & American Life Project*, July 25, 2007, http:// www.pew internet.org/PPF/r/219/report_display.asp.

184 Lev Grossman, "Time's Person of the Year: You," *Time*, December 13, 2006, http://www.time.com/time/magazine/ article/ 0,9171,1569514,00.html.

Chapter Ten

191 John Perry Barlow, "The Economy of Ideas," *Wired*, Issue 2.03, March 1994, http://www.wired.com/wired/archive/2.03/ economy.ideas.html.

191 Spencer Reiss, "Here Comes Trouble," *Wired*, Issue 15.02, February 2007, http://www.wired.com/wired/archive/15.02/ trouble.html.

193 Mike Shields, "Brand Integration Key to MySpace Ad Clout," *MediaWeek*, April 23, 2007, http://www.mediaweek.com/mw/ news/recent_display.jsp?vnu_content_id=1003574609.

194 Stephanie Olsen, "Study: Americans Feel Strongly about Social Ties Online, Too," *CNET News.com*, November 29, 2006, http://www.news.com/Study-Americans-feel-strongly- about-social-ties-online%2C-too/2100-1026_3-6139422. html?tag=item.

195 Clay Shirky, "Tiny Slice, Big Market," *Wired*, Issue 14.11, November 2006, http://www.wired.com/wired/archive/14.11/ meganiche.html.

195 Jo Best, "Is Free the Way Forward for Mobile TV?" *Silicon.com*, February 16, 2006, http://networks.silicon.com/ mobile/0,390246 65,39156508,00.htm.

195 Fred Wilson, "The Freemium Business Model," *AVC Blog*, March 23, 2006, http://avc.blogs.com/a_vc/2006/03/the_ freemium_ bu.html.

197 Steve Smith, "Will Watch Ads for Minutes," *MediaPost's Mobile Insider*, August 23, 2007, http://publications.media post.com/ index.cfm?fuseaction=Articles.showArticle&art_aid=66270.

198 Lexmark International and Ipsos Public Affairs, "Knowledge Workers Point to Benefits of 24/7 Accessibility via Technology in Poll by Lexmark and Ipsos," press release, February 13, 2007, http://www.lexmark.com/lexmark/pressrelease/home/ 0,6930,204816596_653271419_996197944_en,00.html.

200 Henry Jenkins, *Convergence Culture: Where Old and New Media Collide*, New York: New York University Press, 2006.

201 Jeff Leeds, "Universal Music Will Sell Songs Without Copy Protection," *New York Times*, August 10, 2007,

203 Dan Bricklin, "The Cornucopia of the Commons: How to Get Volunteer Labor," *Bricklin.com*, October 12, 2006, http://www. bricklin.com/cornucopia.htm.

203 Paul Icamina, "Wikipedia Reaches 2 Million English Entries; 8.29 Million Entries in 253 Languages," *AHN*, October 11, 2007, http://www.allheadlinenews.com/articles/7008799282.

204 "Call for Participation: Trust and the Future of the Internet," *Internet Society*, http://www.isoc.org/isoc/general/trustees/ headlines/20070809.shtml.

204 Thomas Friedman, *The World Is Flat: A Brief History of the Twenty-first Century*, New York: Farrar, Straus and Giroux, 2005.

205 Stephen M. R. Covey, *The SPEED of Trust: The One Thing That Changes Everything*, New York: Free Press, 2006.

206 "Never Ending Friending," research report, Fox Interactive Media, April 2007.

206 Duncan J. Watts and Jonah Peretti, "Viral Marketing for the Real World," June 29, 2007.

206 Mike Sachoff, "Social Networks Provide 'Momentum Effect,'" *Webpronews.com*, April 23, 2007, http://www.webpronews. com/topnews/2007/04/23/social-networks-provide-momen tum-effect.

207 Ceri Kirkland, "Top Social Networks: Who's Losing to MySpace," *Compete.com*, April 12, 2007, http://blog. compete.com/2007/ 04/12/top-social-networks-attention-myspace-bebo/.

Chapter Eleven

213 Ray Kurzweil, "The Law of Accelerating Returns," *Kurzweil AI.net*, March 7, 2001, http://www.kurzweilai.net/articles/ art0134. html?printable=1.

233 Speigel, "Merkel's China Visit Marred by Hacking Allegations," *Spiegel Online International*, August 27, 2007, http:// www.spiegel.de/international/world/0,1518,502169,00.html.

Index

3Jam, 171
43Places, 173
43Things, 60
50 Cent, 190

Abundant economy, 106–108
ACID, 63
Adams, Paul Channing, 115
Adidas, 206–207
Adobe, 196
Advanced Research Projects Agency
   (ARPA), 32, 52
Affinity groups, 53–54
AFI, 63
Ahmad, Salman, 128
Ahonen, Tomi T., 173
Akgregator, 79
Al Gore's Penguin Army, 44
Allport, Gordon, 41
Al-Queda, 64, 87
Altman, Sam, 113
Alva, Molotov, 114
*A&M Records, Inc. v. Napster,
   Inc.,* 122
Amazon, 201
Amplitude, 106
Anshe Chung, 53
AnswerBag, 60
Anticipation marketing, 82–83
Antimarketing, 80–82

AOL, 82
API, 133
Apple, 96
Application programming interface
   (API), 133
Arrow, Kenneth, 145
AsianAvenue, 60
Assignment Zero, 133
Astronomical time, 95
Astroturfing, 45
Atomic clock, 91
Attensa, 79
Attention, 71–89
Attention consumerist movement,
   87–88
Attention credits, 83–85
Attention rewards, 196–198
Attention Trust, 85
Avennu, 198

Backstrom, Lars, 55
Baghdad, 143
Bandwagon.co.uk, 61
Barabasi, Albert-Laszlo, 29
Bebo, 52, 53, 59
Beme, 38
Best Buy, 150–151
Betamax case, 122
BikeSpace, 60
Bird flu, 35–36

BlackBerry, 112
BlackPlanet, 60
Blade Runner, 23
Bliin, 171
Blinklist, 173
Blip.tv, 173
Blockbuster, 207
BlogBridge, 79
BlogLines, 79
BlueDot, 173
Bluetooth, 111
Blummy, 173
Blyk, 84
BMI, 197
Boole, George, 33
Boomerangs. *See* Bubble generation
Boston University, 58
Boundless self, 115
Bowling Alone (Putnam), 175
Boyd, Danah, 56
Boyd, Stowe, 163, 178
Brand, Stewart, 191
Breen, Bill, 177
Bricklin, Dan, 203
Bubble generation, 163-185
    affiliation, 174–177
    angst, 172–174
    authenticity, 177–180
    characteristics, 167–169
    immediacy, 170–172
    individualism, 180–181
    prepotency, 181–184
Buggy whip makers, 188
Buice, Susan, 106
Burg, The, 78
Burton, Brian, 119–120

Cabinas Publica, 3
Cady, Ted, 62
CafeMom, 60
CalConnect.org, 96
Cambrian House, 203
Captain Copyright, 131
Caribou, 141
Cascio, Jamais, 149
Catal Huyuk, 6, 52
ccMixter, 128
Cerf, Vinton, 32
China threat theory, 223
Chunking, 79
Churchill, Winston, 1

Circadian rhythm, 101
Circuit City, 101
CiteULike, 173
City of Heroes, 175
Clarke, Arthur C., 105
Clarke, Ian, 131
Clarke, Roger, 144
Classmates, 60
ClipMarks, 173
Club Penguin, 60
CNN, 133
Coca-Cola, 83, 194
Codrington, Graeme, 165
Commons model, 203
Complex network, 18
Computer virus, 35
Continuous partial attention, 76
*Convergence Culture: Where Old
    and New Media Collide*
    (Jenkins), 61, 200
Cook, Scott, 147
Coordinated universal time (UTC), 95
Copyright, 119–138
Counter-Strike, 53
Crawford, Karna, 83
CreativeCommons.org, 128–129
Crowdsourcing, 133
Crowdsourcing model, 203
CrowdSpirit.com, 133, 203
CrowdStorm, 133
Cruft, 76
Cruger, Roberta, 121
Crumley, Arin, 106
CSI Miami, 37
Cuba, 136
Cubase, 121
Cult of the Amateur, The (Keen), 134
Cultures Merging (Jones), 137
Curatorial layer, 43
Cyworld, 49–51, 56, 60

DailyMotion, 173
Danger Mouse (aka Brian Burton),
    114
Darknet, 130–131
Dash, Anil, 171
Dave Mathews Band, 63
Dawkins, Richard, 36
Day of two noons, 94
Dayparting, 97–98
DayZLoop, 60

DCI Group, 44–45
DefectiveByDesign.org, 126, 201
DeHart, Jacob, 39
Del.icio.us, 173
Digital rights movement (DRM),
    125, 200–201
Discontinuities, 66–67
Dissociative behavior, 115
Dodgeball, 171
Douma, Collin, 156
Downhill Battle, 120
Draper, Tim, 43
Dreamlords, 175
DRM, 125, 200–201
Dror, Itiel, 77, 79
Drupal, 65
Dunbar, Robin, 64
Dunbar number, 64–65
Durkheim, Emile, 58

eBay, 146, 148–149
eBible.com, 60
Ecademy, 60
Echoes. *See* Bubble generation
Edgerton, David, 69
eHow, 60
Ehrenreich, Barbara, 87
Einstein, Albert, 91
Electronic Arts, 206, 207
ElHood, 60
Eliot, T. S., 211
EMI Music, 201
Eons, 59
Epinions, 151
Ericsson, 11
Erikson, Thomas Hylland, 78
Exabyte, 74
ExpertVillage, 60
Extensibility, 114–116
Eyespot, 173

FabFemme, 60
Facebook, 33, 50, 52, 53, 59, 173,
    194
Fall Out Boy, 63
Falkvinge, Rickard, 132
Famster, 60
FanPage, 60
FanSpot, 60
FastBreakClub, 60
FeedReader, 79

FineTune, 61
Finin, Tim, 38
FIQL, 61
FitLink, 60
Fleming, Sir Sandford, 94
Flickr, 196
Flyff, 175
Fon, 29–30
*Fortune at the Bottom of the Pyra-
    mid, The* (Prahalad), 15
Fotolog, 173
Four Eyed Monsters (Crumley/
    Buice), 106
FreeCulture.org, 126
Freemium business model, 195–196
Freenet, 131
FreshBooks, 196
Friedman, Batya, 145
Friedman, Thomas, 25, 76, 204
Friending, 56, 206
Friendster, 56
Friis, Janus, 191
Frooty Loops, 63
Froppy, 61
Furl, 173

Gaboxadol, 102
GaiaOnline, 59
GameTap, 197
GasBuddy.com, 203
Gates, Bill, 79
Gayeton, Douglas, 115
General Motors, 168
Gibson, William, 152, 159
Gimme20, 60
GLEE, 60
Gmail, 10
Gnatek, Tim, 130
Godard, Jean-Luc, 153
Goldhaber, Michael H., 74
Google, 64, 84, 110, 133, 201–202
Gould, Gordon, 43
GPShopper, 113
Grameenphone, 14
Granovetter, Mark, 55
Greif, Avner, 143
Grey Album, The, 119
Grey Tuesday, 119–120
Grokster, 123
Grouper, 131
GSMA, 11

H5N1, 34
Hacktivism, 202
Hajj, Adrian, 153
Half Life, 53
Happy Birthday to You, 134
Happy Days, 37
Hassan, Robert, 93
Hawala, 212
Hayes, Tom, 237
Hayes Valley, 163
Heinz, 181
Helio, 113, 194
Hi5, 52, 59, 173
Hill, Patty and Mildred J., 134
Hip Hop Summit Action, 121
Hirschhorn, Jason, 195
Hong Kong, 35–36
Horvitz, Eric, 79
Hu Jintao, 223
Hyperlink, 109

iLike, 61
I-Reporter, 133
IBM, 53
ILOVEYOU computer virus, 35
Imeem, 61
ImageShack, 173
*Infringement Nation: Copyright
    Reform and the Norm/Law
    Gap* (Tehranian), 135
InnoCentive, 203
Inpowr, 60
*Institutions and the Path to the
    Modern Economy: Lessons
    from Medieval Trade* (Greif),
    143
Intellectual property rights, 119–138
Intuit, 147
iTunes, 100

Jaiku, 10
Jamendo, 61
Jamglue, 61
Jenkins, Henry, 61, 200
Jiabao, Wen, 223
Jimmy Eat World, 63
Jintao, Hu, 223
Jobs, Steve, 119
Jones, Eric L., 22, 137
Jones Soda, 181
Joomla!, 65

Joost, 191
JumpCut, 173
Jumpgate, 175
Jump Point, 5
Junoon, 128
Jyngle, 171

Kahn, Robert, 32
Kawasaki, Guy, 42, 187
Kazaa, 123
Keen, Andrew, 134
Kelliher, Scott, 197
Kerala, 16–17
Killers, The, 63
Kitson, 39
Knack, Stephen, 145
Koolanoo, 60
Kryzanek, Michael, 166

Last.fm, 61
Leap seconds, 95
Ledbetter, James, 107
LegalForce, 133
Leonsis, Ted, 152
Lessig, Lawrence, 129
LetsBuyIt, 133
Leung, Martin, 72
Levy, David, 86
LicketyShip, 101
Lincoln software system, 13
LinkedIn, 33, 53, 60
Linux, 127
Listal, 173
Litman, Jessica, 129
LiveNation, 62
Long Tail, 207
Loneltgirl15, 179–180
Loopt, 113
Lowell, Francis Cabot, 7
Loy, David R., 78

Mackenzie, Adrian, 93
Macromedia, 196
Mad Max, 204
Maghribi Traders, 143, 146, 156
Magnatunes, 128
Ma.gnolia, 173
Malik, Om, 175
Malone, Michael S., 3
Mangaliso, Winnie, 13–14
Maple Story, 175

Mark, Gloria, 77
Mashup culture, 119–138
MayasMom, 60
McLuhan, Marshall, 37
Mechanical solidarity, 58
Meetup.com, 176
Meganiche, 195
Meme, 36
Merkel, Angela, 223
Metcalfe, Robert, 19
Metcalfe's law, 19
MGM Studios, Inc. v. Grokster, Ltd., 122
Microsoft, 79, 84
MiGente, 60
Millenials. *See* Bubble generation
Minti, 60
Minglebox.com, 61
MIT, 96
Mixi, 60
MMORPG, 116
M&Ms, 181
Mobile phone, 11
Mobility, 110–112
Moblabber, 171
Modafinil, 101–102
MOG.com, 61
Momentum affect, 206–207
MommyBuzz, 60
Moodle, 173
Moore, Alan, 173
Moore, Gordon, 10
Moore's law, 10
Morpheus, 123
MothersClick, 60
Motorola, 11
MP3.com, 61
MSN, 64
MSNBC, 82
Mudflation, 188
Multiplayer online game playing, 175
Multiply.com, 59
Multitasking, 227
MusicHawk, 61
Music industry, 62–64, 125, 201
MusicToday, 63
MuslimSpace, 60
MyChurch.org, 60
MyCollegeDaily, 60
MyDeathSpace, 174

MySpace, 33, 50, 52, 53, 56, 59, 64, 173
MyTeamCaptain, 60
MyTwinn, 181
MyYearbook, 60

Napster, 122
Nelson, Ted, 67
Netlog, 59
Network, 31
Network effect, 30
New growth, 21
NewAssignment.net, 133
NHLConnection, 60
Nickell, Jake, 39
Nike, 168
Nonlinearity, 106, 109
Node, 31, 40, 206
Nokia, 11
Norrath, 187
NYTimes.com, 82

Oddica, 40
Odlyzko, Andrew, 20
Old growth, 21
Olivia,com, 60
Online affinity groups, 53–54
Online social communities, 193–195
Open source, 126–127
Open Source Initiative, 126
Orange, 84
Orb, 198
Organic solidarity, 58
Orkut, 33, 50, 57, 61
OurChart, 60
OurMedia, 173

Pandora.com, 61
Pandenomics, 207–208
Parazz, 173
ParentsConnect, 60
Peer-to-peer file sharing, 122–123
Pepsi-Cola, 83
Perez, Carlota, 5
Personal message bond, 85
Phone ladies, 14
PhotoBucket, 173
Pick-A-Prof, 60
Pickle.com, 173
Piczo, 59

Pietras, Jamie, 174
Pig and the Box, The, 131
Pinger, 171
PirateBay, 123
PirateParty, 132
Plone, 65
Postman, Leo, 41
Postman, Neil, 73
PostNuke, 65
Prahalad, C. K., 15
Preferential attachment, 57
Process accordance, 57
Proctor & Gamble, 168, 203
ProjectOpus, 61
Pro Tools, 63, 121
Psychology of Rumor, The (Allport/Postman), 41
PunkVoter, 121
PureVolume, 61
Purser, Ronald E., 93
Putnam, Robert, 175

Qloud, 61
Qtrax, 197

R, 206
Radical trust, 156
RapSpace.tv, 61
RateMyProfessor, 60
Ratnasingam, Pauline, 155
Reactee, 163
Reed, David P., 19
Reed's law, 19
Reproduction rate *(R),* 206
Reputation, 145–146
Return Path, 85
Reunion.com, 60
Reuters, 153–154
ReverbNation, 61
Revo, 173
Revver, 173
Rheingold, Howard, 52, 54, 78
Road to Oceania, The (Gibson), 152
Rolling Stones, The, 63
Romer, Paul, 21
RSS (real simple syndication), 79
Rumor, 46
Rumor mongering, 40–42
Ryanair, 84
Ryze, 60

Sao Paolo, 81
Sawlogs, 60
Schumpeter, Joseph, 69
Sconex, 60
Second Life, 53, 114, 115, 203
Self-organizing communities, 65
Selfish Gene, The (Dawkins), 36
Seriosity, 197
Shared Phone, 13
Shirky, Clay, 195
Shock of the Old: Technology and Global History Since 1900, The (Edgerton), 69
Shopcast, 177
ShopIntuition, 39
Shopping gossip, 42–44
Shutterfly, 173
Simon, Herbert, 71
Six Apart, 196
Skype, 30
Slifter.com, 114
Slingbox, 198
Smith, Lee, 62
SMS, 73
SNP, 206
Social communities, 193–195
Social networking potential (SNP), 206
Social shopping sites, 43
Sony Corp. of America v. Universal City Studios, 122
SoYouWanna.com, 60
Space Shifting, 182
SparkPeople, 60
Speed of Trust, The (Covey), 205
Splice.com, 61
SportsMates, 60
Sportsvite, 60
Sprint, 113
Starbucks, 139–141
Starwood Group, 203
Stone, Linda, 71, 76
StyleHive, 173
Sugar Mama, 197
Sullivan, Nicholas P., 14
Sundsted, Todd, 148
Suprachiasmatic nucleus, 101
Surowiecki, James, 58

Tabblo, 173
TACODA, 82–83

Takkle.com, 60
Tangiers, 211
TeamBuy, 133
Tehranian, John, 135
Tellme, 12
Terrorist, 87
ThisNext, 43
Thorngate, Warren, 74
Threadless T-shirts, 38–39
Time, 91–103
TiredAndTested.com, 60
Tivo, 198
Toffler, Alvin, 69
ToolsToLife, 60
Torvalds, Linus, 127
Traineo, 60
Truemors, 42
Trust, 139–157, 204–205
TrustedOpinion, 151
24/7: Time Temporality in the Net-
    worked Society
    (Hassan/Purser), 93
Twenge, Jean M., 172
Twitter, 10, 53, 171

Ultima Online, 65
UltraFan, 60
Universal Music Group, 201
University of California Berkeley,
    96
UPlayMe, 61
Urban Outfitters, 39
UTC, 95

Van Alstyne, Marshall, 84
Vanquish, 85
Vans, 181
Varsavsky, Martin, 29
VideoEgg, 173
Vimeo, 173
Video Games Live!, 72
Viral marketing, 43
Viral video ads, 179
Virgin America, 199
Virgin Mobile, 197

Virus, 35
vSocial, 173

W3C, 12
Wal-Mart, 108, 201
Watts, Duncan, 206
Waverman, Leonard, 12
We media citizen journalism, 133
Weak ties, 55
Wealink, 61
Web 2.0, 164
We-Match, 133
Wen Jiabao, 223
West, Geoffrey B., 18
Whyville, 60
Widget, 193
Wikipedia, 55, 203
Williams, Raymond, 49
Wilson, Fred, 195
WiMAX, 111, 112
Winksite, 10
Wired, 133
Wisdom of Crowds, The (Suro-
    wiecki), 58
World is Flat, The (Friedman), 25,
    204
WorldOnDemand.net, 198
Wretch, 61
Wright, Stephen, 94

Xero Mobile, 197

Yahoo!, 64, 96, 110, 133
YouTube, 53, 125, 173
YourSportsFan, 60
YourSpins, 61
Ytterbium clock, 91
Yunus, Muhammad, 14

Zak, Paul, 145
Zennström, Niklas, 191
Zhanzou, 61
Zoomr, 173
Zooppa, 179
Zuckerberg, Mark, 194

About the Author

Tom Hayes has been called a tastemaker for the new Net generation and one of the most influential executives and bloggers in high tech today. He has spent a career making sense out of emerging technology trends, serving as a senior marketing executive at Silicon Valley stalwarts Hewlett-Packard and Applied Materials, and now advises companies around the world on how to succeed in the new information economy. In the 1990s, Hayes was the founding chairman and CEO of Joint Venture: Silicon Valley, the pioneering business network credited with catapulting Silicon Valley into leadership of the Internet Era. Profiles of Tom and his work have appeared in the *New York Times*, *Wall Street Journal*, *Fast Company*, *Los Angeles Times*, *Wired*, *San Jose Mercury News*, *San Francisco Chronicle*, *Boston Globe*, *Rolling Stone*, and publications and news outlets around the world. His often controversial rants and riffs on business can be found on his blog, Tombomb.com. Hayes lives with his family in Silicon Valley. Tom can be reached at tom@hayesmail.com. Read more at www.jumppointbook.com.